Portions of a Life

Recollections and Reflections

Portions of a Life

Recollections and Reflections

Michael Fak

Table of Contents

About the Author

Former Chicagoan Mike Fak currently lives in Lincoln Illinois with his wife Sharon, and son Timothy.

A freelance writer as well as professional home restorationist, Mike splits his duties by working on home repair projects during the day, and writing in the evenings and on weekends. Being an incurable insomniac has allowed Mike to pursue both careers on a full time basis.

A writer since his days in the U.S. Army, this current book is the sixth he has penned, including three in which he acted as ghostwriter for individuals wishing to get their lives and memories down in a printed format. This is his second personal anthology and is being released just months after his new E-book and hard copy CD: "The Inexpensive Old House Repair and Restoration Book" was released for sale on his personal website: mikefak.com

Mike has written over 600 newspaper columns, predominantly for the *Lincoln Courier*, and has begun writing articles for nostalgia genre magazines. This past year his works were included in five issues of *U.S. Legacies* magazine.

Besides various ghostwriting projects, Mike is currently working on a book about the Army in the late 1960,s as well as a religious/science fiction novel.

Mike is currently doing Friday morning radio with his old television sidekick Jim Ash on 96.3 F.M. Atlanta Illinois, and enjoys it much more than television. To quote from one of his columns: "Radio is much better than T.V. You don't have to shave, or comb your hair. You don't even have to change your underwear and no one will ever know. Well, no one but Jim of course."

Foreword

I understand that every time a person picks up something I have written they are giving up a moment of their time in this world. In effect, you have decided to listen to something I am saying. I believe that is the most important thing to a storyteller. It isn't to write the story, which of course is required. Nor to make money, which is a pleasant, although far too infrequent end result. More importantly, it is to know that somewhere, at some given time, a person is reading what you have transcribed. I wish to thank you for this privilege from the bottom of my heart.

This book happened a little by accident. I had decided, with Sharon's approval, to release the 30,000 word story; "Angels on the Ninth Floor". I wanted to include an album of pictures showing the day to day improvement in my son, and this inclusion of so many pictures made the cost of printing the small book too expensive. I took a group of other stories dear to me and included them to give a little more meat to the book, offering more value to the reader, and thus had created my second anthology of short stories.

"The Best I've got...so far", still ended up only being offered as an E-book or hard CD because the cost of printing so many color photos was just too high and I didn't want to hit the streets with a twenty-dollar paperback.

After the newspaper was so kind as to do a feature story on the release, (allowing me to not have to self-aggrandize in my own column) many of you asked me when the book was coming out. I quickly realized many of you prefer the transportability and tangibility a book offers a person.

As I mulled format, a reduction in photographs, going to grayscale rather than color, and everything else a storyteller frets over before going to print, I was struck by two issues I hadn't paid any mind to previously.

First, I noticed that this group of stories and articles were predominantly life experiences. They were tales of what has happened to me and how I reacted. I realized by omitting just a few of the stories, the entire anthology would be about portions of my life, or how I felt or thought about this crazy world I was dropped in to.

The second thing I realized is, although every story in the compilation is one I can honestly say I personally enjoy reading, there wasn't enough fresh material. A "greatest hits" album can just go so far if too many of the favorite songs can be listened to on a previous album. I immediately pulled the E-book version and decided to create a new E-book, and to go to print with a new, more personal compilation of stories.

As if providence decided to lend me a hand, I came across an old story I was certain I had lost a few years ago. Cleaning up the mess around my desk and bookcases, preparing for a visit by my family, I came across a floppy disk behind a few of the books lying every which way on the shelves. Popping it in the computer, I was delighted to find several works I thought I had deleted by accident, forgetting I had backed them up to disk. The story, "The Great Latrine Fiasco" was one of them. Happily adding the short story to the new book, I became convinced someone was telling me something.

I did include five stories from the first book; "One Hour 'till Dawn", because I received so much positive feedback on those specific titles. If this is to be my defining and last anthology, which it will be, I wanted those old favorites safely nestled among what I hope are deemed new old favorites.

"Angels on the Ninth Floor", a full third of this book, is new to everyone as it hasn't been read by anyone save my family.

"Before it was Wrigleyville" was in the first book's collection, but has been expanded by 4000 words over that edition.

"How I lost 50 pounds in 90 days" is all new to readers as is the 7500 word, short story: "The Great Latrine Fiasco." The 7500 word short: "Things that Drive me Nuts" was written especially for all you folks who say you enjoy my writing the most when I'm ranting and raving about things.

I also included a half-dozen columns from the last three years in which I talked about something that had happened to me that also received praise from readers. This new gathering is what I now humbly offer up to you with a confidence that I have created a book at the limits I possess in offering an enjoyable reading experience.

I say this is my last anthology because it is time to stop writing short stories. Oh, my columns will continue to appear in the *Lincoln Courier*, but I have other things to write down in detail that will take up all the time I have left in this world and then some.

There are several books in my head that I have to get down before I and they are gone. They are demanding to be let loose from my mind, so much so, that I sometimes feel like words are falling out of my ears as I walk down the street. They all clamor that they have been ignored too long. I believe I will listen to them this time, and get to work on bringing them out of the mental womb they are tired of being in. I also find myself getting more and more project requests from individuals that continue to keep my writing time occupied.

With all that said, I hope you enjoy this definitive book of short stories and essays by Mike Fak. They are all portions of my life and I can't think of anyone I would rather share them with than you. As I have always said with everything I have ever written; Let me know if you like the story. Let me know if you don't.

Angels on the Ninth Floor

Welcome:

Thank you for deciding to visit a part of our lives. It is hoped you will take something away from this little story that will make you appreciate your lives a little more than when you started to read this journal.

This story was originally intended for our son's eyes and our son's eyes only. My wife Sharon is not as comfortable as I am at telling strangers how she feels, and thus this book was intended to have a press run of 1. I agreed to accept her decision since she is not only co- author, but a principle in this story. One day early in August, Sharon told me she would allow me to publish this book and thus it is here before you. I believe the story has a right of its own to be told, and time will now tell if my beliefs in this story were correct.

You will notice there are no chapters in this story. Each day is broken down so there already is a built in means of reading this book in segments without losing one's place. Secondly, the story is all Chapter 1 of our son's life, and under those circumstances, sub headings don't seem very necessary.

I hope you find interest in our modest tale. I hope if the story is close to you that it will tell you folks you are not alone right now. There are angels with your child and they are very good at their job.

Well dear son, you are approaching your 21st birthday. I am going to assume the best case scenario of all three of us still being together will occur on January 3$^{rd.}$ 2006.

At the time your mother and I were writing this little journal we had no idea how much joy and worry you would bring into our lives these past two decades. The joy is in how you interact with us and the world around you. You are so intelligent with such a quick wit, that I wish I had written down every funny and deep comment you have made over the years. Those words, in book form, would be a national best seller.

The purpose of this journal at the time it was written was to be a gift for you on your 21st birthday. It also gave us something to do besides worry about your surviving or not in those dark, scary, first days of your life.

I'm sure you will expect something more pronounced and no doubt commercial than just this journal on your big day, and I hope your mother and I can come up with something special besides these simple words.

After this was written, it was put on the shelf for two decades. I'm sure you remember us talking about it from time to time, but until recently, no attempt to take the notes and pieces of paper and turn them into a story was made by either your mother or me.

I imagine it was because it wasn't yet time. I think it also had to do with not choosing to bring up some old sorrows as the years went by and you were filling our hearts with so much joy.

I used the word "worry" a little bit ago. I know you think we worry way too much about you. Every day you are at college, your mom and I pause consistently throughout our day, wondering what you are doing and worrying if you are all right as well as happy. Your initial birth into this world ignited these feelings, and perhaps after you read this journal you will understand just how we ended up being such "worry warts".

You see Timothy, we started out worrying about you and we have had so many years of practice that it's hard to break the habit now that you are an independent young man.

For years I pictured this journal with the name "A Letter to Timothy". The name was appropriate since the entire journal was written as a very long letter to you explaining your first remarkable months in this world. Now that mom has given me permission to share this story with everyone, I believe a new title would be more appropriate for this story.

I have chosen "Angels on the Ninth Floor" because that is exactly what you and all your little friends were back then. You were all little angels needing the help of some remarkable and gifted individuals to help you all stay in this world. I also believe there were many of God's angels in that room with all of you; helping you tiny little people make it through another day.

I also believe all the many doctors and nurses who helped you survive those perilous days also are angels. So you see, my dear son, there was nothing but angels on the ninth floor back then.

When I first started typing this journal I thought about re-writing and editing the piece. Twenty years and a million words hammered out on typewriters, word processors, and computers have tightened up my writing since 1985. I left things as they were in these letters however. I think leaving the words and thoughts as we depicted them at the time, is more important than being grammatically correct or having the right syntax. I hope you find this story readable. I hope it makes you understand better why we consider you such a special gift, and most importantly, I hope it tells you why your mother and I have loved you since the moment you were born-so prematurely that is.

Your mother and I were wed in the year 1979. I was 31 years old and mom was 28. Starting a little late in life, we decided to try and have children after only a few years of marriage. We soon found out the possibility of having children wasn't very good. Your mom infrequently ovulated and had been examined by many specialists, including doctors at Northwestern Memorial Hospital, who could not come up with any answers for your mom's problems.

We checked into adoption, but agencies told us it could take several years and we would probably end up being rejected because I would be near 40 years old, and for some strange reason, 40 was a cutoff point for adoptive parents.

In 1983, your mom went to a different kind of doctor. Dan Freesmeier, a chiropractor, also dabbled in Kinesiology, Dan told mom her problem might be an imbalance in her body that could be corrected through vitamin therapy.

In November of 1983, your mother went to Dr. Joe Pineda and he confirmed your mother was indeed pregnant. You have no idea how happy your mother was with this news. I smiled in shock after having five years of people telling your mom she couldn't get pregnant, that something as simple as having her body in harmony was all she ever needed to do.

The winter of 1983 was the hardest time your mother and I ever faced. My father died as did mom's grandmother on the same day, December 13th. Couple these sad events with your mother breaking her foot in early December. Her having to clop around at two funerals made the Holidays not very merry that year.

In January of 1984 your mother had a miscarriage. Somewhere in the tenth week or so, the embryo detached from the uterine wall and disintegrated. Dr. Pineda performed a D and C on your mother and found nothing to show why the miscarriage had occurred. It seemed that we had just been destined to live without children as the long cold winter continued.

In the early summer of 1984, your mother again became pregnant. In the early months we remained guarded against becoming overly optimistic that the pregnancy would last. This time the first six months of the pregnancy were perfect. Your mother was feeling good and getting bigger. You had a strong heartbeat and I remember so clearly going to lunch with your mother as she excitedly showed me the pictures of the sonogram she had gotten that day at Dr. Joes. It was then I decided you were going to be a girl.

Your mom was going through a model pregnancy until Wednesday: December 19[th.] 1984. That day is when your story began.

The Journal Begins

Dear son:

Your mother and I have decided to write this letter or journal as it were, so that you might better understand us and have full knowledge of what happened to you in the early days of your life. The events, occurring right now, will of course not be remembered by you. They are events however which will never be forgotten by us.

Perhaps writing this journal will reinforce our hopes and beliefs that you will in fact survive the next few weeks and come home and grow up and old with us. Maybe it just gives us something to do rather than just watch, and sit, and wait, to see if you will live.

As we write down these words I wonder how long this diary will be. Will it be enough to fill a book? Or as we write this, will a doctor come down the hall to tell us there are no more pages to be written on your life?

I hope the day will come when you are old enough to read this and understand your story. There are so many possibilities that I understand that even hope cannot be a given. A decade from now, or perhaps two, might find you as a young man but will I still be alive? Will Mom? So many things must go right to make the presentation of this on your twenty-first birthday meaningful for all three of us.

All I can say is, in the event the year 2006 does not find the three of us together I hope whoever is alive can remember that in January of 1985 we were together. For at least that one moment in time, we were a family and we loved each other more than anything or anyone else in the world.

Prelude:
Mom's Journal: Dec.19th. 1984

Three months before your projected birth date.

I had lunch at the Chinese restaurant that afternoon and was uncomfortable all day after that. I told myself I was having bad gas from the Chinese food and left work early and went home to lie down in bed. I didn't think at the time there was anything wrong with the baby. Dad came home and he was worried. After everything going so well, my backache and stomach cramps had him very concerned about you. I decided I was going to see Dr. Pineda in the morning to get checked out.

I didn't sleep much that night. I called Ron, my boss at work, and told him I would be late. At the doctor's office, I made an appointment with Nancy for 11:00 a.m. On the way out, I talked to Janet the nurse, and told her I was uncomfortable and having a full feeling, like everything was trying to come out. I told her I wanted to be checked before we went up to Chicago for the Christmas Holidays.

At work I couldn't get comfortable no matter how I tried to sit as I waited for my appointment time. I feared something was wrong with my baby and I needed to know there was still a heartbeat in my womb. At the exam Dr. Joe said he could hear your heartbeat. My relief ended quickly when, with concern in his voice, he said he wanted to do a further check on you. When he checked me, I could see his face become grave. He looked over at Janet and told her I was completely effaced. At those words, Janet also had a concerned look on her face. I asked Dr. Joe what effacement meant, but he said he would be right back and left the room without an explanation.

In a few minutes, he came back in the room and explained to me what effacement was, and what it meant. In effect, it is a changing of the shape of the uterus, and occurs just before dilation. Dilation occurs just before birth, so it obviously was a serious problem.

The effacement meant I needed to rest completely to not cause myself to go into labor, so Dr. Joe advised me a long car trip up to Chicago wasn't a good idea. The news made me very sad, and I was worried about calling and telling my mom. I wanted to see dad right away and knew I was going to cry the minute I saw him. He must have known I wasn't going to be able to come into work to talk to him, because he was waiting for me outside work as I pulled up in the car.

I told him what Dr. Joe had found, but I also believed it was problematic and not a desperate situation. I was fully prepared to quit work and just lay down for two or three months to prevent your being born prematurely. I told myself there was no blood, as with the previous miscarriage, so I believed every thing would still be all right if I was careful. Dr. Joe said you had a very strong heartbeat and the kicks and movements inside me proved I had a living baby. I was determined not to have a miscarriage this time, and was going to do whatever I needed to keep this baby alive. I went home and lay on the bed determined to keep you inside me.

Mom's Journal: Dec. 20th. 1984

Thursday night I couldn't sleep. My stomach hurt with cramps no matter how I laid in bed. I stayed awake most of the night and fought back the need to go to the bathroom. I was afraid to get up because I might find some blood in my urine. I think I thought if there wasn't any bleeding then I would be, you would be, O.K.

At 6:00 a.m. I finally got up to go to the bathroom and I felt the sensation of water running down my legs. It wasn't a big gush and I wasn't positive it was my water that broke, but I had a sad feeling that it was.

I tried to make myself think I was just having trouble controlling my bladder because I hadn't gotten up during the night to go to the bathroom, although I needed to.

I found myself with a strange "flat" feeling. Not really scared, but just sort of detached from the whole importance of what had just happened. I think I was pretty calm as I sat on the end of the bed and told dad I thought my water had broken but wasn't sure. I could see in dad's eyes that he thought it was over and that you were gone.

Dad quietly asked me what I thought we should do and I told him I thought we should go to the emergency room at Abraham Lincoln Hospital just a few blocks away. We both quietly and calmly went about getting dressed. We both thought the same thing. We both thought this last, best chance to have a child was over.

I asked if we should call ahead, but dad told me whoever was on duty would know what to do and that we should just get over there.

The short drive was without conversation as dad pulled up to the emergency room door, let me out, and went to park the car. Walking in,

I told the clerk what had happened, and she called a paramedic on duty to ask for an opinion on whether I should be sent to the E.R or up to Maternity. The paramedic thought Maternity a better choice as he grabbed a wheelchair for me to sit in.

Dad was at my side by now. The clerk told dad to go to Admitting, but the paramedic, perhaps understanding the finality of the situation, told dad he should go up with me first to see what was going to happen.

The nurses in Maternity immediately put me in a room and told me to take off my clothes as they hooked up a fetal contraction monitor to my stomach. The nurse picked up my underpants from the floor and left the room. Dad, trying to lift my spirits, whispered that the nurse had stolen my underwear. I knew they had taken my underwear to see if the fluid was in fact embryonic. It was.

I began contracting every 3 to 4 minutes and had it explained to me that those full uncomfortable feelings I had since yesterday were probably contractions as well.

Dr. Joe arrived by 6:30 a.m. and examined me right away. He said that at least I wasn't dilating yet and paused. I could see he was contemplating what actions he should take to help the situation. I don't remember thinking anything. I sat there just wondering what they were going to do with me.

I remember Dr. Joe was upset with what happened. Until now we had both believed we had a strong chance at this pregnancy being normal and going all the way. When Dr. Joe left for a moment I asked the nurse if he had said. "Oh shit" when he had examined me. The nurse trying to be proper said, "Something like that".

I was given an IV right away to try and stop the contractions. Dr. Joe, coming back into the room, told us he was sending us to St. John's in Springfield because, in the event I was going to deliver an extremely premature baby, he wanted me to be near neonatologists.

Dr. Joe said the obstetrician isn't that important in this case, but that you had to live, and Lincoln just didn't have the necessary facilities. He had called St. Johns to let them know I was coming and he told us about the doctors who I would see when I got there. He was really funny, because after he explained about the doctors and how good they were, he felt it was necessary to "warn" me that Dr. Amankwah was black. He didn't want me to be upset or shocked when I first met him. I laughed and told him to remember I was from Chicago. Dad said something about the name having already given his nationality away.

Waiting for the ambulance to set up, dad went to get some coffee and call in to work. I thought the contractions were lessoning from the medicine they were giving me and was feeling better when dad went out of the room.

I became faint right after he left, and Dr. Joe decided to give me some oxygen. When dad came back I had the oxygen mask on and looked all hot and sweaty. I tried to open my eyes to signal to dad I was alright. Dad later told me he thought you were coming right there and then.

The fetal monitor they had put on me made us both nervous. When you moved, the monitor went crazy. Sometimes it would be very loud and distinct and then we wouldn't hear your heartbeat at all. Then we would again, and then your heart beat would disappear. We didn't know at the time your movement away from the area of the monitor was causing this, and that it didn't mean something was going wrong with you.

Dr. Joe waited with us for the paramedics to come up and get me. As they picked me up to place me on the gurney, I was so stiff, I was afraid they were going to drop me. Once on the gurney, they covered me with a blanket and wheeled me out of the room. The gurney seemed very wobbly and I kept thinking I was going to fall off the side.

Placed in the ambulance, I remember wanting dad to ride with me but the paramedics ushered dad to the cab of the ambulance so that one of them could monitor me on the ride to St. Johns. I believe the two paramedics were not especially fond of each other, and there was a tenseness in the air besides that which your father and I already had.

The ride was extremely bumpy, like riding in the back of an old truck. I was disappointed dad had to ride in the front of the ambulance because I couldn't talk to him. I was worried about dad being worried, and wished I could tell him that you were still with us. I could feel you moving around and kicking up a storm inside me, so I knew you still lived. I knew dad thought you were gone, and I wished I could tell him not to give up hope…not just yet.

9

My first visions of St. Johns were nothing but ceilings as the paramedics wheeled me quickly to Labor and Delivery. I saw people moving and swirling about me as I went through the corridors. Twice I closed my eyes as I was wheeled through the hospital bringing worried questions if I was alright from the paramedics.

When we got to Labor and Delivery, the first nurse I saw looked very familiar. I asked if she was from Lincoln, and she told me she was a member of the same Weight Watchers group I was in over a year ago.

That nurse and everyone else we came in contact with at St. Johns were as attentive and supportive as could be, and I found myself relaxing knowing that I and you were getting the best care.

A female resident by the name of Dr. Samuelson was the first to examine me, and to my relief she said I still had not dilated. She made me nervous however, when she said she thought she saw something unusual in my uterus. She called it a "septum" and it was obvious she wasn't too sure about what that meant to my condition. She briefly took a look at you with a sonogram and advised me she would wait for Drs. Chapman and Amankwah before anything else would be done. A septum is medical jargon for a blockage or wall. Seeing one inside my womb, of course, wasn't exactly a good sign and from the resident's expression, it is not commonplace.

It seemed like hours before Dr. Chapman showed up. Dad tried to reassure me that his not showing up immediately was a good sign that no one was especially worried about what was happening.

When Dr. Chapman came later that afternoon, I immediately became comfortable with him. Dad joked that maybe you were a girl because he couldn't see anything between your legs when they did a sonogram. I thought I saw something, but perhaps it was just a part of the umbilical cord, so I didn't make a guess on whether you were a tiny boy or girl in serious trouble. This was the first time I actually thought you might be a boy because I had so many dreams and premonitions of you being a girl, that I considered it a fact without knowing for sure.

Dr. Chapman acted as if there would be no emergency and explained that the Tributalene IV was to stop or slow down the contractions to prevent your premature birth. He explained the many things that could have caused the water breaking so early, and told me sometimes there is no way of knowing what went wrong until after the delivery. He said they were going to watch for fever and infection and told me he hoped I would not go into labor for several weeks. He explained how each day I could stay pregnant was another day for you to grow bigger and stronger, and have a better chance to live.

That night Dr. Amankwah stopped by. He was very kind and I also immediately liked him. He asked some questions about my family, probably to see if there was something genetic in what had happened to me. He also told me that every day of time that we could give you to grow was going to be important for your chances of survival.

Dad's Journal: Dec 20th

Mom pretty well tells the story of that day. All I want to add is it was a day of real lows and highs for me. I guess I had always feared something happening to you. Our first miscarriage, so early in term, had been tough. But it had happened so fast that we didn't have as much time to mourn the lost possibility. This time you had been our topic of conversation for over six months, and the worry that something was going to happen, coupled with the possibility of actually having a child, flowed and swept through my every waking thought. This time mom was actually getting a belly on her.

This time the empty bedroom I now felt should be turned into a nursery made the worry of something happening more poignant and the thought of another miscarriage cut deep into my heart.

That morning, I was certain that your life was going to end. I thought mom's water breaking meant you had to be born soon, and you were far too young to survive in the outside world. Later at St. Johns, I realized there was still a chance, and that the people surrounding mom gave you that best chance.

Driving home that night I remembered a day from last year. We had lost my dad and mom's grandmother. Mom hobbled about on a broken foot, and then we had the miscarriage in January. I remember dropping her off at Lincoln College and watching her walking up to the door clumping along with a cast on her foot and a now empty womb. I recall

11

never being so sad in my life. I feared I would have a more sorrowful day very soon

Mom's Journal: Saturday: Dec 22nd. 1984

I slept pretty well last night. Dad came in early this morning and Dr. Chapman came in and said they were going to move me out of Labor and Delivery to a regular room on the same floor. I felt like crying. I didn't want to move because I felt safe in that room. I knew they were taking good care of me, and you, and I just didn't want to be moved.

I told dad I didn't want to move, and he tried to reassure me that it was good news because they wouldn't be moving me if they thought something was going to happen soon.

I was moved to room 1124 and found myself with a room mate. I don't know why, but I was terribly sad that day. I also found myself getting scared when the nurses told me they needed to move my IV to the other arm. They had just done the same to my roommate and she had screamed and hollered like she was delivering a baby. I thought it was going to hurt a lot, but it didn't. My roommate must be a wimp.

Mom's Journal: Sunday Dec 23rd

Another quiet day for the both of us. I have been getting a few contractions but not very bad. Dad was rolling his eyes all day. The NFL playoff games were on and my roommate had some fashion show on and didn't think enough to let dad watch the games. Thank goodness his Bears weren't playing that day or I think he would have killed the woman wrestling the remote away from her.

Mom's Journal: Dec 24th

Contractions have started picking up again and I have been in a lot of pain today. My roommate went home, so when dad came we had the room to ourselves. When dad left that night, I had a crying spell. I know dad felt sad too. I was scared because with the contractions increasing I thought you might be born on Christmas. We had decided if you were a boy to name you Timothy Michael after the two grandfathers. We hadn't settled on a girls name yet. We thought we still had months before we had to make a final decision on a girl's name.

I stayed awake wondering if dad would mind naming you Christopher or Noel in the event you were a Christmas baby.

Your Grandma Dell called today and I could hardly talk to her because I was contracting and was terribly uncomfortable. I could hear the concern in grandma's voice and I felt bad that she was so worried about us.

I had told dad that I was getting tired of the contractions and that if I could just get some rest and relief for a little while, I could take some more bad days.

Dad's Journal: Dec 24th

I'm really worried about mom. I can't imagine lying there in bed and then getting stabbing pains every hour or two that just won't let her get any real rest. Your due date is late March or early April, so every day she gives you in the womb is a day for you to grow big enough and strong enough to live.

The toll on your mom is terrible. She can't sleep. She can't get comfortable. I find myself worrying about her as I work on getting the nursery ready for you. I find myself thinking I'm wasting my time.

Mom's Journal: Tuesday, Christmas Day

Poor dad. He said he was going to go out and get himself something to eat, but everything around the hospital was closed. He ended up with a vending machine sub sandwich with a lot of mustard, which he hates, all over it. He also got a bag of pork rinds and some baby bottles of beer from somewhere. That was his Christmas dinner. Christmas day was quiet, with no real bad contractions, and dad and I just watched television the whole day.

Dad's Journal: Christmas Day

I felt sad for mom. She is very close with her mom and siblings, and Christmas with her family is very important to her. I always got her up to Chicago for the holidays, no matter what the weather. This time, the two of us are stuck in a hospital room. In a hospital deserted for the day by as many as possible.

I had talked to my mom and expressed my concerns for Sharon and tried to explain to her that you were too young to make it if the day came soon. Grandma Mary had five children, but also had three miscarriages, one late in term, so she understood. As always, my mom said she would pray to St. Jude for help. Mom always turns to St. Jude when things look bad.

This is a very bad time of the year to have something like this happening to a person. Every radio station is filled with Christmas music and holiday cheer. As I drive back and forth from Springfield, all I do is sing along with the songs, and wipe my eyes as I wonder if I will ever be able to buy my child a Christmas present. First I'm sad, and then I get pissed off at everyone yelling Merry Christmas on the radio.

"What the hell is there to be Merry about?" I yell at the dashboard.

Mom's Journal: Dec 26th

I knew my mom was coming so I was awake early and set my hair and put some makeup on. I wanted to look like I felt good when she walked in the door. The day was a good one, and I was able to sit up and visit with mom and Aunt Norma.

Mom's Journal: Dec 27th

I finally got my hair washed. They took me on a stretcher to the shower room and had my head hang off the end of the table into the sink. It felt good, but I sure wish I could have done it myself. An entire week without standing up once was getting kind of tiring on my back, hips, legs, and everything else for that matter. The bedpan business was also getting very tiring.

Dr. Chapman did a sonogram today and let my mom and Aunt Norma watch. I was glad they got to see it. He said your head was still down, and even though I had been leaking fluid, there seemed to still be enough fluid in your womb.

I had resigned myself to the fact I would be in the hospital until you were born, however long that might be. Dr. Chapman said that if I didn't leak any more fluid for 48 hours he would let me get up to go to the bathroom. I had also resigned myself to the fact this wasn't going to happen. To myself, I realized it was going to be bed and bedpan for the duration of this pregnancy.

Dad's Journal: Sat. Dec. 28th

It was good to see Del and Norma come down for a few days and stay with Sharon. She seemed to perk up with them around, and I noticed the healing power of family had been working overtime the few days they were here. Almost on cue, mom had a couple really bad days after they went back to Chicago. The contractions were getting worse and I feared you didn't have much time left before your birth. My slogan is "one more day" but that is easy for me to say. I'm not lying in a bed getting the crap tormented out of me from a little baby not knowing it isn't time to be born yet.

Mom's Journal: Dec 29th

The Bears just won their first playoff game! Dad was so excited about the game being on today. He had been all nervous about the Bears all season, but they finally seem to be a good team. My new roommate Tina, and her husband Rusty, laughed at the state your dad was in. Dad even brought his Bears stocking cap for me to wear for good luck, and the nurses said they could hear him cheering all the way down the hall. I had a mediocre day with contractions off and on and I tried to doze during the game, but that was impossible with your father.

Dad's Journal: Dec 29th

Yeh, the Bears won a huge game against Washington and yeh, maybe I got carried away a little during the game. I believe it was from a combination of my beloved team since birth being really good for the first time since 1963, plus the need to get something else into my head besides the constant worry I have for you and your mom. Our little secret. My histrionics were staged. Your mom always chuckles when I get excited during a game so I hoped being a "nut case" today would help take her mind off her pain.

Mom's Journal: Dec. 30th

The day started out O.K. I had some "kissy faced" moments throughout the day. I guess I'm starting to wear pretty thin.

Dad's Journal: Jan. 1[st.] 1985

Things are really getting bad for your mom. The contractions are getting very bad, and more frequent, and she is just plain wearing out.

The only thing I could think of today was it is now the year 1985. That would for certain be the year of your birth. I also feared it would be the year of your death. The drives home from Springfield are getting rougher and rougher. They don't make windshield wipers for the inside of cars.

Mom's Journal: Jan. 2nd

Bad day. Contractions throughout the day and evening.

Dad's Journal: Jan. 2nd

Mom is really having trouble. She's as tough as nails, so when she tells me she can't stand it, I know no one can stand it. I'm afraid she has bought you all the time she can, but it is still way too soon.

The Day
Mom's Journal: Thursday, January 3rd 1985.

I awoke about 6:00 a.m. today. I had a feeling it was going to be another long hard day. I was having contractions already and felt really uncomfortable. I always looked forward to my bed bath and clean sheets, but today I just kept sending the nurse away. I just didn't want them to touch me right now. The contractions really hurt today, and I was really cranky. I had been in a pretty good mood up until today, but this was a much worse start then the others.

I rang the nurse's buzzer at one point and when they asked me what I wanted, I said I didn't know but I want "something". I wanted to do "something". When the nurse asked me what I wanted to do, I said I didn't know. I was starting to act pretty weird and found out later I was in "transitional labor".

Dr. Kaufman came in and did a sonogram, and said I was dilated only 1 or 2 centimeters. He didn't act like I was in serious labor and he left after the exam.

The nurses kept telling me to try and rest and to take a nap, which was really getting me mad. Mom and Aunt Norma were down for a visit, and I felt really sorry for them, especially my mom. She looked like she was in as much pain as I was just watching me.

Mom touched my shoulder once and I snapped at her to not press on me. When Aunt Norma asked me if I wanted anything, I told her I wanted to get out of here.

Besides getting really angry at my mom and aunt, in the pain, I found myself getting really angry at myself. I was thinking I wanted the hospital to do "something" and I knew what that "something" was. What I wanted, but couldn't say was for them to take the baby out of me. The thought made me sad, because it meant I was giving up on buying you more time. I didn't want to say that out loud, so I just kept asking for someone to do "something" right now

I wanted the pain to go away. I needed the pain to go away. I asked mom to call dad and he came right away.

When dad arrived, I was crying and moving all over, but I couldn't get comfortable no matter what my mom and your dad said to me. Dad looked so worried and sad, as he watched me writhe in the bed. I wanted everyone to go away so they wouldn't have to see me like this, yet I wanted them to stay with me too. The pain was causing me to be a little crazy.

Dr. Woods came in and gave me a shot, but quickly left. She said she would come back in an hour to see if the shot had helped any. I told my mom to go tell the nurses I didn't want her back in an hour, I wanted her back right now.

Finally Dr. Amankwah arrived and immediately told the staff to take me to the Delivery Room. I immediately felt relieved that they were going to help me, and I started feeling better at just the thought that someone was going to end this pain I was having.

I wasn't scared as they wheeled me down the hall. I remember thinking I might be scared when the time came, but I wasn't at all.

As I was wheeled into the delivery area, I found myself worrying about your dad. He always said he didn't know if he could stand all the blood, and I kept looking at him whenever I could, to see if he was getting pale. He had a surgical mask on, so it was hard to tell, but he appeared to be all right.

When the doctors told me to push, I tried as hard as I could, but I didn't feel like I was doing it correctly. Linda, a nurse, told me I was doing fine and I almost laughed because I didn't believe her. I only remember wondering how long your being born would take, and at being surprised how fast it actually was.

When they took you away to the table, I tried to get a glimpse of you. I was scared and the nurse made me feel better. She explained that I wouldn't hear you cry because the neonatal doctors were working on you.

I felt a huge let down and empty of all feelings. I wanted to see what was going on, but was frightened that I couldn't do anything more for you.

Dad's Journal: The Day

When I got the call from your mom, I dropped everything at work, and just drove like a mad man to St. Johns. I could tell by her voice that it was time for something to be done whether good or bad. When I arrived at the room, I could see by the looks on Del's and Norma's faces that this was it. Mom had been a model patient up to now, but as soon as I walked in the door, your mom turned to me and almost snarled at me to do something.

I waited for about a half hour as Del tells me the doctor is coming. I can't believe the pain your mom is going through right now and I am certain she is in labor.

About 4:30 p.m. Dr. Amankwah walks in the room. I understand now that the delay was the wait for Dr. Amankwah to arrive, and not for Dr. Kaufman. The nurses knew mom couldn't keep you any longer, but they were too nervous to tell you they had to wait for him to arrive. Dr. Amankwah, with Dr. Woods next to him, immediately told the nurses to disconnect mom's IV.

"This woman has always greeted me with a smile." He said. "It is time to deliver this baby."

As mom is wheeled through the hall, Dr. Chapman is chatting with a nurse at the reception desk. Mom is glad to see him and tells him it's time. Although off duty, Dr. Chapman says he is going to hang around to see what happens. That almost brings a smile to your mother's face as they continue to wheel her into the delivery area.

In the Pre-Delivery room, both Dr. Woods and Dr. Amankwah examine your mother's vagina. Blood is starting to show, and soon it is everywhere. Their hands, the sheets, your mother's thighs, are all tinged with thin pink blood mixed with the balance of your embryonic fluid.

Linda the nurse asks me if I want to be in the delivery room while you are born and I say yes immediately. She brings me a gown, a cap, and a face mask as well as plastic booties to put over my shoes.

I go into a scrub room bathroom and begin to change. I am trying to hurry, and that makes me slower than if I just calmly put the stuff on without trying to do it all in five seconds. All the while, I keep thinking how we never got a chance to take the Lamaze classes. We thought we had months to go before you were going to be born.

Struggling with the booties, I finally get them on. I note in my mind that if you have a size thirteen shoe, rather than my size twelve, you can't be a doctor because you could never get these things over your shoes.

When I come out of the bathroom, the room is empty and I start to panic as I rush into the hallway. Dr. Chapman is there and directs me to the Delivery Room and shows me the washing station. Dr. Woods is there scrubbing, and she shows me how to wash. She explains how to use the foot pedal for the water, and tells me not to touch anything, so I don't. I keep thinking that this day is far too soon. I expected these events to happen in March or April not early in January.

As Dr. Woods and I walk into the Delivery Room together, I see Dr. Amankwah is on a stool facing your mother's vagina. Mom's legs are up in the air, her feet resting in the stirrups. There is more blood now and I feel a great concern for your mother's well being. There is a table close by with surgical tools that resemble kitchen utensils more than they do what I had expected surgical tools for a delivery to look like.

Nurse Linda tells me to stand at your mom's right side by her head. I try to talk to your mom but she is too preoccupied right now to listen to my idle chit chat.

In the next few minutes, I take in the whole room. It is about 15 feet by 15 feet, with cabinets along one wall. It reminds me of a kitchen more than what I was expecting a delivery room to be like.

Four doctors come in quietly and quickly start hooking up equipment around a small three foot by three foot metal table with a warming light above it. It resembles something you would see in a restaurant having a brisket of prime rib laying on it. Dr. Chapman, who has scrubbed in to observe, comes in the room and explains the little table is for you, and that the four doctors are the neonatologists who will help you when you come out.

I remark to myself how different everything is than what I expected. It isn't how I have seen these rooms on television but this is reality I tell myself.

Mom looks really happy that Dr. Chapman is here. He is just an observer, so he spends some time explaining to mom what is happening. He is a very calm and kind person, and he seems to be able to relax your mother a little bit. Dr. Amankwah, still on the stool, tells your mom to push as hard as she can the next time she feels a contraction. Out of nowhere, your mom stops having contractions, and after a moment's pause, everyone in the room starts laughing.

To start the contractions again, Dr. Amankwah breaks your fluid sack, and it seems to me that there is syrupy water running everywhere. After he did this, your mom started contracting some and Nurse Linda tells your mom to push.

Dr. Amankwah, with no emotion in his voice, tells us he is going to take you out and grabs a pair of clamps that look like two huge spoons on a hinge, similar to a pair of ice tongs. I look over to where he is, and can now see that they have given your mom what they call an episiotomy, meaning they have cut her open as wide as possible to help get you out. Dr. Amankwah asks your mom to keep pushing while he moves the two clamps inside your mom.

Grabbing hold of you, he tells Dr. Woods you are face down and adroitly spins you around so that you are facing up in the womb. Dr.

Woods continues to cut your mom to make the opening still larger, in order to not have you be under any stress during this process.

Suddenly Dr. Amankwah takes the clamps out and reaches inside your mom with both hands and pulls you out of your womb.

You are very red, almost purple, and covered in blood. The doctors clear your nose, and quickly cut the umbilical cord. Nurse Linda, trying to keep us calm, tells us we won't hear you cry because of your size, and the fact your lungs aren't fully developed.

I have never seen anyone as small in my life as Dr. Amankwah hands you to one of the neonatologists. You are limp, with your arms and legs hanging down off the sides of the Doctor's hands, and I can see that your tiny chest is not moving. I think to myself

"That's it. The little guy didn't make it," as the four doctors furiously work on you.

'Yeh, we won't hear him cry because he's dead. I think to myself.

The four doctors are moving at a feverish pace, and I know they are trying to bring you back, but I feel a wave of finality to the ordeal entering my heart. I can see Dr. Chapman's eyes as he stands near the doctors working so hard on you. I can see in his eyes that you are not responding to treatment, and I start to direct my worry to your poor mom who looks like she was in an explosion.

Dr. Amankwah has continued to work on your mom and he has removed the placenta and holds it in his hands. I have never seen that much deep, dark blood ever, and I am scared now that your mom will bleed to death. Dripping off your mom's thighs are huge blobs of jelly like blood that slowly run off her legs and splash on the delivery room floor.

Dr. Amankwah shows me the placenta, and points to a dark, dried area. He tells me that was the reason for your premature birth. A part of your "home" had ripped away from the uterine wall, causing the distress to you. I look at it with a clinical eye. Nothing I have seen seems to bother me at all. I am here, but I am not right now. I can't explain it any better than that.

I sit down on a stool, and for the first time in my life, I worry for my family. I have a wife who has gone through something I would have expected to see on a battlefield, and I have a dead son being worked on in the corner of the room. Not a very good day I think to myself. I hold back the tears. I need to be strong right now. Mom doesn't need to worry about me right now. There is enough on her plate at this moment.

Dr. Chapman, trying to break the tension in the room, comes over to me and tells me you are a boy. I was so certain you would be a girl that I acted surprised for just a moment, until I fell back on the thought that it didn't really matter, since you weren't going to make it. I don't know why I thought you were going to be a girl, I surely wasn't hoping for one over the other. I guess I just had a feeling, a feeling that obviously was wrong. All I ever really hoped for was a healthy child and right now that looked like it wasn't going to happen.

One of the doctors working on you asks out loud for the time. For the first time he looks at me and tells me you are alive with a steady heartbeat, but had been without oxygen for five minutes. He invites me over to the table, and tells me to touch you. I place one of my fingers in your tiny hand, and immediately notice my finger is broader than your entire hand.

You are incredibly small, and your face is dark purple. Your eyes are swollen shut, and your nose is broken and pressed flat against your face. The Dr. lifts up your arms and legs, but they immediately fall back on the table, limp with no life in them. I understand he is doing a second APGAR on you.

Babies are given an APGAR test at one minute of birth, and if the score is not a seven out of ten they do it again at the five minute mark. We are told the next day your first score was a 1, and your second was a 3. Someone was a biased umpire for your first score. Looking at what constitutes points, I'm sure your first score actually was 0.

The doctor tells me his name is Khanna, and he will be in charge of you. As they wheel you out, one of the doctors is using an airbag to give you oxygen, just like the ones you would see in a CPR unit. Dr. Khanna tells me they won't know anything for several hours, and he will find us when he has news. I nod, and thank him as you are wheeled away.

They wheel you past your mom but they are in a hurry and mom doesn't get much of a chance to see you. I thought under the circumstances that might be for the best anyway.

During all of this, Dr. Woods has been busy sewing your mom back up. Dr. Woods will continue to sew your mom up for almost an hour. I look down once after about 30 minutes to see exactly what she is doing, and I am amazed. Your mom looks almost perfectly normal. Hundreds of inside stitches have brought your mother back together again, and I thought I was witnessing a genius doing the job on your poor mom.

I tell your mom how great she looks, and how good Dr. Woods is with a suture. She gives a half smile in her exhausted state, so I decide to shut up for now. She hasn't asked about you, and I am certain she feels we have lost you, as have I.

At 6:45 p.m. I decide to leave the Delivery Room and go tell Del and Norma what has happened. I go to get my shoes and pants from the other room, but they are gone. I feel silly suddenly, getting worried about where my stupid pants are, but I find a terrible urge to get out of these hospital clothes. It is as if taking them off will make the last hour disappear along with the clothes.

Del and Norma see me walking down the hall and Del rushes over to me. I tell the girls you are a boy and they both shout out congratulations. I feel a rush of anger, for I believe you are dying if not already dead, and there is nothing to congratulate me for. Grandma Del asks me if I know how much you weigh or how long you are and I tell her that doesn't matter right now.

I explain that you are in peril and your chances of living through the night were not very good. I could tell my words weren't sinking in. I calmed myself. They hadn't been there. They hadn't seen you, so the questions they were asking were all perfectly normal ones.

Del says she is going to call Grandpa Tim and Norma tells me she has a good feeling about you being all right. "I'm glad someone does" I think to myself. I step outside and smoke two cigarettes quickly. As I puff on the cigarettes, I think about a funeral for you and where you should be buried.

I tell Del and Norma I am going back upstairs, and will let them know something as soon as I find out what is happening to you. I expect our next visit will be a very sad one.

I get back to the room just in time to see your mom being wheeled out of the Delivery Room to Recovery. I see Dr. Amankwah in the hall putting his trench coat on, his work being done. He comes over and reassures me your mom will be fine, and not to worry about all the blood, as that is perfectly normal during a delivery, even a delivery as abnormal as this one was. He tells me Dr. Khanna is the best there is, and that you could not have better care right now than with him and his staff. He shakes my hand and tells me he will visit your mom tomorrow.

He is smiling as he walks away. I believe it is a smile of satisfaction knowing that he has just done all he could to help your mom and you get through this day. As he walks down the hall, I detect a small strut in his step as he goes along, and it makes me smile to myself. As I watch him go through the doors I can feel the tears streaming down my face. I go into a little hallway bathroom and just let all the emotions and feelings of the last two weeks come out.

I return to Recovery and considering what she has just gone through, mom looks real good. She can tell I have been crying and she holds my hand very tight. She tells me that you are in the best of hands, and not to worry. I tell her all about the events in the Delivery Room and I lose it again.

Del and Norma have come down the hall to see your mom. Nurse Linda comes over every fifteen minutes to check your mom's blood pressure and temperature. She recommends that mom, in her weakened condition; wait until tomorrow morning to go down to the Intensive Care Unit in the Neonatal Center. I quickly agree, believing that will save mom the further grief of seeing you before you die. Mom is exhausted and nods her head in agreement.

Mom will later tell me that she will always regret not seeing you that night. I thought it would be best in the event you died. She on the other hand, said it would have been terrible if you had died before she could see you at least once before you were gone. It looks like I was wrong on that surmise.

Within the hour, Dr. Khanna stops in the Recovery Room. He doesn't pull any punches. He tells us you are on a respirator, and there is always a danger of your tiny lungs exploding while on such a machine. There also is a problem with brain hemorrhages because of your size, and that you are also susceptible to infections, and jaundice. Either of which could be fatal.

He asks us to sign some papers that in effect turn over the decisions on life sustaining measures to him and his staff. There is no hesitancy. We both know he will do all he can, and he shouldn't have to waste any time running anything by us first. He explains that the first 72 hours will be critical in your chances of survival. In the event you can get past those first three days, your chances to survive will be much better. He explains that you presently have no real muscle response, but it is too early to tell how big a problem that is.

Dr. Khanna asks if I would like to go see you and I say yes. He says Del, as a grandparent, is allowed one visit outside of the normal visiting hours, each Wednesday night and Sunday afternoon, and she quickly says she will use that one extra visit now.

When Del and I get downstairs to the Neonatal Center we can feel the heat coming from the room and I become concerned by the sounds of all the beeps and clicks coming from so many monitors all over what the hospital calls the High Risk area.

A nurse shows us where to wash and grab a gown to wear over our clothes. When ready, we walk into the High Risk room and I immediately see several babies each attended by a doctor or nurse inside the brightly lit room. I see you lying on a table with a warming light above you. You have a respirator tube down your throat; a monitor attached to you heart, and another to your legs. You also have an IV that is stuck inside your tiny navel.

A male nurse explains all the wires and what they are for. Your arms and legs lay limp at your sides, and there is no sign of life except the movement of your chest in response to the respirator. Your head is swollen and dark purple. The nurse explains this is from the delivery process, and the fact your tiny body bruises easily right now.

Your eyes are swollen shut and huge gobs of antibacterial salve cover them. You almost look like some type of alien right now, and it is hard to believe you could possibly live through all this. The male nurse tending you right now tells us you are sixteen inches long and weigh 2 pounds 15 ¼ ounces. He advises us you will lose some weight because you won't be able to eat with the respirator tube down your throat.

He tells us the tube in your navel is to give you the nutrients you need.

I can see from Del's face that she now understands the dire straights you are in, and I put my hand on her shoulder as we silently watch the respirator push and pull oxygen to keep you alive. We leave the ward, neither of us saying anything as we go back upstairs.

Your mom is exhausted so Del, Aunt Norma, and I leave for the night. There is nothing we can do, and your mother needs rest more than she needs our sitting around trying to make small talk.

Before we leave, I call Grandma Mary and tell her all that has happened. I ask her to keep praying to St. Jude because I don't think you are going to make it.

At home I lay in bed, my thoughts running between reliving the day's events and prayers to every saint in the universe as well as God and Mary to help my little boy. I can't help believing you won't make it through the weekend. I have just met you and for just a few moments but I am certain I will miss you terribly.

Dad's Journal: Fri Jan.4th

I leave home early and get to the hospital before 9:00 a.m. Your mom is looking really good considering the day before. She told me she called down to the ninth floor about 3:00 a.m. and you were still stable. That is an instant relief to me. I had believed that if you died during the night, mom would have decided not to tell me until I got to the hospital.

Mom is anxious to see you, so we call a nurse who gets a wheelchair for mom and accompanies us down to the 9th floor. We wash up; don our gowns, and holding hands, walk into the High Risk room.

There are nine tiny babies in the ward, 7 girls and 2 boys. You are still badly bruised and I can see how sad your mother is to see you in such a condition. I try to make her feel better by telling her you already look better than you did last night, but I know the words are futile.

The respirator tube is the size of your mouth, and you look so frail and tiny as you lay there. The duty nurse explains everything to your mom and makes us both feel better by telling us she personally had a

27

preemie smaller than you, and she is now a healthy, happy, little girl. She is very kind and compassionate and of course she understands completely what we are going through right now.

Dr. Khanna comes over and gestures us to go outside. He is very honest with us. He says you are stable and that is all. He says he sees nothing problematic happening outside of what he explained to us last night. He gives us no false hope, nor fears. He says you are doing as expected. Nothing better. Nothing worse. I respect his honesty and thank him as we leave.

Mom and I go back up to the 11th floor and I can see how sad she is. You are no longer a baby who was taken out of her and whisked away. She has seen you, and found deep love for you in just a few minutes. The two of you have bonded. The question is for how long. Sadly and quietly we both just sit in the room.

Around 3:00 p.m. we go back down to the 9th floor. We had to wait a few hours because the doctors said they were too busy with some of the babies to have visitors till then. When we got off the elevator I got very dizzy and almost fainted. Mom says I went chalk white and the nurse agreed with mom that I needed the wheelchair more than Mom did. I didn't wait for the chair and went over to the window to catch some fresh air. I cranked the window open and stuck my head out into the frigid, crisp air. I chalked up the dizziness to little sleep and gallons of coffee. For a moment, I feared I might be having a heart attack, which would be just the last straw for your poor mom.

After about 15 minutes I felt better, and mom and I scrubbed up and went into the ward to see you. Inside, Brenda the nurse who had the preemie herself, said you were trying hard to breath on your own and that the respirator was only doing about 1/3 of the work right now. A blood gas exam showed your lungs were working fairly well for a baby your size, and the news cheered us up significantly. She told us we could touch you and we did so very tentatively. You are so soft and frail, I find myself fearful of hurting you, even with just a soft touch from my hand. Brenda says its good to talk to you, and that you will begin to form familiarity in our voices. We talk to you but it seems so strange right now.

When we get back upstairs, Del and Norma are waiting and mom tells them about your trying to breath on your own. With the two girls there, I decide to go back to work, check some things, and to go home and try and get some rest. Work is hard, as everyone wants to know everything, and I have to keep telling the same thing over and over. After an hour at my desk, I go home exhausted from the last few days.

I go to bed, but I just lay there, my brain too active to find any rest. About 10:30 your mom calls and says you had an episode of apnea, which means you stopped breathing. The nurse said as soon as she shook you, you started breathing again. The Doctors asked for approval to do a spinal tap to make sure there wasn't an infection that caused the apnea. Mom says you are otherwise stable as I say goodnight. Now for sure I can't get to sleep.

I go into the unfinished nursery and sit down on a five gallon bucket of plaster. I cry very hard believing there is no hurry to finish your room.

Dad's Journal: Sat. Jan. 5th

I went into work today to make sure everything is all right. Tom Ashley, the owner, has been great about the entire deal. He appreciates me coming in, but anytime I feel compelled to leave is just fine with him. He is being a true friend to me as well as employer. Your mom called and said you were still stable but had lost a couple ounces. The staff had told us to expect this, but it still gives cause for worry.

You got a group special from the Catholic Church today. You were Baptized and given The Last Rites as well. Not many people can say they received two sacraments on the same day but you will be able to.

They have taken you off the respirator and placed you into a little crib with an oxygen tent to help your tiny lungs work easier. Dr Khanna says this is very surprising, and the news cheers us up immeasurably because the doctor is not one to give false hope. He said he expected you to have to be on a respirator for four or five weeks. The probability is you were a few weeks farther along than estimated. You officially will be considered between 8 and 10 weeks premature from now on. Dr. Khanna brings us down to earth by saying you are stable. Nothing more, nothing less.

He tells us you might be able to start eating in a couple days, which is of great concern to us. You continue to lose weight, quickly approaching only two and a half pounds. The doctor explains a part of the weight loss is because of all the fluid loss with the swelling in your head and body going down. Your head is only 2/3 the size it was a few days ago, and you are starting to look like a tiny human rather than something out of a science fiction movie.

You also are starting to have muscle movement in your arms and legs. For the first time we hear you cry. It is such a tiny cry that it sounds like you are next door rather than right in front of us. We talk to you, and try to get you to stop crying. It breaks our hearts to hear your tiny voice, since we can't hold you and comfort you.

I go back to Lincoln to pick up Grandpa Tim at the train station and drive him to the hospital. Mom goes down with him to see you, as Del, and Norma and I wait in mom's room. Del says the first thing grandpa will say is that you look good and that you aren't that small. Sure enough, as soon as Grandpa Tim came back that's what he said. It was the first good laugh I and your mom have had in a long time. I laughed even harder when I saw the look on Grandpa Tim's face thinking we all must be crazy.

Dad's Journal: Sun. Jan.6th

I arrived at the hospital around 10:00 a.m. The doctors had said that perhaps Mom could go home today, but as soon as I came in the room I knew she had been released. She stood there fully dressed and packed, just waiting for me to get there. Considering what she had gone through these past few weeks, she looked really good. Mom wanted to walk out, but a nurse told her she was required to wheel her out to the front door as part of officially being released from the hospital. As soon as we reached the front door, mom got out of the chair and we walked back in to visit you on the 9th floor.

Brenda the nurse said you were doing real well and are in a 32% oxygen environment. I ask when they will start feeding you and she says in a day or two. I worry about your weight loss and not getting any real food, but I tell myself these people are experts, and if they're not worried, it's silly for me to be.

Your head bruises continue to subside and your poor nose is starting to straighten out, but you are so tiny and incredibly thin, that I still fear for your well being. We are talking to you a lot now, and we aren't as tentative with touching you as we initially were. Your mom and I have this sinking feeling about going home and leaving you here, but you are in the best of care and we sure couldn't help you as much as these people if we took you home with us.

That afternoon, I watch a little football, as your mom dozes on the couch. A normal family except for the fact we have a two pound baby.

Dad's Journal: Jan. 7th

Your mom got up at 2:00 a.m. and 6:00 a.m. to pump her breasts to try and get a little mother's milk for you. It's hard, and she is having a tough time getting much, since your premature birth didn't give her a chance to get her body into a lactating mood. Still, the nurses say her milk would be better than anything they could give you, so she will pump her breasts until they fall off if it will give you even one ounce of what you need.

Your mom and I had a fitful night's rest. We remarked to each other how we had strange dreams that were lost to us as soon as we woke up, save the fact that they were odd. Your mom called the hospital this morning, and was told you were a good little guy during the night, but your weight had slipped down to 2 pounds 5 ounces. This new drop in weight really upset me to the point your mom called the hospital back to ask when they would start feeding you. I can't go four hours without eating something, so I couldn't imagine what it must be like for you now in your fourth day without food.

Work went easy today, and at lunch time I came home to check on your mom. She is a lot sorer than she was yesterday and realizes now that it will take some time for her to get back to normal. After all, Dr. Woods said she used approximately 200 stitches to sew your mom back together. We sit in the living room, and quietly sort out our thoughts. I tell your mom that you are on my mind so much that it seems like I'm looking at the world through a transparent picture of you.

Later in the afternoon, your mom called me at work to say Dr. Khanna called when he heard of our concerns regarding your ever diminishing weight. Laughingly, she said he told her you were overweight at birth and it was good that you lost the ten ounces you did. Those ounces were birth fluid ounces, and now you were getting down to your actual playing weight, which they will now try to stabilize. Your mom made me hopeful when she said they might start feeding you tomorrow.

Mom has her first breast milk to give to the doctors for a culture and we bring that with us on our visit. When we arrive at the ward that evening, a young girl behind the desk asks your mom if she is your grandmother. I laugh heartily as the young girl back pedals by telling mom she looks too healthy to have been the mother who went through such an ordeal. Actually she does.

When we go in the High Risk room, you are naked and on your stomach. You look pitiful. Your legs are up, and tucked under your belly, and you look no bigger than a bullfrog as you sleep. Right down the middle of your back is a perceptible line. On the left you are jaundiced, on the right, bright pink.

They have a pair of white cloth sunglasses over your eyes to prevent any eye damage from the bright yellow light being used to cure your jaundice. In my mind, as I look at you, I cross the line and I love you with all my heart with no reservations. I no longer can accept your not living and coming home with us. I look at your mother's face and I can see she too can no longer hold back any reserve. She too is committed to loving you the rest of her life.

A nurse tells us you are on 23% oxygen and breathing well. We watch as she takes you out of the incubator and weighs you. You come in at a whopping 2 lbs 4 ½ ounces. As she is weighing you, she tells us tomorrow you will start to get real food. That makes me feel better. I know everyone here is an expert giving you the best possible care, but in the back of mine mind, I keep worrying that you are starving and just too little to complain about it.

We take some pictures of you, and when we put our hands in the tent, your little hand gives pressure on our fingers for the first time. Before we leave, we stop and say hi to Rusty and Tina, your mom's old roommate. Tina is going home tomorrow for a couple of weeks as her contractions have gone away, at least for now. This is the third time Tina has had to be hospitalized to stop contractions. Fortunately for her and her baby, the staff was able to do so. We both promise to watch out for her and her return. We understand we will be visitors to the hospital for many months. At least we hope so.

We stop and say hello to everyone who helped your mom in December, and we go home feeling the best we have since this whole ordeal started in mid December.

Dad's Journal: Jan 8.th

Good day for the whole family. They have taken you off oxygen and there is only a small tube in your mouth called a gavage tube. They are feeding you 3cc of formula every four hours. It is an incredibly small amount, but a nurse explains that in your tiny state, eating even that small bit of sustenance makes you exhausted. Mom holds you in the incubator and you can just see the hope that you will make it flowing into her. We again take several more pictures as we decide they will be important for this journal. A nurse named Monica says you are doing great and already you are the leading candidate of all the babies in High Risk of getting moved to Intermediate Care. The drive back home with Monica's words still repeating themselves in our minds makes for a happy night at home.

Dad's Journal: Jan. 9th

They have moved you into the Intermediate Risk area. Basically what that means is there is now one nurse for every four babies, rather than one nurse for every baby. Your face is getting much better, with your nose almost looking normal, and only a faint bruise here and there to remind us of how beat up you were that first day after birth. Your weight holds at 1000 kilograms or 2 pounds 3 ounces which is a positive sign. You have stopped dropping weight, and your feeding has been changed to 3 cc of formula every three hours. Just so you understand. Three cc's is about half of a teaspoon.

I see your mother having her head down resting on your incubator and I can see the floor is wet. I ask her what's wrong, and she says you are so little compared to the other babies here in Intermediate Care. They are all around 4 or 5 pounds, and look like giants when compared to you. She says at least in High Risk all the babies were tiny and you seemed to at least fit in with them.

In this ward you look so tiny and helpless, that it's just too much for your mom to bear. I leave her to cry things out. Sometimes you can only build so much up inside yourself, and then you have to just let it go. It's happened to both of us before, so I just stand and wait for the sadness to cleanse itself from your mom's heart.

It does cheer mom up that you are so animated tonight, moving your hands and legs just like regular babies do. At one point you actually lift your belly off the matt with your legs. I tell your mom, although still tiny, you obviously are stronger than before and she half smiles in agreement. We talk to you and tell you it is starting to snow, and that there is a forecast of a bad snowstorm for Central Illinois, so we might not see you tomorrow night.

On the way home, your mother and I both agree that if a thousand preemies were lined up in a row, we could still pick you out. You are developing your own little characteristics, and we both agree your appearance is so burned into our minds that we could never be fooled into thinking some other baby is you. You are most certainly our son, and we want you to live most desperately.

Dad's Journal: Jan. 10th

We had a good snowfall last night, about four inches. The roads were good however, and we were able to still visit you. You were resting very peacefully, and hardly moved during our visit except once to stretch. You looked so funny, as your entire body seemed to stretch out all at once. You had one of your feet resting on the incubator glass and I reached in and placed it down on the little bed. As soon as I removed my hand, you put it right back where it was. I guess this was your first exercise in showing us your independence.

Barbara, the nurse, says you are now at 4 cc of formula every three hours, and are having no problems with your food going down, or spitting it back up. She advises us you are now on full strength formula rather than half strength. Neither I nor your mom knew this until now.

You have stabilized in weight, but have yet to gain any, and your mom is starting to worry along with me about your not getting bigger. Mom leaves a little music box that is inside a pillow, sent by your Aunt Patsy and Uncle Tim. The nurses tell us from time to time they will wind it up for you to listen to. The drive home is upbeat, and when we arrive at the house, your mom starts to pump her breast again. She still isn't getting much, but right now you don't need very much.

Dad's Journal: Jan.11th

It snowed most of the morning, and then became bright and sunny, but it kept getting colder, and the streets are a sheet of ice tonight. Your mom calls me at work to tell you you have gained an entire ounce, and are back up to 2 lbs 4 ounces. You had another case of sleep apnea, but as soon as they shook you, your breathing started right back up. The nurses tell your mom apnea is a common problem in babies your size and I tell your mom now that we can stop worrying about your losing weight, we will start worrying about your apnea.

Early in the evening, a friend of ours calls, advising us I-55 to Springfield is in terrible condition, with ice everywhere. Your mom understands that our being in a car wreck is the last thing we need right now, but she sobs heavily. She has all day to think about seeing you at night, and although she agrees the drive is too dangerous, she misses you very much.

The fact you gained weight, which was my biggest worry, gives me a solid, sound night's sleep for the first time in a month. Your mom on the other hand had to get up at 2:00 a.m. to pump her breasts again. The culture on her milk came back and the nurses told her she can start bringing in her milk very soon.

Dad's Journal: Saturday, Jan. 11th

The doctors advise us you had a brain scan and everything looks all right. One of the biggest problems with preemies is damage to the brain, because your blood vessels are so tiny. The fact you didn't breathe for five minutes, also can give cause for concern. The test results still let lose a series of demons I have had in the back of my mind. I realize now I have not only had a great fear of your not living but of your being healthy mentally as well.

Dad's Journal: Jan.12th

You have gained another ounce today, but you have a tiny wooden board on your left arm to help hold an I.V. in place. They have removed your sunglasses, as the threat of jaundice has dissipated, and that brings relief to both of us. You keep opening and closing your eyes and it looks like you are trying to focus on the world around you. The nurse says it's too early for that, but you can discern shadows and lights right now. One of the nurses comes over and calls you a scrawny wild man. It seems you kick up a real fuss when its time for you to get a sponge bath. She tells us you are up to 5 cc of pure formula every three hours, and you are digesting the formula very well.

Dr Khanna is on duty tonight and his now common, no bones about it report, tells us you are doing reasonably well. He tells us that your brain scan did show some bleeding had occurred in your left lobe, but that it was common to see some bleeding in both lobes. He did perk us up by telling us both sides of your brain looked well formed, with no distinct abnormalities. When we get home, Grandpa Tim and Grandma Del are there, since tomorrow is grand parent's day. The four of us go out to eat a normal meal with your progress being the only topic of discussion at the table.

Dad's Journal: Sunday, Jan. 13th

The four of us go to the hospital and let grandpa and grandma go first, as they only allow two visitors at a time. Grandparents are only allowed visitation on Sundays between 1:00 and 2:00 p.m. and Wed. nights between 7:00 and 8:00 p.m. and that is why they came down this weekend.

While your grandparents are visiting you, I walk down the hall craving for a cigarette. Off to the right, away from all the beeping and bright lights, I see a baby all by itself in one of the rooms. Its head is almost the size of its body, and although not a doctor, I understand the child has hydrocephalus. The baby is looking at me, but it is obvious it isn't seeing me. With all your problems, I know you are in better shape than this poor little child. I say a prayer for the baby and I ask God why there has to be a need for the 9th floor at St. Johns. I'm not questioning His decisions. I'm just telling Him I don't understand any of this.

You are really active today, have gained another half ounce, and now come in at a burly 2 pounds 7 ounces. Your mom tells me she can see the 3 ½ ounce weight gain, but she must have better eyes than I do. You smile today for the first time when we start talking to you and that is like the first ray of sun after a violent storm. It is improbable you smiled because you heard us, but it is something special that your mom and I will never forget.

I softly rub your tiny head and you seem to really like that. The nurse tells mom she can change your diaper, and she does a pretty good job through the hand holes of your incubator in her first attempt. You are so small. I smile at your little butt. A butt so tiny, it could easily fit into the palm of my hand with plenty of room to spare. Your penis looks a mess right now, all black and blue and covered in gobs of antiseptic gel. I laugh to myself that I can add your having an ugly penis to my list of worries regarding your health.

Afterwards, Grandma Del says you look great compared to last week, and looking at the pictures, we all agree you have made a remarkable transformation in your first week on Earth.

When we get home, I start to work on your nursery again for the first time in almost a month.

Dad's Journal: Jan. 14th

You are up to 2 pounds 8 ounces today. Mom chides me because I can't see the weight gain like she can, but I tell her I'm relieved you are getting bigger and that is enough for me. They are feeding you 10 cc of pure formula now every three hours. Ten cc's is the same as one whole tablespoon in case you were wondering.

Mom winds your little music box and it appears you are listening to it. Mom wonders if you are able to recognize our voices yet because you seem to respond to them so positively. I scratch your head and nose for you very softly, and as before, you really seem to enjoy this a great deal. Every time your mom or I do this, you seem to relax and smile.

I tell you I have gotten back to work on your room and not to worry. I will have it all done before you come home. You seem tired today, and one of the nurses tells us you kicked and fussed about all afternoon and are just worn out from the activity. On the way out we ask about an apnea monitor, which one of the other families who had a preemie went home with this week.

The machine sets off an alarm in the event you stop breathing when we aren't with you. A nurse tells us not to worry about that now, as apnea sometimes disappears after a preemie gets to be about 4 pounds or so. The conversation is a positive one. We are talking about when you come home with us, not if you will come home.

Dad's Journal: Tues. Jan. 15th

You are gaining weight on the fly. Another 2 ounces gained puts you at 2 pounds 10 ounces. I have to admit to mom I can now see the difference. You almost have a little meat on your scrawny arms and legs. Mom says your neck will be thick like mine and I agree since I am positive you look just like me, without the bruises of course.

While we are there, your apnea bradycardia monitor goes off and mom starts crying. The nurse tells us it sometimes goes off when your movement disturbs the wires, and that you are just fine. Mom is terribly nervous about your apnea now. She is so tired from working and making the drive, plus getting up every three hours to try and get her breasts to produce enough nourishment for you.

She wishes she could hold you as do I. We have so much love for you, but can't physically demonstrate it right now, and that is tough. Instincts tell a parent to hold their child, and right now we can't do that. We have visions of holding you and feeding you. I picture you and me wrestling on the floor, and playing catch, and my helping you do homework. All these things I pray for every moment of every day.

Dad's Journal: Jan. 16th

A female doctor named Gonzalez talks to us today. She tells us you are doing "good" and are out of the woods concerning infection and jaundice. She says they have to continually monitor you for possible brain damage and pneumonia but that right now, all is well with you.

Dr. Khanna also stops by and for the first time he seems upbeat while he talks to us. Always very grave and deliberate with his conversation, the doctor doesn't even discuss you. Instead he goes on with a little diatribe how clothing companies that make clothes for preemies have a real racket going with the prices they charge for such tiny clothes. As he starts to leave, he smiles and tells us you are doing a good job. Those words from him mean the world to us.

Dad's Journal: Sat. Jan. 19th

A very cold day is settling in to the area. The weathermen say we might hit 20 degrees below zero tonight. Maybe you are lucky to be in an incubator at a balmy 90 degrees right now. Grandma Mary has come down with Grandma Del and Grandpa Tim to see you for the first time. She can't wait to see you. When I got off work at 4:00 p.m., she and mom came racing down the steps to get into the car. Tim and Del stay at home because tomorrow is grand parent's day, but Grandma Mary can use her first visit today, and no one on God's green earth is going to tell her to wait until tomorrow.

Since I saw you with Grandma Del's first visit, I thought it was fair to let your mom go with Grandma Mary this time. I kidded your mom that Grandma Mary would tell us you were just beautiful no matter how you looked today. Grandma Mary is a very emotional person. She cries all the time. She cries when she is sad. She cries when she is happy. That's just the way Grandma Mary is. When she came back, I asked her about you, and she told me you were "perfect". Now that's a grandma for you. Two and a half pounds, beat to crap, and grandma thinks you're perfect.

Looking at your early pictures, I'm sure you will agree that there was a lot to be desired in your appearance. But you know, Grandma Mary's positive attitude is rubbing off on me as I have to admit you are cute. You're just so damn tiny.

For years I have always said people who walk around showing baby pictures. and telling baby stories drove me nuts. Now I find myself being a charter member with these folks. Your mom and I go around showing pictures of you, and telling stories about you to everyone we run into. The one difference, of course, is our stories are about your struggle for life, and not in trying to crawl or something else.

Tomorrow Grandmas Del, and Mary, as well as Grandpa Tim, will come back to visit you .Your Grandpa Mike of course, has died, and the fact he is not here to see you, holds a fury in my heart. A fury I don't think I will ever let go of. I hope someday I will be able to tell you stories about him. The Lakota's believe a person doesn't die until all memories and stories of the person also are gone. That is why

Indians pass on so many stories. In effect it gives a temporal immortality to people, and I like that thought. I just hope I get the chance to tell you all about him someday. Damn it. I wish he was here.

Dad's Journal: Sun. Jan 20th

27 degrees below zero, with a wind chill of 77 below. This is the coldest day in Illinois history. Grandpa Tim's car wouldn't start, so I loaned him a car from the dealership, since we all can't get down to visit you in one car. It is so cold that some of the house pipes have frozen, and we have no hot water right now. My head cold is getting worse, so I come in just to see you, but stand away from your incubator. Your grandparents take so many pictures of you; one would think you were a movie star or professional model.

The staff has moved your IV to your head to give the tiny veins in your arms and legs a chance to heal up a little bit. Mom doesn't like the looks of that at all. You have hit 3 pounds 2 ounces, but the nurse says you are starting to retain a little water, and they are going to give you something to help pass the water out of your system. I advise mom not to be disappointed if you drop a little weight, or don't gain any for a few days after you pass the water out of your body.

You have a bradycardia episode today, and Mom scolds you and tells you to stop doing that. She is very nervous about your forgetting to breath as well as your heartbeat going below 60 beats per minute every once in a while. This is her first baby and you aren't exactly what a person would call normal, so her concerns are understandable.

Dr Khanna is on duty, and he spends a minute or so with us. As we talk, the IV is taken out of your head and placed back in your left leg, which makes both your mom and I feel better. Dr. Khanna says your legs are still swollen because of a lack of protein, and an amino acid imbalance that is common in preemies. He tells us there is nothing to worry about, and that in time, your body, through nourishment, will handle the situation on its own.

Afterwards, your mom mentions how he didn't seem overly concerned with anything, and she takes that as a good sign. On the drive home I tell your mom how I can understand a woman having a closer tie to their baby than a man can have. A woman is the one who feels the baby growing inside, and I can see how women can take having a baby, and being concerned with their baby so personally over how a man can feel.

Dad's Journal: Jan. 22nd

You have stayed the same in weight, which is probably a good sign since you have been losing the unwanted fluid in your body. Your feet still look huge compared to the rest of you, but they continue to get better, so I'm not overly worried. Your mom brings in a small vial of breast milk as they now are giving that to you along with formula. Mom tries so hard, but after all day, she only has a few tablespoons worth of mother's milk to give to you. We kid about it and tell the nurses we have brought you another snack to go along with your formula.

Mom brings a bunch of cookies for the staff, and they all really appreciate the food. Mom jokes that she wants to stay on everyone's good side so you get the best care, but we both know you couldn't be getting better care anywhere.

Everyone has been moved to Nursery 5 and we laugh that you seem to have graduated with the big kids who have been your room mates for the last week. We are told you will have a brain scan tomorrow. We don't talk about it. We keep the fear of the results internally.

Dad's Journal: Jan 23rd

You are still at 3 pounds 2ounces today. You have not had a case of bradycardia or apnea in three days and that perks us up a lot. Most nights, when we come, you are sleeping but today you are restless and fussing about. It looks like the IV board, now in your right arm, is making you mad, since it restricts the movement of your arm. You keep frowning and fussing and when you start to cry mom cries as well. She says she can't stand to not be able to hold you and comfort you, and that this helpless feeling just sets her off. I told her there is nothing wrong with those emotions and she doesn't need to explain herself to me. I try and comfort her and tell her you soon will be at four pounds, which will be enough for the staff to allow her to hold you.

The ride home is quiet. Thoughts of you and praying to God that you be well fill the hour drive.

Dad's Journal: Jan.24th

You're still at 3 pounds 2 ounces, but you look good tonight and that really brightens Mom's spirits. You are on your stomach again, which seems to be your preference. You keep smiling tonight when mom talks to you, and I am convinced you recognize her voice and somehow know it is your mother talking to you. Who knows what extra sensory bond develops when two people share the same body for so many months. I just wish you had decided to share moms a little longer than you did.

Next door in High Risk, a little girl named Lisa is having a rough time. The staff tells us she is only a pound and a half right now and from the glass doorway into the room, I can see how tiny she is. I can tell the way doctors and nurses are moving around the tiny infant that she is in dire straits right now.

I find myself crying for her and her parents. I have become a member of a community that only someone who has gone through these circumstances is allowed to join. No one volunteers to be a part of this kinship, but once it happens, you develop a feeling of empathy for others that I wish I could explain to you. I only hope the day never comes where you are forced to become a member yourself. I pray that you will never be forced to understand the feelings your mom and I have right now.

Mom touches my shoulder and remarks how, for all our worries, we could have it much worse than we do. I nod in agreement, but I can't keep the tears from coming.

A nurse says it's been five days since you had a bowel movement and that they are going to give you something to help you pass a stool. I tell your mom it probably means another day with no weight gain but she already knows this. Your mom remarks how it seems like we have had you for a lifetime, and she has trouble remembering what it was like without you in our lives. I agree completely. In my mind the two of us have already grown up and older with each other. I am positive that we have known you forever.

Dad's Journal: Friday, Jan. 25th

We take a day off from visiting you today. We both need to try and get some sleep. Mom was asleep by 8:00 p.m. and I hoped she would get some needed rest. The hospital called to tell us no new problems showed up in your brain scan, and that has been a huge relief to your mother and me. You lost a half ounce, but you passed your bowels, so the weight loss makes sense. It seems so strange how we have gotten caught up in your weight gains. I can lose or gain pounds in just a day, but now we are concerned with grams and ounces as we track your personal progress.

Dad's Journal: Sat. Jan. 26th

Grandma Del and Grandpa Tim come down again for their weekend visit. I imagine they will come down every weekend until you come home. They are really something else. They already have five grandchildren but you have become special to them already, and they live for mom's phone calls every day on your progress.

The IV is in your head again and that really bothers your mom and me. I don't know why. Perhaps it's just because it looks so bad and covers your little face. You lost another half ounce, but your swelling is now almost completely gone in your feet so the loss makes sense to us.

I look in High Risk and can see little Lisa. She has wires and tubes everywhere on her tiny body to the point you can hardly see her. Mom and I have decided to include her in our prayers. Looking at Lisa, and then at you, makes us understand just how lucky we all are today. It's so strange to look at you and consider ourselves fortunate, but there it is, and yes we are.

On the way out, a nurse says you have been doing so well with eating that tomorrow might be your last day with an IV stuck in you somewhere. That little bit of news sends your mother's spirits soaring.

Dad's Journal: Jan. 27th

A good day for the entire family. They have taken your IV out, and you seem to revel in your new found freedom. Now you only have the apnea-bradycardia monitor on, and God knows we don't want that taken off of you. You are up to 33 cc of formula and mother's milk at each meal, and mom jokes that she can't possibly keep up with your eating habits anymore. Poor mom pumps herself sore but can only muster about 60 cc's a day. Still every little bit helps, and your mother is on a mission to get every single drop of milk she can for you.

This is the third day in a row you are awake when we come and you do a lot of smiling when mom talks to you. No one can convince me you don't know the voice is your mothers. You are scooting all over the incubator, especially when mom lays you on your stomach. You dig your toes in and start moving everywhere. It's so funny; we both are smiling and laughing at your antics.

Mom and I both have begun talking to you like you are a twenty year old. We tell you what's going on in our lives as well as yours. I ponder for a minute what will be the first memory of your life you will remember. I remember thinking I believed right then with all my heart you would be coming home with us someday.

Dad's Journal: Sun. Jan. 28th

Of course Grandma Del and Grandpa Tim are down. Grandma spends another roll of film taking pictures of you, and I can see through the window your scrambling around the incubator is making them smile. You haven't gained any weight again today, but you look better than ever, so we write the sudden lack of weight increase on your body continuing to replace unwanted fluids with muscle and ligament tone.

While grandma and grandpa are in with you, I look in High Risk to see how little Lisa is doing. I don't see her, nor her name on the outside wall that shows who is currently in the room. Your mom asks the desk nurse if Lisa died, and the nurse tells us she did last night.

The rest of the day is a mixed bag. We are so upbeat about your progress, but it's tempered with the fact one of God's tiniest babies didn't make it. I wonder if it had something to do with your genetic makeup, or maybe moms or mine that gave you enough strength to get this far. Did God spare you because he has plans for you later in life? Was it mom being so tough that she kept you inside her for two extra weeks when you refused to wait for your proper turn? Or were you just lucky and will you continue to be lucky. I'll never know the answer but I think it's probably a combination of everything that has gotten you to this point.

Dad's Journal: Jan. 29th

When we get to the hospital, Dr. Khanna is in the lobby having an animated discussion with several nurses. When he sees me, he calls me over and asks me if crickets have brains. I tell him I don't think they do, and believe they have a nerve response system like most other insects. He quickly asks me why then are the crickets in his house so smart. He explains to all how he can't catch them, or even find them, and they chirp all night driving him crazy.

The nurses seemed embarrassed by his story telling, but I understand. He is using the tale to break some of the tension that always pervades the 9th floor of the hospital. He has nothing to say about you, and your mother and I have learned that no news from Dr. Khanna is always good news.

When we go in to see you, you are in your favorite position, on your belly, legs tucked up into your chest. We rub your back and talk to you, but you are out cold today. The nurse tells us you weigh the same, but that plateaus in weight gain are standard fair for you little people and not to worry. She tells us once you take off again, you will be four pounds in no time, which makes your mother very happy. She talks all the time about how when you hit four pounds she will hold you all day if they let her.

Dad's Journal: Jan 30th

Real bad snow storm tonight. We get to Elkhart but decide to turn back, as the roads are getting bad in a hurry. In front of us, a dumb semi driver, going too fast for conditions, ends up with his trailer sliding completely parallel to his cab and that's enough to tell your mom and I we need to turn back for home. The daily phone call your mom makes told us you have started to gain weight again and went up an ounce.

That night I wonder if you will see life differently than so many other people do. You have been brought to life and sustained by Jews, Gentiles, Africans and Indians as well as Spanish and Chinese nurses and doctors this past month. I imagine those people have every imaginable faith in God in their lives as well. Dozens of people from all walks of life have been dedicated to helping you survive this momentous period in your life. I know I will never teach you prejudice, just like your grandfather taught me never to judge someone until you know them, but I wonder. Will you have a sense of all those around you who have helped you. Not consciously of course. But is something being instilled in you right now that will form a trust in your life for all good people regardless of race, creed or color?

Dad's Journal: Jan. 31st

Big day for your mom and me. You are up to 3 pounds, 4 ½ ounces. The nurses surprised us and said that was enough to let us hold you. I let mom go first, but if I hadn't, she would have knocked me down and gone first anyway. Sitting in a chair, a nurse handed you to mom and I never saw a person look so happy in my life. I promise you son, there was such an aura around your mother right then, that I believe I could have lit a cigarette off of it. You, of course, decided to sleep through the most important moment in your mom's life, only occasionally opening an eye to see what all the fuss was about.

When mom gave you to me, I couldn't believe how light you were. It was like holding air in my arms. I believe the staff decided today, being the end of your first month of life, deserved something special, like letting mom and I hold you. I smiled to myself, full knowing now that your mom could hold you that we would be here more than ever after today.

Your mom made cookies and brownies for all three shifts on the ward, and its fun to see everyone make such a fuss over such little things. Again I believe it is a mechanism these marvelous people use to break the tension of how serious their jobs are here on the ninth floor.

On the way out, a nurse told us you might be able to go home in two or three weeks. This sent your mother's spirits soaring as she quickly replied she thought, in her opinion, it might take a little longer.

Dad's Journal: Feb. 1st

You gained an ounce to 3 pounds 5 ounces. Mom lets me hold you first and again you sleep the whole time we both hold you. I can't help but laugh when mom tells me she can tell you are heavier than yesterday. Every once in a while the bradycardia monitor shows a distinct slowdown in your heart rate, but a doctor tells us until you go past four pounds, they don't consider the event anything to worry about.

I still worry about your heart and breathing problems, and so does mom. Its nerve racking to be on edge for your every breath and beat of your heart, and we both hope you grow out of it. Having to bring you home with a monitor will send us up the walls. I joke that I will just stand over you, and watch you until your ten years old or so to make sure nothing happens to you.

Dad's Journal: Feb 2nd

Grandma Del and Grandpa Tim come down as well as your Aunt Kathy and cousins, Jimmy and Mark.

The temperature is still very cold, hovering around zero to 10 above at the most, and I find some comfort in you not having to be out in these elements, even if just for the moments of being transferred in and out of a car. You are asleep when we get there, and stay asleep the entire time your mom and I hold you.

Dad's Journal: Feb 3rd

Today, when mom holds you, you set off the monitor several times. The nurse on duty says they wait to see if you come out of it on your own, and you always have the past few weeks. You stay awake and even when the alarm goes off, you don't seem to have any problems going about your business. The worry of you needing a monitor at home is very real to us now, and your mother and I joke that we will take turns staying up all night watching you. We don't laugh. In a way we are dead serious about actually doing so. We have both talked about SIDS, and the worry is like a fearful giant lurking over us every moment of every day. I can tell that night your mother is having trouble going to sleep as am I. We don't say anything to each other, but I know we are worried about the same thing.

Dad's Journal: Feb 4th

Another ounce gained today. We get to the hospital a little later than normal and you are awake. Monica, the nurse who had preemie twins, is on duty tonight. Mom likes her a lot because there is nothing mom is feeling or going through right now that Monica doesn't understand completely. When she takes you out of the incubator for mom to hold, she disconnects the wires to your monitor. She answers our surprised looks by telling us a few minutes without having to listen to the constant beeping will do us all a bit of good. She got that right. Mom is so happy tonight, that she just starts talking to you about the whole day.

People walking in and out look at your mom as she explains her job to you, but she doesn't pay a moments notice to anyone, as she just talks and loves you as she rocks you in the chair.

Mom must have bored you because as soon as I held you, you fell sound asleep. So much for being interested in what dad has to say.

Dad's Journal Feb 5th

You have jumped up to 3 pounds 13 ounces. You are awake for us tonight as we hold you. Monica is on duty and she turns a few lights off, and you really start to look around. Through experience, she knew your vision would improve without the bright lights glaring in your eyes. You seem so quiet and passive even with a wet diaper. I tell your mother that's a good sign that you will be a good baby for us and no doubt never cry or stay up all night. Yeh, it will be us staying up all night watching you and listening to the damn monitor.

We both tell you how our day went, and you look at us like you are taking it all in, but you can't be of course. Or can you?

Dad's Journal: Feb. 6th

When we arrived at the hospital, you had just eaten and we were told that wasn't a good time to hold you. You are starting to really look good. You are filling out, and your face actually looks a little chubby. You still have absolutely no rear end. The staff tells us as soon as you reach four pounds they will start nipple feeding you and stop giving you aminophylline for your heart.

The news, that should have been good news, makes us feel that some anxious and nervous days are ahead of us.

Mom's Journal: Feb. 8th

Today dad and I decided not to go to see you at night. We both need to get some rest. Gail Petro told me she was going to Springfield at 11:00 a.m. tomorrow and would be there until about 5:00 p. m. and she offered to drive me down and then pick me up in the afternoon. I took the day off from work so I could spend the day with you.

You look so good now. Your face has really cleared up, and there's just some small bruising in your one eyelid. You had just finished eating when I arrived, so I went to get something to eat myself while you were digesting your food.

I went up to the 11th floor to check on my old room mate Tina Vernor. She had her baby on Tuesday. A 6 lb. 11 oz. baby girl they named Kate Ashley. Tina told me she and the baby were going home tomorrow, and I had tears in my eyes because I was so happy for them, and I was relieved things had gone so well this time. I briefly saw Kate Ashley as they were bringing her in for feeding as I was saying my goodbyes.

When I came back to the room, Steve, a male nurse, wrapped you up for me and told me to sit down before he would hand me to you. Steve is always very particular about how he wraps you and is a stickler for the rules. You were awake and angry and crying a little bit.

Jan, the other nurse on duty, asked what all the fuss was about but I had no idea. When she walked away I loosened up the blanket around you a little bit so you could move around, and that made you quiet down. I think you felt a little too confined being wrapped so tight, and just wanted a little space to move around a bit.

When you dozed off, I put you down and went into the other room to pump my breasts. Up until today the milk had come out in droplets, I didn't produce any greater quantity, but the milk came out faster, almost in a spray rather than just in drops. The nurses told me it was because I had been holding you and you had been crying a little and this caused the milk to "let down" as it is supposed to.

When I was done pumping, I went back to your isolette and started wrapping you up so I could hold you again. Nurse Steve had just returned from taking a room mate of yours by the name of Gabe to radiology, and he thought I had been holding you all this time and was just putting you down. I got real defensive and explained I had put you down earlier, and now I was picking you back up again.

It was time for you to eat again so I held you while Steve put the gavage tube down your throat. You gagged a little bit, but not too bad, and Steve told me to hold the tube steady while he poured the formula into the bottle. He explained you would cough the tube out if I didn't hold it in place as he poured. The formula ran very quickly through the tube and as soon as your stomach was full, you fell sound asleep.

I just sat there holding you for the next hour and a half, watching you as you slept. Finally, I put you down in your isolette. I just stayed there watching you sleep. I finally left and waited for Gail to call saying she was ready to go back to Lincoln.

When she called, she said her and a couple of her nursing students were across the street at the Quality Inn having a few drinks. I went across and had a couple glasses of wine as we visited.

I didn't make it home till around 8:15 and felt kind of drunk although I only had three glasses of wine. I was so tired I plopped on the couch and went right to sleep.

Mom's Journal: Sat Feb. 9th

Dad and I had a short visit with you today. I let dad hold you first since I had so much time with you yesterday. You seemed sleepy and weren't very social. Monica was on duty, and I asked her about the wine I had the night before and if that would have any effect on my milk. She said no, but that night I decided to pump my breast but not keep the milk just in case. I didn't keep the first milk from Sunday morning either, just to be sure.

Your dad and I had invited Jerry and Annie Shockey, as well as Bill and Libby Turner over for dinner. Grandpa and grandma were down again of course and they helped me get things ready.

When we got home from our visit, grandma said that Monica had called to tell us after we left, she started talking to you, and you smiled and laughed out loud. It was so nice of her to call and tell us this, but I wish I could have been there to hear and see you laugh for the first time. I just can't imagine how you would sound laughing. You are so quiet and even your cries sound like they come from a little squeak toy.

Mom's Journal: Feb. 10th

You look so wonderful today. Dad and I came to see you a few minutes before grandparent's visiting hour started. I put a little sleeper on you that my friend Kelli had sent us in the mail. You looked so cute in it. A nurse came over and combed the few strands of hair you have on your head just to finish off your getting dressed up for grandma and grandpa.

You are very alert now, and stay awake for long periods. Grandma, grandpa, dad, and I visited with you the whole hour, and when other visitors for the other babies left, I asked the nurse if we could pick you up while grandma and grandpa were still in the room. She said yes, although that was against the rules. Dad held you while grandma and grandpa got a chance to see you close up.

Most of the time, it was me and grandma in the room with you. Your grandpa stayed outside looking in through the window in the door to your ward. We wanted to keep the two person rule because the nurse had already been kind enough, and we didn't want to break any more rules.

You smiled for all of us today and really looked good. When you fell asleep I went to lay you down and planned on leaving the little sleeper on you rather than disturb your sleep. I checked your diaper, and seeing it was wet, decided it was best to change you. I took the sleeper and diaper off and you didn't move a muscle. I guess I hogged changing you. I didn't ask dad if he wanted to do it, even though it was his turn.

Mom's Journal: Feb. 11th

You finally broke the four pound mark. I called in at 11:00 a.m. and Steve said you had gained 40 grams and now weighed 4 pounds 1 ounce this morning. There are predictions for a major snowstorm today for Central Illinois, so I doubt we can get to see you today. I feel all right about that because Gail is going down to Springfield for the entire day again tomorrow, and I plan on spending it with you. I tell Steve I will be down early tomorrow, and he tells me he will wait for me before he gives you your bath.

Grandma Del called just after noon, and said Chicago already had four inches on the ground. She said it was O.K. for it to snow during the week, just as long as it didn't snow on the weekends.

The storm did come, and the roads were too dangerous for a visit tonight. I called the hospital and was told you did a real good job nippling the baby bottle. This made me feel good. Another step in the process of your coming home with us had been reached

Mom's Journal: Feb. 12th

I rode to Springfield with Gail Petro, who had to teach a nursing class today, and got to the hospital around 8:30 a.m. I had told Steve I would get there early, and he asked if I wanted to give you your bath. I declined and said I would watch how he does it this time, and do it the next time myself. I assumed they were going to dunk you in a basin of water or something. It turned out all he did was wash you off with a damp washcloth. I could have done that.

At 9:00 a.m. I fed you your bottle. You did well, but were a little slow today getting all the formula down. Around 10:00 a.m. Dr. Khanna came in and said "This baby looks fine" This is the first time that he has been that positive with his words, usually telling me you look "O.K." or "reasonable". He told me he was going to move you to Newborn and explained the course of action for reducing your medication. He said if you gained an ounce a day on average you would be released in about 15 days. Although Newborn is on the 11th floor, he said he would continue to check on your progress.

I became upset at the news. I was worried that the people up on 11 wouldn't know as much as these people down on the 9th floor. I also hate change no matter what it is. The fact it seemed forever for someone to come and get you, just made me more and more nervous. I had a doctor's appointment, and I was to meet Kelli downstairs at 11:30 a.m. and go to lunch with her before she drove me to the doctor. I decided she would have to wait, since I wasn't leaving you until you were situated in your new surroundings.

Finally around 11:20 a.m. nurses from the 11th floor came down and moved both you, and your little room mate Melanie up to your new home. Melanie has been a room mate of yours back in High Risk at the time you were there, and you were both moving up to the "normal" baby ward together.

Once I saw you being situated in Nursery B, I left for lunch and my doctor's appointment.

I had a nice lunch with Kelli who has a little girl named Breanne. Bree was very good and slept through the whole lunch. Kelli drove me to see Dr. Amankwah. He was pleased with everything and gave me a clean bill of health saying Dr. Joe could take over from here.

When we arrived back at the hospital, I looked in Nursery B but you weren't there. If they ever tried to give someone reason for a nervous breakdown, they were trying to do it to me today. A quick question and I was advised you had been moved to the less crowded Nursery C.

I went in to Nursery C and picked you up as soon as a nurse wrapped you up for me. I took you over to the big picture window so Kelli could see you. Kelli stayed for a long time, content on just watching us.

It was time for your meal, and they let me feed it to you. This time it was my breast milk, and you seemed to feed more quickly than you did this morning. I think my milk goes through the nipple easier and that makes it less work for you to get it out.

After you were done, I put you back in your little bed and went to say goodbye to Kelli. I then used a breast pump to get what I could for you and followed that with a little walk before coming back and picking you up again.

I held you for about an hour as you slept. Later around 6:00 p.m. when it was time for you to eat again, you kept falling asleep instead of drinking your formula. The nurse said you were just tired from all the sucking, and she would give you the balance of your formula, along with the rest of my breast milk later tonight using the gavage tube, since the process of sucking was still a little tiresome for you. I held you until dad arrived around 7:00 p.m. You slept the entire time he held you.

Everything worries me so much. I worry about us being able to call down here anytime of the day or night like we could on the 9th floor. I worry if I can feed you whenever its time up here. How will grandma and grandpa react to not being able to come into the nursery and having to look at you through the plate glass window? Most of all I worry about you being pulled off your medication for your apnea problem. I was very emotional today, and was teary eyed when dad arrived. I think he got upset with me and told me they wouldn't move you if they had any doubts that you weren't ready for the nursery. His words don't help. I hate changes. I especially hate them when I have become comfortable with how things were before.

Mom's Journal: Feb. 13th

After spending the whole day with you, it is very difficult to go into work and keep my mind on my job. The more I get to know you, the more I miss you when we are apart. The day is very long, and I am worried if we can get to the hospital tonight. The roads were terrible last night and I'm afraid we won't make it to Springfield. When I call your father to see if we are going he says; "You bet we are". Dad tells me you have been waiting all day to see him.

The roads were poor, but better than the night before. When we arrived you had just finished eating. They wrapped you up anyway and let us hold you. That probably wasn't a good idea, as you spit up a little of your food while dad held you, and when he started to pass you to me, you spit up quite a bit more. We decided to put you down. We both rubbed your little back as you soundly went to sleep.

I hate leaving you and I wish we weren't so far away. Every time we leave the hospital, I thank God for keeping you alive another day. In the morning, after I check in on you, I thank Him again for getting you through another night.

Mom's Journal: Feb. 14th

When we arrived tonight you had been moved to a bassinette. Norma, the nurse on duty, was taking care of you and said she had just finished feeding you. After last night, we decided not to pick you up and have you lose some of the formula you need to grow bigger and stronger. Norma acted surprised that dad jumped right in and changed your diaper when you went pee in it. She smiled and told me to make sure I keep dad involved when we all get home.

There is a little Valentine's Day card on your bassinette from the hospital. It is your first.

Mom's Journal: Feb. 15th

I left work early enough today to get to the hospital in time to give you your 3:00 feeding.

When I arrive, you and Melanie are in "isolation". Cheryl the nurse says it's because you both came from an "outside" ward and environment and both of your stool cultures showed "outside bugs."

Of course I get all freaked out, and ask what kind of bugs you have and are they serious. I start to imagine all kinds of crazy things, but Cheryl says there is nothing to be worried about, and the incident is quite common when babies are transferred from one ward to another.

When Suzie, a nurse I like comes on duty, I ask her if you have anything "bad" but she says not at all. I still worry of course. I can't bear to see you having any complications when you are so close to coming home. You have been doing so well and I have finally started to relax.

I feed you before dad comes, and after you are finished, I put you down so you can digest the formula and get the rest you need. I hate leaving you at night. I am getting so used to being with you, that it is becoming harder and harder to leave.

Dad's Journal: Feb. 15th

Your mom is worried sick again. It seems a nurse used the word "bugs" when describing why you and Melanie had been isolated from the other babies. I imagine saying something like "non viral microbes endemic to floor 9 were found in your stool and just to be safe you were being isolated". Instead someone had to say the word "bugs" to your mom. They might as well tell her they dropped you out the 11th floor window. We now have new worry number 857 on the drive home.

Dad's Journal: Feb.16th

Your Aunt Patsy and Uncle Tim come down for the weekend. We tell them they don't have to, but they come anyway, and immediately pitch in helping me get your nursery ready for you. Getting your room done hasn't been easy. After work and on weekends, we are down in Springfield with you, so progress has been poor. I see myself really getting it done once you are home. I can really get into it once there is no need to drive anywhere to see you.

You weigh 4 pounds 4 ½ ounces today. It was a lot of fun showing you off to Uncle Tim and Aunt Patsy through the nursery window. Patsy says you are beautiful, and your mom and I agree. In the event your mom and I somehow die while you are still a child we have asked Tim and Patsy if they would take care of you, and become your legal guardians, and they quickly say they would.

Here on the 11th floor, with the big windows, everyone can see into the nursery and see us holding you. I tell mom I feel like a zoo animal, but of course we don't mind showing you off to everyone who stops to see this tiny baby in a room full of giants. If only these people knew just how small you used to be. If only they could have seen the greatest triumph I have ever witnessed, as you came from death to the point you are right now.

You are my hero regardless of your size, and nothing I have ever been through in my life will ever inspire me as much as your struggle to remain in this world has.

Mom's Journal: Feb. 17th

You weigh in at 4 lbs. 8 oz. today. A super 3 ounce gain in just one day.

Grandma Del and Grandpa Tim are down for their weekly visit, of course, and we all arrive around 11:00 at St. Johns. I got to feed you at noon, and we all hung around a little while. Dad and grandpa went home to continue working on your room, and grandma and I went shopping at the mall to find some material for your cradle.

Grandma and I get back to the hospital so I can give you your 3:00 feeding. When I asked a nurse if you had eaten yet she said yes, even though we arrived just before feeding time. I could feel my eyes well up with tears because I thought I had missed a chance to feed you. Just then the nurse came out with your bottle, and I found out she thought I had asked if you were ready to eat, and not have you already eaten and that is why she had answered with a yes. You ate faster this time, at least for a while, and then you slowed down. Grandma watched through the window and I know she is dying to hold you.

People talk about postpartum depression. I'm not sure if that's what's wrong with me, but I have been so emotionally up and down that I wonder. I am just so worried about you. Every little thing makes me nervous and I am worried that the nurses will watch you close enough now that you're in the regular ward.

Another part of my depression is I let myself gain too much weight before and now after your birth. I'm not feeling attractive anymore to your dad, and it's not just the weight that makes me feel like I'm no longer his lover. It seems we aren't a couple anymore and that really bothers me. Working and then running home every three hours to pump my breasts also is wearing on me. Not getting enough milk for you also makes me feel inadequate. Not being able to carry you full term also makes me feel that your problems are all my fault. I worry about the bills, groceries and all the other expenses we have and I feel like crying all the time.

I bolster myself up. I make plans in my head to do better, and then outside influences remind me of how I look or what I can't do. For example, last Sunday I tried to eat a reasonable breakfast at the smorgasbord without over eating or eating things not allowed on the Weight Watchers Plan. As I was returning to the table, a waitress asked me when my baby was due. You are already six weeks old and I still can't get into anything but maternity pants. I felt my eyes tear up at the waitress's remark, and I feel like a blimp, but I try to be cheerful and get through breakfast without feeling sorry for myself. Well at least not anymore than I already do.

When we got to the hospital, I used the breast pump to try and get some milk for you. I usually don't get much in the morning, but I got a little bit more than usual. The nurse on duty asked me if my milk was diminishing, and proceeded to give me all kinds of advice on how to improve my flow. I had heard all her suggestions before from every other nurse, and I just kept smiling as I backed away from her. She kept trying to give me pointers, and I kept moving away from her. I felt a lump in my throat again, and I felt compelled to get away from her before I broke down.

As we leave dad asks me what's wrong and I say "nothing". He angrily says he knows better and wants to know what is wrong and then he's pissed because I'm still dwelling on the poor quantities of milk I'm able to produce. He's mad if I don't tell him what's wrong and he's mad if I do tell him, so I'm always wrong, no matter what. I guess I'm supposed to be strong and happy, no matter what I feel inside, and it's very hard these days to get it all together.

Some days, I wish I could just go some place by myself and cry and cry and cry. The one thing that really makes me forget about all the things that make me sad, or cause me to worry, is when I see you and your little face and you break out in a smile. Then and only then does my sadness leave me.

Dad says I'm "gloomy" and taking a special time and making it miserable and he resents it. I wish I could explain to him how I feel and I wish he would understand. I want your coming home to be a special time for us too but I don't feel very special.

I wanted to do everything right for you and so far I couldn't carry you long enough and I can't supply you enough milk. Those are very personal things that I don't think a man can understand. Now I feel like I can't even be happy in the right way to make this time special for the three of us. I love you so much and really want all of us to be perfect together. That's probably not possible, to be perfect that is, but I don't want to be a "crummy" mom.

Dad's Journal: addendum

I read your mom's thoughts today. I admire her honesty. I have always had an easier time telling people my true feelings than she. Needless to say, dear son, your father feels like a complete asshole. I certainly don't love your mother any less than before, and to be honest, I haven't given it a moment's thought to at least show her some affection lately. It seems my life has centered around you and you alone and that is so unfair to your mom.

There is nothing to the fact I think she has gotten too fat. I think the waitress who knew us and that mom was pregnant just asked about a due date, and really hadn't been looking down at your mom's stomach.

Just six weeks ago, your mom looked like a casualty on the Normandy beachhead, and I have been fearful to bother her, plus I was afraid she would think badly of me worrying about something other than you. She is right about my not paying enough attention to her. I'm not paying enough attention to anything, including my job. Tom hasn't said anything, but I know I'm not carrying my weight at work right now.

I look at people and I nod my head, but I don't hear a thing they say. My brain can't get free enough of you to think about anything else, and with all your mother's worries, it looks like I have created several more for her that she really doesn't need right now.

I did go off on your mom one night driving back home. I was frustrated that all the positive things, like you being moved to the regular ward, and being taken off medicine, and Dr. Khanna not thinking we needed a monitor at home, had all been joyous things I desperately wanted to share with your mom. I accused her of turning everything positive into a negative. I was sorry later for all I said, but I failed to understand that right now, a single, harsh word carries more weight than a thousand kind ones. I'm not making any excuses for my not being sensitive enough to your mom's condition.

Yes I haven't been paying enough attention to her. I haven't been paying enough attention to anything but you, and I have to learn to measure my focus before I drive myself nuts and make your mother sad again. You will find over the years I don't make excuses. I screwed up and was a lousy husband. There is no other way to cut it.

It is so strange that mom thinks she was inadequate in not carrying you to term. The one thing I admire most about your mom is how she lasted those extra fourteen days when most mothers wouldn't have had the strength or courage to do so. I am so completely positive that giving you that thirteenth and fourteenth day in the womb saved your life that I am shocked she feels she has failed somehow. You came into this world right after your lungs had formed enough to breathe.

A few days sooner, and this entire story would have been unnecessary. How strange it is that she thinks she did something wrong during the pregnancy. She never smoked nor drank. She studied what foods would be good to eat, and she stayed away from those that might not be good for you. In every single day, in every single instance, she did every thing right to bring you as far as she could before you came into this world.

My God, she saved your life and she feels like she failed. I have to fix some things son, and they are not in your nursery. I can't change the past, but I can direct my efforts to show I can be a better husband. Being a better father I will leave for later, since I am certain your mother will do a job well enough for the both of us.

Mom's Journal: Mon. Feb. 18th

You weigh 4 pounds 8 ounces today. That's the same as yesterday, but after the big gain yesterday, I wasn't worried at all.

Today is President's Day so I didn't have to work, and I rode down to Springfield with Gail. I got there around 11:00 a.m. and was able to help with your noon feeding. You had a sleepy kind of day, and were not really awake most of my afternoon visit.

Dr. Khanna was here today. He looked sort of harried when I first saw him. I asked him a bunch of questions about your care after he released you, but he told me Dr. Joe could look after you. He planned on changing your feeding schedule to every four hours in the next day or two, and was going to decrease your medication in that time period down to nil.

You have been doing well, without having any heart or apnea problems, and he believed it was time to see if you had "outgrown" the problem. He explained that if you were off medication for five days with no episodes that he would be able to release you and send you home with us. We set a goal date of next Sunday for you to come home and I find myself very excited, but very scared as well.

I sometimes feel so inadequate about being able to take care of you. I used to baby sit a lot when I was younger, and there have always been little kids around me my whole life, but everything seems so different now. Maybe it's because you are so special to me and I never realized how special babies were when I was younger. Dr. Khanna says if we were uncomfortable about taking you home without a monitor we could arrange to take one home with us.

When dad arrived that night, I told him what Dr. Khanna had said about the monitor. He asked if I would be able to sleep at night if you weren't on a monitor, and I told him I wouldn't. He said he wouldn't be able to either. Tomorrow I'll tell Dr. Khanna we want to have a monitor come home with us.

Dr. Khanna also told me I should try to nurse you before giving up on the idea entirely. He said that direct nursing is different than using an electric pump and my milk might increase with you stimulating my nipples. I told him I would try. After all, I have been using a breast pump for six weeks and I want to do whatever is best for you if I can.

Cheryl, the nurse on duty, helped me try to nurse you around 3:00 in the afternoon. I think I made her late getting off work since there was a shift change at 3:00. You did pretty well, except your weight before and after was the same, which meant you hadn't been able to get any milk out of my breasts. I fed you a bottle after that and told Cheryl I would try again at 6:00 p.m. to see if I could nurse you.

The 6:00 p.m. nursing attempt didn't work out very well. Suzie was the nurse on duty and she didn't help like Cheryl did. In fact, after she weighed you, she went to lunch and left me in the room alone with you and your little room mate Melanie. I had just brought you up to my right nipple when Melanie's monitor went off. I placed you back in the isolette and went to the adjoining room to make sure a nurse was coming over to check on your little friend.

When I came back after that little nerve racking interruption, I tried to position you again on my breast but it wasn't working, and I could see you were starting to get mad. I grabbed the bottle and fed you, deciding not to be discouraged or uptight about the situation, because that wouldn't do either of us any good.

Mom's Journal: Feb.19th

Today was a very good day. Irene Bloch said she had to run her son to Springfield and was leaving work around 3:00 p.m. I told Ron I also was leaving work early to catch a ride with Irene. When I first got to the hospital, you were sleeping, so I just sat and watched you for a while. The nurse came in and asked if I wanted to hold you, but I told her I would let you sleep instead.

After Irene dropped off her son Andrew, she came back to the hospital to see you. When she arrived, I started to un-wrap you from your blanket so I could change your diaper and hold you up to the window for Irene. You were really cute. I kept talking to you and you kept making smiley faces. Irene remarked you were much cuter than your pictures and that you looked exactly like your father. She also said I looked like a "real mother" and that after looking at us together she expected me to quit working after you come home.

She is right. I am not going to be leaving you with a babysitter. At that moment I knew I wasn't going back to work after you came home with us.

Dad's Journal: Wed. Feb. 20th

Mom feeds you an ounce of breast milk again plus a couple of ounces of formula. We take turns feeding you. You have had no apnea problems since they stopped giving you aminophylline, and that cheers us both up. The nurse tells us you are doing an excellent job and perhaps you can go home on Sunday. Mom and I try not to get overly excited. It won't be five days without the drug till Sunday night, and you might not be at five pounds just yet, so we both measure the nurse's words for now.

Dad's Journal: Feb.21st

We both watch as the nurse gives you a bath in a metal pan not much bigger than a paint pail. You look so small when you are naked, and you still have absolutely no butt. The water seems to shock you, but as always, you don't seem to mind and you don't cry.

A Lamaze class is in the hall, and they hang around the windows to watch you. I am certain many of those babies inside their mothers are already bigger than you are. You have become a celebrity on the 11th floor. Everyone who visits anyone is brought over to the windows to see the miniature person now in the nursery.

Mom feeds you and you eat quickly tonight. Most probably the bath woke you up to the point you can stay awake for the entire meal. Your monitor keeps going off and it concerns us greatly. The nurse says you look fine, and it might just be a loose wire, or this monitor might not be sensitive enough to pick up signals when you move around so much. I look at your mother and nod without her saying anything. Yes we are bringing home a monitor with you. I'm not going to screw up any more than I already have.

Dad's Journal: Fri. Feb. 22nd

We don't see you tonight. Mom went up to Chicago for a baby shower for you. I hope this perks her spirits up. The amount of stuff she got is so amazing that Del and grandpa won't be able to get it all in the back seat and trunk for the ride back to Lincoln. Of course mom is coming back right away. She won't go two days without seeing you even if the Atlantic Ocean is in her way.

Dad's Journal: Feb. 23rd

You come in at 4 pounds 11½ ounces today. Mom is there early and I come after work. The nurses are talking about you going home next Wednesday and I think that is probably right. Aunt Mary Ellen and Uncle Mark have come up from St. Louis and brought a crib as well as two boxes of baby clothes.

Mom has temporarily turned the dining room into a nursery till I finish the room, but looking at all the stuff, I don't know how it all will fit into your room. When I arrive, you are asleep of course. I don't want to pick you up when you look so peaceful, so I just look at you for a while. The nurses say that every time we leave, you wake up.

Dad's Journal Sun Feb. 24th

4 pounds 12½ ounces today. Another day, another ounce closer to your coming home. The head nurse says there is a chance of Tuesday being the big day. Del and Grandpa Tim are here of course. Your poor mom has been working so hard and has had so much to do. She works, and then she comes here, and now she is trying to get the house organized for your coming home.

Add the fact she gets up every three hours to pump her breasts, and I am surprised she can stay on her feet. She is nervous about being a good mother to you and I vow to continue to tell her she's the best I have ever seen, with all due respect to your grandmas.

She already has been incredible, just giving you life, but I vow I will tell her how good a mother she is for the rest of our years together. I am hoping your coming home and mom being able to be with you all the time will help her finally get some peace of mind.

Just to make things more nerve wracking today, you decide to upchuck all of your food all over the place. Thanks little guy. That's just what your mother needed.

Dad's Journal Feb.25th

A world record. 4 ounces in one day puts you over the hump at 5 pounds ½ ounce. The nurses say tomorrow you probably will be released. To add to our joy, we meet your little room mate Melanie's parents. She is now 4 pounds 13 ounces and her parents have been told she can go home by Sunday. The two of you have been together from the start, with little Melanie weighing almost the same as you at birth. She was born on January 2nd so you beat her out the door by a few days.

Melanie's mom held back her birth for fifteen days, just one more than your mom. We share our joy with her parents and the day is really upbeat for your mom and me. We of course are rooting for your little roommate, as her parents are for you.

Both your mom and I have trouble going to sleep knowing tomorrow should be the big day.

Tuesday February 26th. The Final Day.

Mom gets up at 5:00 a.m. I get up at 6:00. Mom and I catch breakfast and then it's off to St. Johns. We get there about 8:30 and mom gets to give you your 9:00 a.m. feeding. Shortly after you eat, a social worker named Andrea comes and shows us how to work the home monitor. The one she is giving us doesn't beep; beep all the time and this is a great relief to your mom and me.

67

After being instructed on how to work the monitor, we have to go downstairs and receive a crash CPR course. I received plenty of such training in the service, but I'm not arguing with anyone about anything right now. I'm not going to delay our taking you home today. The CPR training is a bit unnerving because it brings to light the fact we might have to use it on you someday, and we both hope we never do. We both agree it would make no sense to have you on a monitor and then not know for sure what to do to help you if the monitor goes off, so we take the lesson very seriously.

After the CPR training we go downstairs to catch a cup of coffee. Both your mom and I are a little unnerved about possibly having to give you CPR one day, so we take a few minutes to gather ourselves before going back upstairs.

Dr. Khanna is there to sign your release and is busy filling out a report for us to give to Dr. Joe. Your medical file is at least three inches thick and brings to a head just how long and how much had to be done to get you to this day. While we are getting you dressed, he continues to work on the report. He explains he is synopsizing your treatment into a page or two, which is remarkable considering all the pages they have filled out on you these past two months.

You decide to go to sleep rather than say goodbye to anyone, so mom and I say thanks to everyone for you. So many people, so good at what they do, have brought you to this day. I know they are doing their job but it has to be a special feeling for them when a day comes to let one of their preemies go home.

The entire ride home you sleep. When we get home I open the door for your mother and as she walks in with you, you start crying like we have never heard you cry before. It appears you are telling us right now who is going to be in charge of this family.

Dad's story:

Well dear son. That is your story. I hope it told you something about your mother and I as well as yourself that you found interesting. This journal was just the first part of chapter one in your life of course.

Many of the chapters you are more aware of, being the principal in them, than we are. We have decided we should add a few home stories of those early days.

It appears our reading our words have rekindled some memories of those first years together with you that you might not have ever been told before.

Yes you came home with us, but if you think that calmed us down any, you are sadly mistaken. Oh there was the joy of you being with us all the time, but it was tempered with our not wanting to leave you out of our sight for even a second.

I started your tenure at home all wrong. After we came home, I told mom I now could consider you as safe, and left to go pass out cigars and pop a few with the boys. Mom was pissed because she was scared to death, and I left her and you right when she needed reassurance from someone that everything was going to be alright. I guess I had told mom not to have grandma down just yet, so the three of us could have some time together, and then I buggered out on you two. My first shot at being a good dad went right down the drain along with the nicotine and beer. Mom is stilled pissed at me for that night.

In the next few months, the fetal monitor we brought home with you would drive us both up the wall and onto the ceiling. It almost made us crazy. The monitor, you see, would go off whenever you started doing baby things, like wiggling or moving around. The monitor also went off when power was disrupted. Yes at least four times that winter the power did fail in the neighborhood.

Your mother and I continually smashed each other's shoulders as we both tried to get through the doorway of your room at the same time to make sure you were alright. Always when we checked you, you were fine, either talking to yourself or discovering your toes or something.

The false alarms didn't stop us or slow us down of course. Every false alarm brought your mother, or I, or both, at the run with total disregard to what we were doing at the time.

The monitor became a hateful thing to your mom and me. When we were certain you were alright, and didn't need it anymore, we still had a hard time giving it up. It had become a crutch you see, that although not needed, was still leaned on until you were ten months old. As I look at the whole affair now, I am partly surprised that you aren't still wearing the damn thing when you are home with us.

Mom told me a story I had never heard before. It seems as winter was finally breaking it's strangle hold on us, your mom decided to take you out for a buggy ride. She bundled you up, but as soon as she did, the monitor started going off. She called Gail Petro and amidst her tears, lamented she didn't even know how to take her baby for a walk without something going wrong. Gail, a qualified nurse, told your mom to take the damn thing off of you. She explained to mom you would be in the buggy with mom looking right at you, so what did mom need a monitor for.

The early days were nerve wracking to say the least, but they were tempered with so much fun having you around. You were so funny, and even as a baby you loved to laugh. Your mom used to get furious with me when I made you laugh. For some strange reason, every time you started laughing, you got an enormous case of the hiccups that just wouldn't go away. They were loud, and mom would really get mad because you couldn't eat until they stopped, and they sometimes lasted for half an hour or longer.

At an early age, about six months, you started using the little baby walker, and you loved that thing. As soon as we put you in it, you were off to somewhere. Crashing into walls and cabinets you would push yourself around in that little wheeled seat until you were exhausted. At the time we noticed you were up on your toes, but your mother and I didn't understand what that meant. We were uninformed and naïve I guess.

I didn't worry about your not being able to walk and constantly being up on your toes until after you were a year old. Medical people had explained preemies were always behind the curve in growth and motor skills, because they not only had been born before their time, but also would be behind just because of what they went through at birth.

You had been so quick to use the walker and started so early to stand up using something to hold on to, that the concept of something not being right never occurred to me. My lack of knowledge would cause further stress to your mother who believed something wasn't right. She has told me how very frustrated she became with me and grandpa and grandma, who kept telling her every thing was fine when she knew that it wasn't.

I will let your mom take over from here because she remembers everything about those days like they happened yesterday.

Mom's Story:

As most new mothers, I wanted my mom to come and stay with me and my baby as soon as you came home. Dad talked me into telling grandma that we were bringing you home one day later than we actually were, because he wanted some time for "just the three of us" to be a family. Dad already told this story but I want to tell it again. As we walked in the door, dad put down all your stuff from the hospital and said, "I'm going to go see the guys and pass out cigars."

Great, here I am with an itty bitty baby wearing a heart monitor and crying his lungs out...we just sprung you from a 2 month stay at the hospital where people knew what to do to keep you alive...and now I have no mom here, no husband and "just the family" consists of only us two. By the way, I think we managed very well.

Dad wants me to recount some of the "doctor stories" during your first year. Most of the time, it was "just the two of us" when we went to the doctor. Of course Dad was working and there was really no need for both of us to take you for regular doctor visits. Dad always tried to make the big ones though.

During the first few months, I read a lot of books about taking care of babies, preemies, etc. I didn't like some of the things that I read about some of the situations preemies sometimes run into and that aren't always recognizable early on.

When we went for your first visit with Dr. Khanna, he indicated that you were doing well and when I asked if we needed a pediatrician for your care, he said that our regular general practitioner in Lincoln should be adequate to follow your progress. He also suggested that because you were a preemie we should take you to the 0–to–3 clinic at the health department to help identify any "delays" in development that you may experience. I did take you to the clinic every so often

71

(whatever intervals they determined necessary) and every time the report came back "developing at age appropriate level").

I don't know if I read too much, babysat too much as a teenager, or just had a better knowledge than some of those nurses who were looking at you at the clinic, but I did not think that their reports were correct and was uneasy about not doing more for you.

When I would try to voice my concerns to anyone, Dr. Pineda, dad, grandma and grandpa, and whomever else, I would always get the "he was so early, you have to give him time to catch up" line.

Dad didn't want to hear my concerns that I thought something was wrong, I'd start by telling him that I read that sometimes preemies had brain damage from loss of oxygen (you didn't breathe for the first 5-6 minutes when you came out) and he'd yell at me…"There's nothing wrong with his brain." You were so smart and funny even when you were real little that everyone thought that brain damage was out of the question. Well I read the books and I knew that "brain damage" could mean that "the little bleed" you experienced in your head during the first few days, the loss of oxygen, etc. could result in a myriad of consequences from being retarded, having cognitive delays, having physical delays, having many problems or only one problem, but NO ONE wanted to hear that anything could be wrong. Now this is really funny…..IF THERE WAS ANYONE ON EARTH THAT WANTED EVERYTHING TO BE PERFECT---IT WAS ME!!!!!!!!

Did people think I wanted there to be some kind of problem???? I wanted to HELP you develop correctly. I wanted someone to help me help you. I felt very alone at this time, because everyone kept telling me not to be nervous, not to look for problems where none existed and to be happy that you were O.K.

I had a friend at Lincoln College, Judy Horn. She was the student health department nurse.

Actually she was the entire student health department. Sometimes you and I would go up to her office just to visit her. I told her my concerns and she played with you a little and I think she noticed some of things that I was concerned about were probably true. She said I should make another appointment at the 0–3 clinic but that I should go when they had a physical therapist there doing the evaluations. Judy happened to know the therapist coming that month from Macomb. Her name was also Judy, Judy Strong.

We went to see her and she played with you for a while, evaluating your movements and such and then she went to another room and wrote up some notes and said that she wanted to talk to me. When she came back, she was very stern and jumped all over me because "you need to be getting your son some help, he is very developmentally delayed physically and there are exercises and treatment he should be getting."

I was crying and kind of in a way relieved at the same time. I said "I KNOW!" I think she thought I was nuts and I'm sure she thought I had been neglecting you for months by not taking you to see a doctor or therapist. Actually we were probably at the doctor more than most babies. Besides the regular check ups, you had throat and ear infections all the time and every time we went I asked about your progress and Dr. Pineda just looked at me like I was bothering him with the same old questions and gave me the same answer…give him time to catch up.

Okay, now we are getting somewhere. Judy Strong had us set up an appointment with a Dr. Mazur in Springfield (Orthopedist). There was a young resident on duty who did the intake questions. He examined you and looked at us kind of weird and asked what we were told of your situation.

Dr. Mazur came in and examined you also and asked the same question. When I say examined, both of these doctors only spent maybe 5 minutes with you compared to the many, many visits with Dr. Pineda and the nurses at the 0–3 clinic. I went through the "he has to catch up" responses and told them my concerns and Dr. Mazur said, "I'm not a neurologist and I think you should see one for a diagnosis but I think what you're dealing with here is Cerebral Palsy and we can get you some help for his development.

We immediately set up some appointments with physical and occupational therapists there at Memorial Medical Center.

Dad's story:

Like I said, mom remembers things very well. Needless to say you were diagnosed as having C P primarily in your lower extremities, but with some hand eye coordination problems as well. I remember quite well Dr. Mazur's young intern looking at us and not knowing how to tell this fearful mother and exceedingly dumb father that their child had Cerebral Palsy. When Dr. Mazur dropped the number on us, I recall so many ideas of what life was going to be like with you going up in smoke with just the two words "Cerebral Palsy" going through my mind.

C. P. isn't understood by most people. In fact I wince when I watch the C. P. marathons on T.V. and hear so many people fail to correctly pronounce the term itself. C. P. is the same as having a stroke. In some cases, the results are minor. In others the end results can be as debilitating as ending up in a non-cognitive vegetable like state for the duration of someone's life.

Your official diagnosis was Cerebral Palsy with Spastic Diplegia. The technical term means you had a stroke and your legs don't work worth a crap, but the medical term although more alarming in its words isn't as harsh sounding as mine.

A new plethora of concerns would follow us the next few years. Health Department visits, people from the local United Cerebral Palsy coming to our home to make sure we were giving you the proper care, and visits down to St. Louis to an odd young lady who was deemed an expert in physical therapy for kids with C.P.

For several years you wore plastic leggings called AFO's on your feet. These molded plastic contraptions went from the bottom of your feet up the back of your calf and were held in place with Velcro straps. The purpose of these things was to stretch your heel cord down so that you would get off your toes and stand with your foot flush to the floor. You had several sets of those the first six years of your life.

Once, when you were about three, your two legs were put in casts to help stretch your heel cords down. That was a tough time on your mother, as now she had to carry a baby with an extra twenty pounds of casts on your legs.

We were referred by a friend of mine to the Shriner's Hospital in St. Louis when you were about five and they recommended a heel tendon reattachment and a hamstring release operation to alleviate the problems with the spasticity in your legs and the problem you had placing your foot flush to the ground. The operation would change your physiology of course, and your mother and I agonized over the decision to allow the operation. In effect your foot would fall flush to the ground because it would flop down. Although many C. P. children have had this operation, your mother and I had started to see improvement in your legs with the therapy and exercises we were doing with you, so we finally opted out of the operation.

When you were about six or seven we went to see a doctor at Memorial Hospital in Springfield who was an expert in a new operation called Dorsal Rhizotomy. The doctor explained to your mom and I, and Grandma Del who came down for the consultation, that they would open up your spine and leave it exposed for several weeks. The doctors would find out what nerve endings were directly related to your problems and then cut those nerves to alleviate the bad nerve signals your body was getting which help precipitate your problems.

I remember as clearly as yesterday the doctor telling us about all the potential side effects, including meningitis, plus the fact you would be laid up for months as your spine and back healed. We considered the whole idea a bad tradeoff when he gave his last best pitch to us. The doctor, with pride in his voice, told us to date no one he has operated on has ended up any worse than when they started.

I had expected him to say the operation would mean you someday would be a quarterback or a dancer on Broadway, but all this doctor promised after months of healing, would be no worse than what you are now. I remember looking at Grandma Del and she had the same look in her eye that I did. This guy is goofy.

It appears the operation has grown in use and frequency over the past two decades. Now that you are 21 years old, you can make the decision yourself if you ever want the procedure.

Over the years I have often wondered if we should have had one of the operations, or perhaps both done to you. I believe our choices on opting out were correct under the circumstances, but I will leave it to you to decide if your mother and I failed you back then or did you justice by relying on physical therapy instead of the operations.

Well son, there you have it. The rest you pretty much know all about as we have told you stories about your growing up over the years. I know with the memory you have that much of your young life is remembered by you without any outside influences needed to stir recollections. I hope this journal fills in the early blanks in your life as much as you have filled in our lives with your being our son.

Early in this journal we both wrote how we seemed to have known you forever when you were just a few weeks old. That emotion has never left your mom or me over the years. You have been the love of our life. Then, now, and forever.

The Graduation

Timothy, as you all have just read, was born months premature. His initial playing weight before he decided to grow was two and a half pounds. As with many "preemies", Timothy was born with Cerebral Palsy and this is the story of his eighth grade graduation.

The Metcalf School, located 45 minutes from our home, was a better fit for Tim than the local school just two blocks away. Metcalf, besides being geared for disabled students, had a swimming pool and offered daily therapy for our son that wouldn't be available locally. The years of commuting had been hard on our son but now with graduation day around the corner, a big part of his life was coming to an end.

As graduation day approached, Timothy was very excited. Actually he wasn't excited about graduating from grammar school. Instead, he was excited about George Lucas finally releasing his first Star Wars prequel in nearly twenty years.

I kept asking Tim why he wasn't fired up about graduation. He had been a good student, but his interests in life certainly never included going to school. Tim is like most kids of today. In subjects he loved, like history and social studies, he was a straight "A" student. In subjects he disdained, such as math, he did just well enough to get by.

Timothy, quite nonchalantly, stated that graduating from eighth grade was no different than any other day and that I was making a big deal out of things…again. I asked if he was excited about going to high school just a mile from the house. He seemed disinterested in the fact he wouldn't have long bus rides ever again. He had been very quiet lately. A quiet his mother and I had learned to respect.

There was something deeper in my son's thoughts about why he showed no emotion for this big event in his life. I had asked him for his thoughts. He didn't care to express them. I had learned over the years that handicapped children carry a great many feelings inside themselves. When it was time to talk about something like his graduation, we would sit down and talk about his feelings. Now just wasn't the time.

I had surmised that perhaps Tim was a little nervous about going to a new school, with new people. I also felt that perhaps graduation for him meant the ending of relationships with friends at Metcalf that had lasted half of his short life. I also knew that right now wasn't the time for Tim and me to discuss his obvious lack of interest in this whole affair.

As always, my wife Sharon was in charge of making sure everything on graduation day went smoothly for the Fak family. Sharon had decided since we were traveling to Chicago for the Memorial Day weekend, that a party for Tim up there, where all of our family members still live, would make the most sense. Only she and I, and the two grandmas would go to the ceremony at Metcalf this Wednesday night.

The morning of graduation, Timothy still had school. He laughed that it was just a goof off day. That the only thing the class was going to do was practice the graduation ceremony and mill around the school telling stories of the past eight years.

It was during this morning conversation that Tim laid the bombshell on us that he wasn't going to use his K walker for the ceremony. He said he was going to walk up and receive his diploma just like everyone else.

Timothy's Cerebral Palsy has given him a cup half filled, not half empty. His mind is as sharp as anyone's. His hand eye coordination is good, although nothing to brag about. Like thousands of children with C.P. Timothy just can't walk without outside assistance. He also has no sense of balance.

As a practice exercise, Tim tries to stand in the middle of a room with nothing to use for balance. To date he can't do this for more than a few seconds. My son needs help to walk. That is why his decision to not use his walker was so unnerving to his mother and me.

We both told him that there was nothing shameful in his having to use his walker. He had spent all his years at Metcalf using either a walker or a wheelchair on longer excursions. Our son was adamant. He was going to graduate using just his own two legs and nothing more.

Although both Sharon and I feared Tim would have an extremely difficult time doing what he felt he had to do, all we could do was support his attempt. I think that in his mind, just this once he wanted to be like the other kids who were graduating. Just this once he was going to be "normal".

Two of Tim's classmates, Cody and Christine would graduate in their wheelchairs. They didn't have a choice. They both have Spina Bifida, which makes those wheelchairs a part of their lives. Tim felt that he had a choice and he was making it.

That evening, as Tim and Sharon and the two grandmothers, Mary and Del, got ready for the drive to school, I asked Timothy again if he was sure he didn't want to use his walker.

"Dad I did the rehearsal today without the walker. The only problem I had was getting by the podium, which is right in the way of the stage's stairway". He replied.

"Great", I thought, nothing to worry about but my son falling down the stairs at graduation. I found an anger welling up inside me. Why on a day when everyone else will be celebrating their child graduating from grammar school, will I be living in fear of my child being hurt or badly embarrassed? I tried hard to quell the anger. I knew it was a demeaning thing to have running through my mind. The long drive to Bloomington was filled with thoughts of why couldn't Tim be just like everyone else.

I dropped the family off at the front door and drove the two blocks to the parking area. All the time driving there and walking back, my mind was filled with my dear sweet son, falling down during the ceremony. I saw Timothy falling down and not getting back up. In my mind, I saw him lying there for what seemed like an eternity until someone "normal" came over to help him back up.

My eyes had filled with tears. I hated everyone who was in that building that night. I hated how normal they all were.

As I entered the vestibule of the school's theatre, I saw Tim sitting on a brick ledge in the lobby. His classmates were flitting about the place, checking out what each other was wearing and acting excited and silly as the time for the event of their lives was about to occur.

I went up to my son and asked him if he was all right.

"Yeah, I'm fine. Mom and the girls are in the auditorium waiting for you."

I debated asking Tim one last time if he wanted a walker. Instead I just stuck out my hand and said good luck. As I walked in the auditorium looking for the girls, I opened my eyes wide to fight back tears. You shouldn't have to say good luck to your son before a graduation ceremony I thought.

Walking down the aisle of the auditorium towards where the girls were sitting, I noticed how pitched the floor was. It wasn't that gentle angle that you find in today's theaters. It was deep, and caused a person to keep moving faster as the ground kept going away at a seemingly steeper and steeper pitch.

"Great", I thought. "Another thing I have to worry about".

The seats we had were good, based on the fact that we were a full half hour early for the event. I spent the initial time surveying the obstacle course my son was about to attempt to conquer.

The auditorium was excellent for a grammar school. Holding about 600 people in comfortable seating, the front stage was deep and wide. Before the stage was where the band was set up for tonight's music. On stage, in three rows, were the fifty-two folding chairs that would hold tonight's graduates. I pondered which one my son would be sitting in.

On the left of the stage was the podium. I surmised that this was the one obstacle my son had told me about this morning. I wondered what others he had decided to keep to himself. To the right, off the stage, was a piano. I noticed how little room was allowed for access to the stage stairs on that side and decided that there was no easy way for Timothy to get up on stage.

At the piano, as family milled about looking for seats, Tim's classmate, Mike played. The songs were classical and did not ring a bell with me. That isn't important. What struck me was that Mike was playing the music without fail, without error. As I watched the young man, I wondered how many in the audience noticed that there was no sheet music in front of Mike. I wondered how many seated in the auditorium knew that the reason there was no sheet music was because Mike was vision impaired.

What a powerful mind this lad must have, I thought. I wondered as I listened, if Mike was the one who was handicapped, or was it the rest of us who could never accomplish what the young man now did so easily.

Finally, as the time for the ceremony to begin approached, the band began to play a march. Down both the left and right sides, the students hurried toward the stage, and I mean hurried.

Tim's Grandma Del remarked.

"Why are they going so fast?"

The idea that the students were at a near trot towards the stage made me sink deep into my chair. We all watched the left aisle, as we knew Timothy would be coming down that side. There as if on cue, we saw Tim's head bobbing and weaving as he hurried down the steep aisle, trying to keep pace with his classmates.

This was an easier task for Tim than might be expected. The outer walls of the auditorium were perfect for Tim to run his left hand along and maintain balance. It was the speed the children were going at that made the Fak family clench their teeth…and pray.

As Tim approached the stairs to the stage, my son went down. You could see the young girl behind him, put out her hands and debate whether she should help him up or not. Before she could process her decision, Tim was on his feet and up on the stage stairs.

Approaching the podium, he slowed while he fought to maintain his balance. Like a man on a window ledge, desperately struggling to not fall off the building, Timothy edged his way past the poorly placed obstacle. I squeezed my eyes tight for a second and asked God to help my son.

When I opened them, I felt a wave of relief. Tim was past the podium, and in a mad dash, made for a front row seat in the middle of the folding chairs that awaited the class of 99. Immediately, he sat down, a look of exhaustion as well as triumph on his face. As Tim reveled in his victory, he remembered that the students were to remain standing until all were on stage. Rather than feel he had accomplished enough, Tim stood by his chair. He had his legs bent deeply. His body twisting awkwardly as he used his right hand to steady himself on the far too low chair seat.

Within a few minutes, the dash by his classmates was complete. As the students all received the signal to sit, you could see my son plop down eagerly in his chair. With a deep breath, the girls and I relaxed for a moment. Part one of this adventure was over. Part one was a victory. Timothy was sporting a smile the size of the Grand Canyon on his face.

As teachers and students came forward to speak, my mind wandered back to a Christmas pageant many years ago. Timothy was attending Zion Lutheran School for kindergarten back in Lincoln. He had told us at the school play, his class was going to be on stage for a Christmas song. I laughed as I remembered how he told us he was going to be in costume that day, (he was to wear a cardboard crown on his head). He said that he would wave at us so we would be able to recognize him. I smiled within my soul as I recalled how Tim came down the aisle that day, the only child with a walker. I thought how cute he had looked with the oversize crown pressing the tops of his ears outward like one of the seven dwarfs.

Upon seeing us, Tim had waved at us in the stands. You could tell his lips were saying: "It's me". I remembered that when he reached the stage stairs that everyone had forgotten he would need help. Undaunted, my son shed his walker, climbing the stairs on his hands and knees. As Tim reached the top stair, his teacher rushed to help him as a classmate gathered his walker. Without a moment's concern, Timothy got into his place on stage and proceeded to steal the show during his class's skit.

There are days when Tim gives up on life skills too soon, or doesn't even try at all. There are days like that day at Zion, and now tonight at Metcalf, however, where he shows the determination and courage that I wish I could have just once in my life. Living in this world for Tim is a series of challenges, of victories and defeats. When you are disabled or are the parent of a child disabled, you simply are made more aware of them than others who are blessed with all their functions.

My attention came back to the ceremony as Molly, one of my son's classmates, began to play the violin. I cringed and again tried to hide my body in the deepest recesses of my chair. On stage, as the young girl played, my son sat staring intently at the performer. His mouth was open so wide in a gaping look that I was tempted to stand up and yell:

"Tim, close your mouth".

I felt that all 600 adults in their seats must have been staring at my son. Finally, taking my eyes off Tim, I noticed several other boys had similar expressions on their faces.

I smiled, realizing that the impressiveness of the young girls playing as well as perhaps a boyish thought that the young lady was cute was what was happening to the young males on stage. Yes, my son looked funny up there. Yes, but he was not alone. This time, Timothy was being just as normal or abnormal as his classmates. Some things in life, it seems, are universal.

Finally the time for diplomas to be handed out arrived. I tensed as I looked over at Sharon. I knew whatever fears I carried in my heart were magnified ten fold in my wife.

Timothy is the world to Sharon. From birth they have had a special bond that no one, not even I, can match. I felt sad for my wife. She shouldn't have to worry every day about every little thing. She does, however, with no complaint. It is the principal reason I admire her so much.

As the Dean of Students stood at the podium, the first row of students rose from their seats. As she called the student's names, they filed down the aisle, past the podium, to center stage where the principal, superintendent and assistant superintendent waited to dole out diplomas to the class of 99.

This open area movement for Tim was going to be the real crux of tonight's challenge. Watching Tim go down the aisle, he bounced his hand from seat cushion to seat cushion. It placed his body again in an awkward position. An awkward position that he felt was far less uncomfortable than the option of falling down. When Tim made the turn at the podium, there was a brief delay in front of him.

There at that point in time, at that point on the stage, Timothy's struggle with life was defined. He was caught in no mans land. There was nothing around him to use for balance. For perhaps five seconds that lasted in my mind for hours, he struggled to stay on his feet. I could see him raise his hands from his sides as if to catch a breeze to keep him aloft. I felt tears welling in my eyes. "He's going down", I thought.

Then, just at the last second, the D S at the podium extended her hand and called Timothy Michael Fak's name. Touching her hand ever so briefly, Tim had regained the sense of balance he needed to amble across the stage. As Tim walked, his five foot two inch frame dwindled to probably four feet. His knees were bent forward terribly as he bobbed his head back and forth to maintain motion. You could see that as he reached to shake hands which each school dignitary that he used their handshake to steady himself and move on to the next.

Finally he was at the end of the stage and bouncing back to his seat. Again a smile of accomplishment beamed from his face. I had sensed the whispers in the crowd as my son had made his triumphant march. I knew some of the murmurs were from many of the parents who knew my son and knew what he had just accomplished. I also knew that some of the mumblings were from people who did not know my son, and were making judgments about him that were terribly incorrect.

I felt a deep urge to stand up and lecture the crowd in that hall. I felt like' telling them that at the age of ten my son had scored an IQ of 139. I wanted to tell them that he consistently scored as a college senior in many of the Iowa tests the school administered. I needed them to know that my son was witty and charming and a wonderful person to spend your life with.

Instead, I just sat there. My emotions interchanging from great pride in Timothy to the sorrow that many times more in his life, a first impression would shortchange his opportunities to show who and what he was.

Suddenly, I was back in the present. The ceremony was over and the students were leaving the stage. With a feeling that nothing more needed to be accomplished, Tim sauntered off backstage instead of tackling the stairs and the aisle again. He had already won this battle. There was nothing more to prove.

I smiled again at my son's intelligence." You would have been too dumb to think of that", I thought.

The students and adults were to meet in the gymnasium for a cake and punch reception. Following the reception, there was going to be a graduation dance that Tim refused to stay for. We had already told him too many times that we would leave and come back for him. He was getting frustrated telling us again and again he didn't want to stay for the dance.

I rushed ahead of the girls to get to the gym. I had this desperate urge that I needed to hug my son. I needed to tell him how proud I was of him right now and not in a few minutes.

Walking in the gym, I immediately saw Tim sitting at a table drinking punch. As I walked towards Tim, classmates flitted by, giving Tim pats on the back or high fives. I knew he would kill me if I bent over and kissed him, so I just stuck out my hand and said congratulations.

With out much ado, my son said thanks and asked where the girls were.

"They are right behind me", I said.

"I took the shortcut backstage and down the back hall to get here", my son said triumphantly.

"That was a good move", I replied.

With that, the three girls were at the table hugging and kissing my son. We would have a "guy talk" about this later, I promised myself. Tim stayed at the table as some of his classmates came by to visit. Sharon was busy taking pictures of them with Tim as I stood watching the reception going about its business.

The kids were all wired. Running from table to table, person to person, I understood why Tim didn't think he would enjoy a dance tonight. These kids were all going to go to University High School together. Tim was going to his own hometown school. Perhaps that had something to do with his obvious disinterest in the whole affair.

Standing in the middle of the gym, I noticed one of Tim's classmates talking with his father. The young boy was tall and straight as he laughed with his dad. I found myself hating those two people as I watched them. I found myself hating their being normal and told myself what jerks they probably were.

I then took a breath and apologized to God. Here I was, a person who didn't want people to judge my son on his appearance doing the same thing to this boy and his dad.

The kid is probably a great kid I thought. The dad is probably a better dad than I will ever be.

"You are a real jerk." I thought to myself. Here you are making judgments on people you don't know because they are normal, but you don't want people to do the same to your son because he's not.

I went back to the table and sat with my son until he asked if we could go.

The drive back home was fairly quite. Timothy had made no big deal about his journey into the world of regular people, so none of us did either. During the drive, I felt the weight of the night's worries being taken off my shoulders. I knew there would be many more. The thought no longer bothered me. Timothy was my son who I loved so much.

Tim is who he is because of how he is. Sharon and I will be there for him, and love him always, just the way he is. I hope the world will get to know my son and all the others like my son.

They will be better for it if they do.

Note; Tim Fak will be completing his junior year at Illinois State University in Normal Illinois in the spring of 2006. He uses an electric scooter for traveling and occasionally uses a walker or cane for short distances. His father can no longer beat him in a game of Jeopardy.

I was born in 1948 in Chicago Illinois. Until 1960 I lived at 3824 North Sheffield, just a block and a half from Cubs Park. The following is a compilation of memories that, for whatever reason, I found myself compelled to turn into this story.

I wrote "Before it was Wrigleyville" at 2:00 a.m. after an evening of fitful dreams. No longer being able to sleep, I typed a huge jumble of thoughts and recollections triggered by my subconscious before they were lost again forever. This little grab bag of memories lay in a folder I promised to someday rewrite into a cohesive story. Every night for several years, as I lay waiting for sleep to end my day, I had a pang of regret that I had not compiled, sorted and brought those pages into story form. It seemed to be of no consequence to me whether the story was any good or not. I only knew that I had to bring it to life, regardless of it having any quality or value.

In 1997, I did just that. On a night where sleep was a stranger to me, I took the folder out and started typing. This is how the story you are about to read came about. It is about my life as a young boy growing up in the shadow of Wrigley Field in the 1950's. As is the case with such stories, it has continued to evolve and grow over the years, now being 4000 words longer than the original.

Before It Was Wrigleyville

The Near North Side in the 1950's

It is just one of those things that from time to time happen to all of us. I had a dream about my childhood. I am not sure what exactly triggered this one. I don't recall seeing someone I had not seen in a long time. Nothing I can recall seeing in print or on the T.V. was the culprit. I guess it was just brought on by something I ate. Anyway, I had this dream about my childhood.

The first scene in this vision had me at Wrigley Field in the middle of a snowstorm. The half dozen friends who were with me, sitting along the third base line, were a compilation of many people I have met over the years. As with everyone's dreams, since they were not important to the text, they in a sense remained nameless as well as faceless. The point of my mind's journey was that I was back home in my first playground. Although there was a snowstorm, the day itself was sunny and bright. I understand this is not possible, but reality has little domain in a person's dreams.

I believe the winter storm that wasn't cold was done for effect. There were no ballplayers on the field, or anyone else in the park save my small group in the stands, as I sat and looked and smelled all that was Wrigley.

The fake storm had been the catalyst for the next scene, I now found myself under the stands at the corner of Addison and Clark sipping a coffee, looking in the window of the autographed baseball store which has never been there. Baseballs with the signature of every ballplayer you could imagine were lined up stitch to stitch in the display cases. As I shuddered and sipped my coffee, an elderly clerk with glasses dangerously close to the end of his nose, waved at me through the store window, beckoning me inside.

Walking into the brightly lit store, the dream changed again. The small store was now empty except for a single glass case on a walnut pedestal in the center of the shop. In the case was a single baseball with the autograph of Ted Williams perfectly discernible across its face.

I recall having no surprise at the ball carrying the "Splendid Splinters" name. Ted Williams was my favorite player over all the Hall of Fame players I saw in Wrigley Field during the late 50's and early 60's. That might seem strange, since I never saw him play. My opinion, based on memories of my dad having family arguments or just preaching to me about Ted being the best ballplayer ever, convinced me Williams was the man. I recall my dad saying that if Ted hadn't given up five years of his career to serve his country in World War II and Korea, that his career totals would have been unsurpassed. I was a young boy. He was my father and his word was gospel. My favorite player, like dads, had to be Ted Williams.

Staring at the special baseball, I noticed a card requesting $200.00 from whoever wished to purchase the souvenir. As I stared at the perfect signature, a hand rested upon my right shoulder.

"Forget it kid. That's way too much to pay for that ball".

As I turned to see who was talking to me, the dream shifted into the third person.

I watched from a distance as I became a young boy again, standing and talking to Ted Williams, my hero. Without explanation, which is never needed in a dream, I saw myself walking away with Mr. Williams. I knew as I watched the two figures leave the ballpark that they were going somewhere to talk about my youth around good old Wrigley. With their backs turned to me, I heard myself say to Ted,

"You were my dad's favorite ballplayer."

"I know". He replied.

As the two figures dwindled in the distance, I saw the young boy reach to hold the man's hand. Gently, you could see the older man return the gesture.

Within a moment, a completely new vision had formed in my dreamful mind. I was sitting on a sofa in a room that carried no substance. It was like no room I had ever been in, yet it was similar to all the rooms I had called home in my life. Ted Williams was sitting in front of me on a straight back chair, with hands folded, his body hunched over towards me. I felt like I was being questioned by a doctor about some malady I had claimed to have.

I kept asking Ted to tell me stories of his playing days. I wanted to know if he really could pick up the rotation of a ball as it left the pitcher's hand. Could he really know if it was a fastball or a slider or a curve like people said he could? I wanted to know what went through his mind that last day of the season, when batting 400: he refused to sit out the last doubleheader games of the season and went 6 and 8 at the plate. All my questions to Ted were brushed aside by him.

For every question I asked, he said:" No, I want you to tell me about your days in the old neighborhood first."

Suddenly the point of my dream became obvious. All of us have things locked in our minds since childhood. Things that we remember but never have had occasion to recall. Some of those memories are sent into deep corners of our mind because they were sad or hurt to remember. There are many good events that also have been tucked away in corners of our recollection. These thoughts have helped shape our life's character, yet have become lost in the innumerable files of memories past. A thousand of these little vignettes of my youth now came forward to be recounted. Things I thought I had forgotten as well as things I had forgotten that I ever remembered now came across my mind's eye.

I recalled the old neighborhood explicitly. I mean to the point that I could draw you a detailed map that would be 100% accurate. Every building, every store, every nook and cranny of the one mile radius around Wrigley Field was there for me to see. Each element, like a miniature film that carried its own story to tell, one after the other, flew before me.

The neighborhood was, and is, made up of innumerable six flats called brownstones or greystones built within a few inches of each other, or in some cases having no space between them at all. This strange trait had caused gangways to be cut through the underbellies of the apartment buildings, so that residents could go from back yard to front steps without having to walk all the way around those long city blocks. In some areas, homes rested comfortably a few feet from each other, but that was not the case on the thirty eight hundred block of Sheffield which was lined almost entirely with six flats on the west side of the street.

I remembered the Hotel Carlos in the middle of my block on Sheffield. I recalled Mom telling me not to go in there 'trick or treating" at Halloween because the hotel was full of transients. The word scared me. I never asked what it meant.

I thought back to the busy corner where Sheffield turned into Sheridan Rd. as a person heads north. The tough Irish cop who was there every morning and afternoon to help school kids cross the intersections, ruled the corner like a feudal tyrant. Step off the curb before he waved you on, and you would find him crouched down on his knees, his face in yours asking you,

"Who told you to step in the street? You wait till I give you the signal to cross or I'll whack you on the noggin with my night stick."

All of us got yelled at once a year. None of us got lectured twice.

As we crossed the street thoroughly scared, the old cop would rub us on the head and tell us to do a good job in school.

Our quick movement crossing the street would cause the hundreds of pigeons on the huge sidewalk to get spooked enough to take flight momentarily until the leaders of the flock would signal that it was all right to land again and return to checking the area for food scraps. The neighborhood was densely filled with families, but the pigeons outnumbered us ten to one in those days. I recall how everyone in the neighborhood just considered so many big birds as part of life on the Near North Side of Chicago.

The memory of my walking down Sheridan in my brand new black suit, going to my First Holy Communion came back to me. Proudly walking the four blocks to church, I remember a lesser mannered pigeon dropping his waste on the left shoulder of my brand new suit. I remember that being the first time in my life that I cursed out loud.

The next memory on Sheridan going to school was Hanover's Delicatessen. They had a son my age named Larry. He didn't go to St. Mary's with the rest of us because he was Jewish. Larry was a great guy and an integral part of the gang. Even when we were just in third grade, I remember Larry having to work around the store before he could come out and mess around with us. That was no problem. At the age of ten, I had a Herald American paper route after school and so did my other buddies. A job, some type of job, was a given if you were a kid in the fifties. Want money to spend? Then earn it, was the rationale of all the families in the Near North.

I recall my mom sending me to Hanover's to pick up a pound of boiled ham for dad's lunches one day. Larry was outside sweeping the wide sidewalk and I set the neatly wrapped ham down to give him a hand. After working and then visiting, I said goodbye and went home. As I walked in the door it dawned on me that the ham was still laying on the sidewalk. Before mom could ask me where the ham was, I ran out the door and down the street. Larry, smiling as he leaned against the store window, flipped the package to me, as in full gallop, I circled and continued my mad dash back home. At the age of eight I had just had my first senior moment.

A little further down the block was the old Mode theatre. An old timer even in the fifties, the Mode showed movies that my dad would say were already on that newfangled invention, the television. You could always find Foy, Fak, and Flynn in the front row on Saturdays however. That was the fifty cartoon day plus a couple Three Stooges shorts, and an old movie classic like King Kong or The Creature from the Black Lagoon.

For some strange reason, we always tore the popcorn boxes in a certain way so that they fit on our faces like some type of goggles. I'm sure the three of us were a strange sight. Sitting in the front row, popcorn boxes affixed to our faces as we mouthed the words to shows we had seen a hundred times before. It actually made sense back then for little kids to sit up close to the screen. Women wearing huge hats, that they refused to take off in the theatre, could make it impossible for a small fry sitting behind them to see the movie. Besides, all the theatres allowed smoking, and if just a few adults came to the show with their kids, the plumes of smoke filtering in the air could make it tough to see the movie, unless you were in the front row of course.

The show cost a quarter to get in. Popcorn was a dime. We drank from the water fountain to save money.

The rest of the way down Sheridan Rd. was inconsequential except for the Elevated train station just before Irving Park. Under the tracks was a great candy counter as well as the home of the second most important item in our lives, the comic book stand.

A short, gaunt man, with a perpetual cigarette in his mouth, always stood behind the counter. He didn't seem to mind our spending so much time reading all the comic books. He knew we would never steal any of them, and although we might have read the comic, we would still buy it. A good comic was worth owning and reading over and over and over again. They cost a dime back then. When their price skyrocketed to 12 cents, we had our first lesson in inflation.

One of the only debates that put any stress on the friendships of the gang was the argument over whether Superman or Batman was the coolest superhero. Anyone who came up with Green Lantern or The Flash as their choice was quickly admonished by the rest of us.

Going down Sheridan Road, the next two blocks had many apartment complexes in a U shape formation. These buildings, called courtyards by us back then, made the neighborhoods still more crowded than the six flats, as they allowed twice as many apartments in the same amount of space. Parking would have been a nightmare back then if every family had a car, but most didn't. I recall never knowing anyone back then who had two vehicles.

The walk down Sheridan finally brought me to the corner where my school and church, Saint Mary of the Lake was located. I always did the last half block to school at a run because I had to first go by Konitzer-Rowland funeral home to get to the streetlight. Both Grandma and Grandpa Fak had been waked inside that building and I carried a great fear of the structure all my years in the neighborhood.

St. Mary's Church was a huge classic limestone building with broad sweeping stairs leading up to its three sets of massive doors. Behind this awesome structure was the convent and beside that the school that I went to until seventh grade. I remembered how the playground was a forest with dozens of trees until a sixth grader during recess fell out of one of the trees and broke his arm. The next memory I have of the playground was nice, neat, completely harmless asphalt. I guess even back then a lawsuit here and there would raise its angry head.

The memories of my time at St. Mary's Grammar School revolved around two events. First the news that the Russians had launched the Sputnik satellite into space in 1957 scared everyone with the thought of nuclear weapons raining down on us from the stratosphere. I recalled how we would scurry into the hallway or be told to get under our desks and put our hands over our heads as we practiced air raid drills all the time. I remember by fifth or sixth grade wondering what good it would do to be under my desk if the Russians dropped an atom bomb on the school, but I followed directions explicitly lest I catch a whack across the back of the head from a nun.

I also remembered the Our Lady of Angels fire when I was ten years old that had the entire city in mourning. The West Side school, being old and not properly alarmed, like most schools back then, had burned down early one winter's day. The fire took 92 children and three nuns to their deaths before the blaze could be extinguished. Not much for news reading back then, I remember the Chicago American printing the pictures of all 95 victims on the front page a few days later. Even to a ten year old, the enormity of the tragedy hit home with all those young faces looking at me as I stared at the paper.

After OLA burned, we had fire alarm drills several times a week. Nuns in the hallways with stop watches would time the evacuation procedures, looking to shave off precious seconds all the while telling us to move quickly but not to run.

Going north past St Mary's was rare back then, except for occasional jaunts to the Lawrence Hotel. We went there sometimes on Saturdays to swim all day in the hotel's indoor pool. A buck back then, which is what it cost to get into the pool, was an extravagance that we only incurred when the heat of summer made spending a dollar more comfortable than sweltering through another summer Saturday. The neighborhood the Lawrence was in was called Uptown. Not being our domain, it could be dangerous as the early formations of gangs more interested in violence than playing baseball together were starting to rear their ugly heads. This was especially true in Uptown around Lawrence and Halsted.

Curiously we never used the beaches off Lake Michigan back then. I know our parents couldn't have come with us, as the dads were always working and the moms were raising other kids in our families. Perhaps our younger age meant we were told not to go there by ourselves. The St Lawrence pool always had a lifeguard and I believe that was why our folks didn't mind us going all the way over to Uptown.

The strange area of the lake front called "The Rocks" popped into my dream. Huge stair stepped walls of great stones along a deep part of Lake Michigan was where my father took me smelt fishing a few times. I didn't like to fish and after dad had spent a huge sum of money on all kinds of fishing gear, he realized he didn't like to fish either.

I remembered looking out at the dark, foreboding waters of Lake Michigan and having a terrible fear of being thrown into those waters as my father had been by his brothers many years before. The Fak brothers, Eddie and Kashmer, had thrown dad in because it was time for him to learn how to swim. Dad said he almost drown until Eddie went in after him. Looking at the waters kicking up waves of cold, frosty foam upon the rocks, I couldn't imagine being within twenty miles of this place if that had happened to me.

On summer days, a right turn on Sheridan going east, would take us on a mile and a half bike ride to the lakefront. For some strange reason we would climb into the bramble bushes that fronted and grew up and over the fence line surrounding the Waveland Golf Course. I can't recall if we thought we were Tarzan in the jungle or some type of soldiers in the bush, but for several years, we would park our bikes at Sheridan Rd. and crawl through this growth on our hands and knees for nearly a mile, all the way to Belmont. When we walked back, our unlocked bikes were always still there, and we were always filthy from head to foot. A few years later, unlocked bikes would disappear in a matter of minutes if left unattended.

A left turn at Sheridan off Sheffield would mean that we were now going west on Dakin. A trek up Dakin would take us to the railroad tracks and Graceland Cemetery. We were always being told to stay away from the trains. Story after story from our mothers, told us of some boy we never heard of getting maimed or killed by pretending the huge machines were toys to play around. We never knew if the stories were true or if our parents were trying to prevent us from hoping on and off the slow moving rail cars back then.

True or not, the stories didn't work until a kid we knew from another neighborhood got his leg cut off by a slow moving railcar. That bit of fact did work, as we never road the railcars again.

The cemetery, now considered a tourist attraction due to all the governors, and mayors, as well as famous people entombed there, had a long fieldstone wall about four feet high running all along the Irving Park Rd. side of the cemetery. We had to walk that wobbly old wall whenever we could. Slips, followed by cut knees, elbows, and an occasional tooth knocked out, never slowed our enthusiasm for walking on top of that wall.

Graceland Cemetery itself, started before the civil war, wasn't a place to play in. Huge looming statues of fierce looking angels guarding graves, and dark, above ground crypts made the place too scary even on the sunniest days for ten or eleven year olds.

Off Dakin, heading back south to Grace was a very strange, one block long street called Alta Vista. Cobble stoned with dimly lit streetlights, this one block of homes was an anachronism in a neighborhood full of subtle incongruities. Many of the tightly joined homes had gothic, and to a youngster, foreboding embellishments.

From stone statues of lions and gargoyles, to iron fences with tall sharp spires, Alta Vista was a street to stay away from at night. I recall an early test of manhood was to be able to slowly walk down the street alone at night as your friends watched from a safe distance. I recall now that I was eleven before I could make that trek. I also recall that I was scared crapless the whole time.

A few blocks up Sheridan to the east was Marigold arena. Then it its death throes, the Marigold had been famous for years as a coliseum to professional wrestling. A strange character of the 50's called Gorgeous George had helped put the Marigold and Chicago pro wrestling on the map. A huge twelve chair barbershop across the street from the arena was adorned with picture after picture of George in his heyday. I saw and heard so much about the man, that after a while, I was certain that I had seen all of his thousand or so choreographed matches.

I remember once going to the Saturday night matches and watching a tall, thin Jamaican called Beachcomber Rockhead get pummeled for about 20 minutes by this bad guy with hair on every part of his body except his head. Finally Mr. Rockhead had enough and knocked the bad guy out. How did he do it? He did it with a head butt of course.

Across the street from our apartment was Horace Greeley Grade School. The huge four story red brick building took half a city block. The gravel covered schoolyard, all the remainder except for the Hubbard Storage building on the northern corner. The rear of the school facing the playground was chalked with a dozen batters boxes on its walls. A game called fast pitch with a rubber ball was all the rage back then because you only needed two people to play. The small rubber balls cost a dime back then and every store in the neighborhood carried them. The constant bouncing off the school wall, plus the wear and tear as the balls skidded along the harsh gravel meant they didn't last more than an hour or two at best.

I remembered how we had to be a team when we played fast pitch. If the next batter was a lefty, you had to bat lefty. We even kept statistics on our team's players. When we really needed a hit, we would put in a pinch hitter from the team to make sure we ended up batting in our natural stance when the game was on the line.

When there were enough of us for a "league" game we would switch to a hardball and use the diamond that had been etched into the ground by thousands of games played by as many kids over the years. It took no time at all for the ball to need a wrapping of electrical tape to keep it from disintegrating. Getting balls, which cost a buck and a half, was a constant concern to all the neighborhood kids. I remember that there were four sports back then on the Near North. There was spring baseball, summer baseball, fall baseball, and winter baseball.

Moving west on Sheffield towards the ballpark at the corner of Sheffield and Grace was the Antiseptic Laundry building. More like a factory, the doors were often open to dissipate the heat from the huge pressing machines. I always stopped for just a second and looked in on all the people sweating and toiling in the steam. I vowed never to do that kind of work when I grew up

One more block and you were at Sheffield and Waveland where the turnstiles for the bleachers were. Earliest recollections of the big sign over the gates stated 75 cents for a seat which quickly went to one dollar. My dad thought the Wrigley's had gone crazy with their prices. Especially for a team that seemed to have little problem losing a hundred games a year.

Still, the bleachers at a dollar, was cheaper than the upper decks at $2.50. I can't recall what the box seats were in those days. They probably cost a buck or two more, but why sit there when the bleachers were the place to be.

Past Wrigley, with a left turn on Addison, were the old pawnshops that littered the area all the way to Halsted. As long as I can remember I was fascinated by all the World War II souvenirs in all the windows. I often wondered why anyone would hock in a medal they had received from their country for being in the war. I never realized the sign of poverty and need that pawning those medals probably meant.

Around this area, nearly six blocks from my home, was the music studio where I took three years of accordion lessons. I truly hated that accordion. Weighing a quarter of my own weight, the trek to the studio was exhausting. To rub salt in the wound, the studio was on the second floor at the top of a set of stairs that seemed to never end. I remember mom saying I could switch to the piano, but dreading the thought like the plague. When it dawned on my fourth grade intellect that I didn't have to push a piano all the way to the lesson and back, I switched in a heartbeat.

I also switched music teachers. I recalled I started taking lessons from a nun whose name escapes me even in this dream. I do remember she was as frustrated as the lay music instructor because I refused to practice my piano lessons. I do remember the nun cracking me on the hands every time I hit a sour note. I always came home from a lesson back then with a pair of stinging hands.

A little further south, at Seminary and Belmont, was my grandparents, John and Mary Treacy's neighborhood. Like my own, it was a microcosm of the city. Within a few blocks, one of each type of little store that served that specific neighborhood etched itself into the landscape.

Grandma and grandpa were just three decades off the boat Irish and grandma never did get used to the fact she had a refrigerator and freezer. Every day she would walk the block to the corner butcher shop and buy just the food needed for that day's meals. I recall when I went with her how I hated to see the chickens outside the store in cages, waiting to be chosen for beheading and plucking. The old butcher always showed grandma the meat as if he was trying to sell her a car. He would tell her how he had saved just this selection for her and didn't it look lean and tender. He wasn't doing this just for show. On the occasions that grandma cooked up an inferior hunk of meat for grandpa, the butcher darn well knew he would get chewed out the next day.

Also on Belmont and Seminary was a department store that was called The Blue Store. The old building housed everything that the small neighborhood stores didn't offer including shoes. My grandmother would always tell me with a laugh of the time she took mom and me to The Blue Store to buy me a pair of baby shoes. I wouldn't shut up for anything, until grandma pulled a stuffed teddy bear off a rack and handed it to me while the shoe salesman laced up a pair of white, high top shoes on my feet. When the fitting was over, the shoe salesman almost lost his fingers trying to wrestle the bear away from me, so grandma bought the teddy bear along with the shoes. The bear still has a place of honor in my home as he watches me type this story.

The one thing I recall hating about going with grandma to the stores was our trek over to John J. Cooney's Funeral Home on Southport just off Addison Street. The funeral home handled all the Irish in the neighborhood who passed away, and grandma considered it very important to go in, see who was being waked, and for us to say a prayer or two regardless of whether she knew the person or not.

I remember grandpa, a big barrel-chested man, sitting at the kitchen table eating incredible amounts of food in his tee shirt with a towel draped over his shoulders.

"You're not eating if you don't break into a sweat Michael" he would always tell me.

Grandpa Treacy was a dandy. The small house on Seminary that he and grandma purchased when coming to America, had a crawl space under it and Grandpa and mom's uncle Pat decided it needed a full basement. For two years they dug a seven foot tall, full basement out from under the house...by hand. At night when it was dark, grandpa would take bucket after bucket of dirt across the street to the grammar school playground until finally the basement was completed.

The old basement was a fearful place for a youngster. The lights were all individually strung, and a person needed to walk into the shadows to get to the next pull chain that would be on the end of a wire swinging a foot off the ceiling. To the front of the house, and to the end of the basement as you came down the stairs, was grandpa's tool shed. It was a frightening experience lighting your way to the shed, but the neat, old tools worth playing with, made me overcome my fear. Well, most of the time.

I recalled many more memories of my grandparents, the Treacy's, than I could my fraternal grandparents, Anthony and Louisa Fak. Grandma Louisa died when I was six and Grandpa Tony a few years later.

I recalled for the first time in decades, the little apartment at the back of a closed up hardware store on Halsted Street. The apartment couldn't have been more than six or seven hundred square feet with two small bedrooms, but at one time, all five Fak children plus

Grandma lived there. Grandpa Tony went out for a paper one night, and didn't come back for twenty years. I laugh now how I recalled when I asked my dad or uncles where Grandpa had disappeared to, they said they didn't know because no one ever asked him.

My most vivid recollection of Grandma Louisa was of her in her casket and that is a shame. I remembered with more fondness Grandpa Tony always telling mom to burn his toast. I also remembered dad getting yelled at by nursing home staff because grandpa was ruining all the jig saw puzzles. It seems he didn't have a lot of patience, and when a piece would almost fit, he would take out his pocketknife and whittle it until it did.

There was one of those years, where the 17 year locusts came out, that I vividly recollected. Both Faks were buried together at St. Joseph cemetery, and the family, as was the case back then, was there for a frequent visit to tidy up the graves.

The locusts were everywhere and the constant, deafening sound was something I was surprised I had forgotten about. After locust after locust landed on me, I ran into the car, and with my little sister Mary Ellen, sweltered in the summer's heat as the locusts climbed all over the windows. Mom and dad never said a word as they finished their jobs, flicking away the creatures that were like a swarm of gnats that day.

Abruptly my dreams changed again. I was back in the room with Ted. He was smiling and said.

"Those are good memories of the places around Wrigley, Mike, but I want you to tell me more about the people you remember. I want you to tell me about the sights and sounds of those days"

As he said his last word, a new series of specters formed in line for me to recall. I saw the sharpener man walking down the street, pushing his huge grinding wheel cart, calling out his services to all the wives abandoned for a day of housework in the countless apartments.

Tony, the fruit and vegetable man, his panel truck with baskets hanging over the sides, would slowly drive down the alley, stopping every hundred yards or so to swing out his huge scales and yell,

"Fresh fruit and a vegetables."

The moms would all come down and judiciously select a few perfect fruits for the family table. You could see by the way they smiled and visited with each other, that hanging around Tony's truck, finding out the latest in neighborhood gossip, was a special respite from the day's activities. Tony's fruit truck was more than a traveling store. It was an event.

I remembered the coal trucks driving down the alley and then dumping their coal. All the apartments back then were coal heated. The huge trucks couldn't get closer than fifty yards to the coal chutes so they got as close as they could, dumped their load and drove on. Soon, down the alley would come this lean, chiseled, black man pushing a wheelbarrow with a janitor's broom and shovel inside. Back and forth the man would go, shoveling the coal into the barrow and then wheeling it to the apartment bin. The job was always done by this same man as best I can recollect. In all the times we saw him, and played around when he was working, he never looked at us once.

He never said a word. Just back and forth, load after load, until the mountain of coal was gone. A brief sweep of the alley and he was down the block, repeating the job of making the next mountain of coal disappear. I remember trying to catch this man's glance, to say hello or just to confirm our existence together. Always though, his eyes were down, without a glimmer of life. A backbreaking job had taken the life out of this man and the spark out of his eyes. It now dawned on me how hard this man worked. I found myself hoping that his personal life wasn't as difficult.

As the coal man slaved away, we often played in the cave like gangways. The gangways on Sheffield were an integral part of our lives. They were shelters in the winter from the cold and snow as well as a cool shaded place to be in the summer. It was in these tunnels on hot summer days that we sat and read our mountains of comic books or organized our shoeboxes full of baseball cards. We would swap and study the statistics the back of each card told us. The goal every summer was to get the complete four or five hundred cards to complete the year's set. The victory was in this achievement alone. I recall never talking about how much one or another card was worth.

I wish this dream had been kinder to me. I remembered putting hundreds of cards folded up on the spokes of my bike to make noise, especially several Mickey Mantle rookie cards that I had no use for at the time. As with most childhood treasures, the comics and cards as well as the toys all lost their importance over the years and were mercilessly disposed of. How different my life, all of our lives would have been if we still had all those cards and comic books.

Other visitors down our alley were the garbage men. I recalled how everyone had heavy 55 gallon drums to throw their garbage in. There were no plastic, light weight, garbage cans back then and I remembered how I admired how these huge men would balance the cans on edge, spin them to the truck, and then lift them up to dump the trash into the truck's hopper. There was no such thing as a little garbage man. They were all huge men that in the summer sported enormous arms that stretched their tee shirts to the limits.

I remembered when Mr. Green on the first floor died and his daughter from another state came to clean out the apartment. Each tenant had a storage shed in the basement and after she had checked it out for valuables, she told us we could have whatever was left. I remember an awesome chemistry set that was left by her. With beakers and flasks and all kinds of things to make messes with, we all played with that chemistry set. Dad set up a sheet of plywood on saw horses in the coal bin that had been abandoned after the building switched to oil heat and for a year that was our secret laboratory. We always had to be together when we played with that stuff as the basement was dark and scary when left alone.

Regrettably, I also remembered that we found a shoebox full of old baseball cards in the piles of stuff left by Mr. Green's daughter. They were stupid tobacco cards, of baseball players long retired, with just a picture and name on the front with no statistics to read. Agonizingly, I remembered how we just threw them in the trash. There were hundreds of them in mint condition.

I recalled Tuesdays at 10:30 a.m. That was the date and time each week when the air raid sirens would sound. At the time it wasn't a question of if we would have a nuclear war with Russia. It was a question only of when. As the sirens wailed I watched adults, who when they thought no one was looking, took a quick glance up in the sky, just to make sure it was a test. My dad always told me that the Russians weren't dummies. When they did decide to attack us it would be on a Tuesday at 10:30 so that they could catch us all off guard. Watching the adults take quick peaks at the sky, I wondered if they had talked to my dad.

In 1959, the year the Chicago White Sox won the pennant, a poor misguided soul set off the air raid sirens that night to celebrate the Sox victory. Dad was a die hard White Sox fan and I remember him later laughing and saying that all he could think of was that his beloved Sox had finally won a pennant and the Russians were going to blow us up before they could win the World Series. Ten days later the Sox went down in six games to the Dodgers and my dad wished the Russians had bombed us. He was disconsolate.

I remembered the huge summer festivals at St. Mary of the Lake. Not a carnival like today, but more like a giant two day family picnic. In 1958 the church had a big raffle with the all new Ford Edsel as the grand prize. I remember my dad and I walking around that car on the church lawn and his telling me all about the new technology this auto offered. He talked how some day we would get a new car instead of always driving around in a junker. At the time, neither of us knew that would never happen.

I recalled how for several years, half of the dining room was a train layout on two full sheets of plywood. I remember dad continually buying new buildings or tiny streetlights or Lionel cars that did special things when you threw a switch. I also remember mom being mad at dad for spending so much money when there were other things she deemed more important than another building for the miniature city. As I grew older, I came to realize it wasn't my train set but dad's that he continually worked on. Somewhere in his childhood he had dreamed of having a train layout like this one, and I being born had been the perfect excuse to go and spend a fortune on these toys. I recalled looking under the apron of the layout at what looked like hundreds of feet of wires and considering my father a genius.

I remembered always having a birdcage in the corner of the kitchen. Canary after parakeet filled those cages as well as the cages of almost every other family in the neighborhood back then. I remembered Happy and Chirpy and a mean nasty little parakeet that thoroughly enjoyed biting people even when they were putting food in the cage. I don't remember that birds name but it should have been Lucifer.

I recalled the catwalk running across the back yard from the second floor rear steps to the roof of the six car flat garage that was home to clothesline after clothesline of freshly washed clothes. There was no fence around the perimeter of that roof, and I wonder why after so many years of playing on that roof, no one had ever fallen off and broken something.

One day for no apparent reason other than age, the roof of the garage caved in causing Mr. Green to lose his model T car that had been stored in one of the stalls for over 30 years. When the garage was completely torn down and removed, we had a great new ball field to play the new game of whiffle ball. Whiffle ball was a huge hit because the ball didn't travel very far and was perfect for the crowded neighborhood.

I remembered a very stupid incident when I was about eight years old. A bunch of the older kids were playing Tarzan in the back yard. There was an old oak tree that had a huge branch running parallel to an equally old fence. The boys had wrapped a rope around the big limb, and climbing up on the fence, they would swing off and land several feet away and then beat their chests. I thought this was great and asked if I could try it but I was in a different, younger, gang and I was told to beat it.

Later that day, after the boys had left; I grabbed one of mom's clotheslines to repeat the feat myself. I made one serious mistake however, as I tied the rope around the trunk of the tree rather than the limb. When I jumped off the fence, I was drawn back into the old tree of course, and rammed it point blank with the top of my head. I knew something was wrong as blood started running down my face, but it didn't hurt, so I casually went upstairs to tell mom I needed another cleanup.

When I walked in the door, mom started screaming. It seems there was a piece of the old oak tree sticking out of my head and a great deal of blood was matting my thick hair smooth.

I couldn't remember much more of this story except mom put a stocking cap over my head (I guess she didn't want people seeing me with a hunk of tree in my head) as she threw baby sister Mary Ellen in the buggy and the three of us trotted the seven blocks to Dr. Purcell's office. I do recall the number of stitches was seven. Seven out of what eventually would total more than one hundred over the years.

I thought of the old refrigerators that from time to time popped up in the alley. There had been horror stories of children going inside them and suffocating when they couldn't get out. People were told to remove the doors of any abandoned fridges to prevent this. I remember one of the dads coming out into the alley with a sledgehammer and smashing the door mechanism off of a refrigerator abandoned behind one of the apartment buildings. The look on his face told me he would have used the sledge on the person who had put the fridge there if he knew who it was.

In a way, the abandoned refrigerator was an early harbinger of what was happening to the neighborhood. People who didn't care about how they lived and how to keep their property clean, were moving into the neighborhood, and things were becoming filthy as well as dangerous. It was getting near the time to leave the Near North.

As other vignettes in my life moved up in line for their turn in my sleep, they were all whisked away by Ted's voice bringing me back to the room.

"Mike, those are some wonderful memories, but I don't want to leave out old Wrigley from this dream. You're starting to stir and I wouldn't want this dream to not be complete."

There, across my sleeping mind's eye, appeared the famous red Wrigley Field sign at the corner of Clark and Addison. The park was empty now, and I found myself walking around inside the even then old ballpark. Under the Clark Street stands was the concession counter that always saved us the ends of the popcorn machines offerings. A poor crowd or a rainout gave us boxes and boxes of free popcorn, plus a hot dog or two. I wish the venders at that counter had a face. They were the kind ones. The other stand's employees would shoo us away, and smiling devilishly, throw the food in garbage cans as we watched. We never needed the food. It was just that we loved freebees.

Looking out from the stands, I could see on the Waveland side of the park the one truck firehouse, where, when certain teams with right handed power hitters came to town, we would sit and wait for two things to happen. First we would listen on the firehouse radio for the signal that someone was in the process of parking one over the catwalk and into our waiting gloves. Sometimes when we had missed a few games, one of the firemen would give us a ball that had bounced into the station and ask us where we had been that day.

Every once in a while somebody like Mays, or Clemente, or Musial, would clank one off the fire engine's grills. Those were keepers to the firemen. We understood. We never asked for those special balls. A baseball to us was for play, not a souvenir.

The second thing we waited for at the firehouse was the fourth or fifth inning. By then it was obvious that no one was going to pay to see the game and the Andy Frain ushers would smile and walk away from the turnstiles. In a heartbeat, we would go under the bar and scoot into the upper deck to watch the end off the game. Some of the Frains were better than others about freeloaders in the park. I don't think Cub management minded, because attendance back then was not very good during the week. I think maybe the Wrigley's were embarrassed when a foul ball was hit down the right or left field stands, and those new fangled TV cameras would show the sphere clanging around and about completely empty sections of seats. Maybe we helped make the place look closer to the always exaggerated attendance figures that Jack Brickhouse and Vince Lloyd would announce every day.

Two areas that were strictly off limits were the box seats and lower stands. These seats were where the season ticket holders sat, and no one was going to let them think that freeloaders could see the game the same way that they could.

The bleachers were our favorite area back then. Usually half filled, a good seat could still be found except on double header Sundays. I recalled that sometimes when there was a twin bill or a special team was coming to town, we would actually pay to get in. We would arrive two hours before the game so we could get front row seats on whichever side of the field we thought a home run was more than likely. We also got there early because sometimes during outfield practice, the coaches, hitting enormously high fungos to the fielders would answer our waving plea to them to hit one a little too far. The result, of course, would be another ball for us, condemned to the gravel playing field of the Horace Greeley schoolyard as soon as we got home.

In those days roller skating was very popular, and Wrigley was made for the sport. The smooth concrete walks around the ballpark were great for a maximum head of steam. Sometimes when the Cubs were out of town, the fences around the turnstiles would be open for delivery men. A quick zoom under the bar and Wrigley's great concrete ramps were before us. Walking up to the upper level we would put on our skates and zoom down the great ramps. Catch the bar at the end of each level, and you could whip your self in the opposite direction at a still greater speed. The noise of our skates of course, would bring someone to chase us out. A quick duck under the turnstile and we were gone. We never once got caught.

I remembered how in the fall, the great metal gates on Sheffield were open. Mountains of new turf would lie on the sidewalk waiting for the grounds crew to sod the ballpark for the next Bears season. When crews were on breaks or weren't near the gates, we would gingerly walk into right field. The inside structure of the ballpark was a playground. The field itself was a different matter. We would walk reverently in the outfield, dreaming of a day when perhaps the stands would be filled with fans cheering for us. Hope against hope of being a major league ballplayer filled our minds as we felt the grass under our feet. Thoughts of all the great ballplayers that had walked on this very soil made each step an event. The Wrigley Field complex was a place to goof around in. The field itself was hallowed ground to be loved and revered. Eventually, someone would see us and yell at us to get out of the ballpark. We would run away, back out the great doors.

One after another of the great memory making players that I had seen in Wrigley lined up to vie for favorite memory in my recollections. I remembered how the players parked their cars by the ballpark along the railroad tracks off Clark. They needed no special security area. People would always wave and say hi to them, but they were never harassed back then, at least not by the Near North kids.

It always made us laugh when, before a game, we would see people hanging over the walls asking any ballplayer to sign something for them. To us, the players were a daily fixture in our lives. We felt no need to collect remembrances or gather souvenirs of the moment. Like our childhood, we thought both would last forever.

Ernie Banks was always the best. Every time we saw him we would yell, "Hey Ernie". The man would always acknowledge us with a huge smile and that constant classic retort of his.

"Hey, how ya doin?"

Although he said it to all the kids he saw, the genuineness of his manner made every kid feel like they were a personal friend of Ernie Banks.

It probably was a better time for all the ballplayers back then. They could walk over to the stands, spend a few minutes of idle chatter with us, and not get deluged with people shoving things in their faces to sign. I think they knew who the Wrigley kids were. So many adoring faces, in so many towns, they couldn't remember us individually, but they acted like they knew us. This simple if false recognition by our heroes was everything to us. It allowed us to pretend we were friends with our idols. It validated our lives.

Pushing itself to the front of my dream was a remembrance of a day in right field. We must have paid to get in that day because we were in the front row, our drinks precariously resting on the aggregate wall that was the border between a long out and a home run.

A young Cub rookie, who was having a horrible time not only at the plate but also with the glove, was on the field in front of us. During the game, the rookie was backing up to the wall and having all kinds of problems judging the flight of a hard hit ball in a swirling wind. As we watched in horror, the rookie almost got hit on the head as he dropped the ball for a two base error. The fans, who loved their lovable losers, never did seem to warm up to this young man. In a few years the Cubs gave up on the young player and he was traded. Fortunately the young man never gave up on himself. His name was Lou Brock.

I remembered coming back to Wrigley in 1963. I had been gone for over two years and the distance from the old neighborhood to where I lived now was akin to being in another state at the age of 14. I had come to hang with the old gang and catch a doubleheader against the Mets who were one of the few teams the Cubs could beat back then. Jimmy Piersall, primarily an inhabitant of the American league, had a brief stint with the Mets at that time. During batting practice we watched in our favorite front row, right field seats as Jimmie made behind the back or between the legs catches of impossibly high fungo hits. Whenever he caught one, he would turn to the bleachers, wave the ball at the crowd, and then fire it at the scoreboard or somewhere else where hands waved in the air like the beaks of newly born sparrows. I would bet that Piersall caught twenty balls that day during fielding practice. I don't recall any of them making it back to the batters box. Lord, he would have made a great Cub. How the fans would have loved to have cheered for him.

I didn't know it at the time, but that would be the last time the gang would have Mike Fak hanging around with them.

Suddenly, I was back in the room.

Ted said: "Hurry, it's almost time to wake up. Tell me your most memorable thoughts about Wrigley Field."

I knew what the recollections were immediately, although I hadn't thought of them in almost forty years.

Once, the gang was sitting in the front row of the bleachers in left field just off the catwalk. The Cubs were playing the Giants with Willie Mays at the plate. I watched as the Cub pitcher threw a slow curve or change up that had Willie completely fooled. Amazingly Mays stopped his motion, re-cocked his bat, and nailed the pitch high and deep, right at us in left field. I felt that great rush that anyone feels who has ever gotten near a ball in the stands. I recall pounding my glove (which I always brought to the games) and bending my head straight back as the ball soared over my head, onto Waveland, and into the firehouse full of scurrying firemen. A homerun on a near second swing of the bat! For weeks when we played ball, we tried to double hitch on a pitch. We couldn't do it. Finally we had to resign ourselves to the fact that only Willie Mays could do what we had seen.

I also remembered sitting way up in the upper deck one Sunday with my dad. About twice a year dad didn't work on a Sunday and it was a special treat to go to the game together. Koufax was on the mound for the Dodgers and I never saw anyone pitch as great as he did in my life. I remember, even way up in the upper deck, I could see how his sweeping curveball had hitters bailing out of the batter's box only to see the pitch curve back over the plate for a strike. Dad would laugh and tell me that I was watching the greatest pitcher in the history of the game that day. I still believe he was right forty years later.

My dream was ending. Ted's voice in the background was saying goodbye. I quickly asked Ted what had been his greatest thrill in baseball. He said we could talk some more but first he wanted to give me his phone number before he had to leave.

"So we can keep in touch", he said.

As he started to hand it to me, I woke up.

For several minutes I felt a deep depression as I lay in bed. I'm not sure if it was because of what I had experienced or because I was saddened that the dream had come to an abrupt end. I tried to go back to sleep, to see if this was one of those dreams you could get back into, but it wasn't. It wasn't because I couldn't get back to sleep. It was because still more memories of those days went racing through my mind. The dream had been a key. A key that had opened the door to those days past and although the dream was over, the door remained wide open.

I remembered when the Duncan yoyo champs came to St. Mary's. It was such a big event that the nuns gave us a double recess to watch these grown men do amazing things with a piece of wood and a string. I now remembered that for years I wore a mitt on my left hand and carried a yoyo in my front pocket.

I remembered the sand box dad had made out of plywood. Day after day we would build fortifications for our plastic soldiers and then either shoot at each others troop deployments with rubber bands or bottle caps to knock the soldiers over before our own were considered killed.

Often you would find six shooters around our waists as we played other games. Cowboys were kings back then with Hopalong and Roy Rogers and the Cisco kid not to mention the dark and mysterious Lone Ranger.

Every "Five and Dime" back then had an entire aisle of cap pistols and caps back then. I smiled as I remembered wasting so many nickels taking entire rolls of caps and slamming an old brick on top of them. The noise was a loud as a cherry bomb. Unfortunately, our being so close, made our ears ring for hours after we were done.

When I was six, I remembered going all day in my new cowboy boots without wearing socks and firmly believe I have never had a set of blisters more remarkably large and painful than those given by those boots. Even the blisters on my fingers when I decided to see if my first wood burning tool was hot yet, paled in comparison to those babies all over both the tops and bottoms of my feet.

From time to time, our ball caps were laid aside to don a coonskin cap or two. Davy Crockett was big in the late 1950's. No doubt bigger and more famous than he was when he was alive some hundred plus years before. After watching Fess Parker's image of Davy swinging his gun, "Old Betsy" back and forth at the evil Mexican soldiers and fading off the screen in Disney's super popular, three part series, I entered my first curious sojourn into the world of research. I recall being a very disappointed young frontiersman when the books all told me Davy probably surrendered and was killed unceremoniously by a firing squad. The idea of determining fact from fiction with every thing I see or hear has been a trait I carry with me to this day thanks to Mr. Crockett.

Once in a while, the ball glove, caps and pistols were taken off to be replaced by one of our mom's biggest bath towels. Tucked into the back of our tee shirts, the gang would whoosh around the block as Supermen, saving the world from villain after villain. George Reeves as Superman was our first huge television hero who wasn't a cowboy. When the news broke that he had allegedly shot and killed himself I recalled realizing for the first time that even our heroes were temporal.

I recalled getting in serious trouble with mom and dad while helping out Tom Terrific one Saturday morning. I drew a boat on the T.V. picture tube to help Tom get away from some dastardly villain. I was supposed to have a Winky Dink set that included a plastic film to be placed over the picture tube in order to do this, but I didn't. For many years the family saw their favorite television programs with a faint vestige of a poorly drawn boat still indelibly smeared on the 10 inch screen.

I remembered the hula-hoop block parties, and the haunted house on Kenmore. I remembered going to Cricket Hill with my dad to fly a kite or play croquet. I remembered playing football, first with my uncle's old leather helmet that I could tuck in my back pocket, and later a great plastic Bears helmet that had the newest good idea, a facemask.

Most of all I remembered the freedom we had at such an early age. A freedom to play within several square miles of home without fear to either our parents, or ourselves, that any harm would befall us. I remembered though how slowly, almost imperceptibly, the neighborhood had changed for the worse. Changes that caused us to move to the Northwest side when I was twelve years old.

It has now been nearly forty years since I have walked those old familiar streets. I wonder if my thoughts have been accurate. I will have to go back someday. I have to find out.

A Return to the Old Neighborhood

The Near North is Now Wrigleyville

My wife Sharon and I got up at 5:00 a.m. on Thanksgiving Day Eve, November 23rd 1998. We had come to Chicago for the holiday a day early so I would have time to make a jaunt over to "Wrigleyville". Sharon, ever being the supportive spouse, had said she would be happy to go with me and take some pictures. She didn't ask why after over twenty years of living together that I now had to go back home. I'm glad she didn't ask. I really didn't have a compelling answer to why all of a sudden I had to visit my old stomping grounds.

I had decided that a dawn raid on the neighborhood was best for two reasons. One, the area is now a mass of humanity and traffic, and I wanted to drive slowly through certain areas. Secondly, I also knew that walking around the area with my head bobbing in and out of alleys and buildings could look suspicious to residents. I didn't care to have to explain myself to the inhabitants of Wrigleyville, or worse yet, a Chi-Town cop or two.

Driving east on Addison, the day's first light was illuminating the sky. My grand entrance back home would be at dawn. I felt myself tense as the great red shield of Wrigley Field came into view.

It was all wrong. The park didn't look right. The building was the same, but the huge towers of lights on the roof just weren't supposed to be there. Wrigley didn't have lights until, strangely enough, the night of my 40th birthday. I recalled how the neighbors around the park had heavily contested their installation. They didn't want night games to further crowd the already densely populated area every summer night. I found myself wishing the lights weren't there for another reason. They had crushed one of my childhood pictures of what Wrigley Field was supposed to look like.

Driving past the south end of the park, we took a left on Sheffield. Immediately, I noticed that the Sheffield side doors were gone. The huge green iron gates had been replaced with modern ribbed aluminum entrances. They also didn't look as big as I recalled. In fact the huge sidewalk of my youth didn't seem as large as it once was either.

I was shocked as my old block came into view. I had heard that Horace Greeley School had been razed many years before, but I was not prepared for what had taken its place. Nearly the entire east side of 3800 Sheffield was a huge four-story brick structure. With only small glass block windows sparingly placed on the Sheffield side of the structure, the monolith came within just a few feet of the street. Allowing only enough room for the standard four foot wide sidewalk, the huge building made the whole block still dark a half hour after first light. My home block, so open and bright with the schoolyard across the street, now looked like it was part of a passage through a giant cavern.

I turned left on Dakin, still shocked by what I had driven past. Once again, I noticed that the entire block was not as long as I remembered it was. The street also was a lot narrower than I recalled.

We found a parking spot all the way up Dakin where the old railroad tracks were. The area, in fact everything, seemed condensed. Apartments snuggled close to the little street that ran adjacent to the tracks and Graceland Cemetery was just wide enough to get a car through.

I wondered how long these residents had to drive around to find a place anywhere near their house to park. One thing the Near North or now Wrigleyville never did have was enough parking spots for the huge amount of apartment dwellers in the area.

I found the cleanliness of the old tracks remarkable. Along them, the great brick buildings stood clean and neat as pins as Sharon and I began walking the neighborhood. First up going back east on Dakin, was Alta Vista Street. It is a remarkably beautiful, one block long street with house after house looking a year old instead of a century. With brightly lit streetlights and an impeccable asphalt street, Alta Vista wouldn't scare anyone today.

The two old lights on the whole block. The cobble stoned streets, the gargoyle statues and gothic fences are all gone now. With them I felt a little of Alta Vista's unique character also has been deleted.

As Sharon and I walked toward Sheffield, I soaked in the sights of all the buildings we were walking past. I had this strange feeling that things were the same only different. I was saying hello again to an old friend I hadn't seen in four decades. I knew I was different now and so were these man made markers of my life so long ago.

Reaching the alley back of Sheffield, I started feeling more excited. The great back yard at the corner was still there. I had played in that yard a thousand times. It felt good to see it was still the same except, instead of a field of dirt created by a thousand ball games; it boasted a marvelous lawn with manicured bushes and trees. It obviously had taken the years a lot better than I had.

Walking down the alley showed just how much renovation had taken place since the early 1960's. The old cracked alley was now a smooth clean path of concrete. The old back stairs of the apartment buildings, exposed before to the elements, like a strange scaffold covering the homes, now were mostly enclosed with walls of new siding or brick.

The few buildings that still had outside rear porches boasted redwood or cedar milling that showed great pride in ownership at no small expense. The days of garbage, abandoned stoves, and deadly refrigerators and graffiti on a garage door were now gone. I didn't mind. I was proud of what had become of my old friends.

As I came to the back of my old apartment building, I had to pause for just a second. The flat roofed, six stall garage was gone of course, but the back of the building had enclosed stairways shielded from the elements that weren't there many years before. The yard had become a parking lot with signs on a fence by each marked stall, explaining whose car belonged in which spot, and what dire consequences would befall a vehicular interloper.

As we finished our walk down the alley, I understood the huge investment that had indeed been made by the area's residents. When we had moved away in 1960, the Near North Side was deteriorating badly. It was becoming unsafe. It was, to be honest, a dirty place with more and more undesirable elements moving in on a daily basis. Looking around, I realized the neighborhood had indeed been reborn. I no longer felt contempt at the "yuppies" for renaming my old haunt. It was beautiful, and deserved a new name. I found myself saying good morning to Wrigleyville.

A turn east towards the front of the block brought us to the corner where the old Antiseptic Laundry Building still stood. The only seemingly abandoned building in the area, boarded up windows with graffiti seemed to tell the tale of an ill-fated nightclub venture. Perhaps it was a thriving place and the look was for ambiance. Either way, this old friend, like me, was out of place in this neighborhood. I laughed at the thought that the laundry and I both had aged rather poorly compared to the rest of the structures around us.

I found myself shaking my head as we walked to the middle of the block where I had lived. The block, now a full hour after dawn, still was dark from the strange building hovering over the entire block. The new brick building still troubled me. I thought how unfortunate it was for all those upper apartments to loose their front window views. Views I had of an old school with an old schoolyard with the elevated tracks as a backdrop.

Perhaps the new view was in fact better. Perhaps I was just starting to hate so much change to the pictures I carried in my memories. I know I was upset that the gangways cut into the underside of the buildings now carried locked iron gates or doors on them. I knew it was a sensible security decision, but I hated seeing them lost to view. A few looked like they had been bricked over for good.

Remarkably, the greystone at 3824 Sheffield had a "for rent" sign on the door. The apartment my family had rented for $98.00 a month, utilities paid, now commanded the price of $1,920.00 per month, plus utilities. In my mind I quickly asked myself if the neighborhood was now twenty times better than when I lived here.

"Not with that damn building across the street." I decided.

At the time I was looking at the "apartment for rent" sign with Sharon taking pictures of the block, a thin black man came out of what once was the Hotel Carlos. Looking strangely at us, he went about his task of sweeping the sidewalk in front of what now was called the Sheffield Inn. I smiled at myself and wondered if the inn was still a home for transients.

Sharon and I decided to walk a few blocks down Sheffield going north. The corner where the tough old Irish cop ruled now looked like any corner intersection in any city. The deli was gone. All the little stores were as well. In their place were small professional storefronts for dentists or lawyers.

Starting to feel totally out of place, I quickened my pace to get to the elevated station just before Irving Park Rd. I thought if anything was still as it was, the el station would be that place. The elevated system in Chicago had changed little over the years. I felt certain the Sheridan Rd. station would be no different.

Going in the big glass doors, I felt a wave of recognition. It was as I remembered it. A little more modern, the interior was laid out exactly as it always had been. The newsstand to the right with papers, magazines, candies, and gum could have produced a photograph interchangeable with one from the 1950's.

As Sharon took pictures of this one mental toe hold of my past, the young man behind the counter stared quizzically at our rapture in admiring the inside of this old station.

"Tourists" my wife said to answer the man's look.

Back outside the station, a quick glance around told me that I had found my one landmark in this area. It was time to get back to the car and drive up Sheridan Rd. towards St. Mary of the Lake.

Driving the three blocks to the church, I paid no attention to the buildings going by, save one. The beautiful Jewish Synagogue was being replaced. A huge sign touting condominiums at the location for under $200,000 was displayed over the front of the building.

As we came to St. Mary's, I pulled over to let Sharon take some pictures of the huge greystone church. I felt a wave of sadness. St. Mary's hadn't received the attention the other structures had in the area. Its grey blocks of limestone were heavily stained with the wear of a century. Its huge triple front doors needing refurbishment and a new coat of varnish. In that moment, I felt fifty years old for the first time in my life. Looking at this venerable, time worn church, it soon became apparent how long ago I had worn the robes of an altar boy in a magnificent looking church of an era now lost forever.

Later, after I told my family of these thoughts, my brother-in-law told me he and my sister, Mary Ellen had visited the inside of the church and it was still one of the most magnificent cathedrals that they had ever been inside. I laughed as I thought how St. Mary's and I were brother and sister. Both still had a lot going for us inside, but our exterior appearance left a lot to be desired.

Quietly, I drove back to Sheffield and made a right turn on Waveland at the north side of the ballpark. Shaking my head again at the light standards on the ballpark's roof, it felt good to see the little fire station where it always was.

Stopping to let Sharon take pictures of this pristine little one truck station, a young fireman walked out the door and looked at us. I thought of getting out of the car for a minute to explain myself, and then realized there was no explaining what I was doing, let alone what I was feeling.

Quickly I drove off.

Driving back up Addison, Sharon asked if we were going over to Belmont and Seminary where my grandparents, the Treacy's, had lived. Feeling fortunate that I was wearing my sunglasses, I whispered to Sharon, "It's time to go home."

When I wrote: Before it was Wrigleyville, I had forgotten all about this event. I call it an event but that is being kind. A better word would be "terror".

I'm not sure when it started to happen. I imagine I was perhaps 7 or 8 years old when the dream started visiting me almost every night. My mind has deleted and expunged as much of the timeline as possible from my memory, so the exact period this dream controlled my sleep will forever be a surmise.

I'm sure experts in the field would call this a classic first person night terror. It was a classic all right. It haunted me for many of the early years of my youth.

The Turn at the End of the Hall

It all started after a visit to the Lincoln Park Zoo. I don't know why I asked for that Bushman Bank. The foot tall replica of Lincoln Park Zoo's most famous ape was brought home by my parents. I must have asked them to purchase the plaster cast bank of Chicago's most famous zoo animal of the past century. The ape had died a few years before and had been immortalized by being permanently placed on display at the Field Museum. I don't know if I saw the 500 pound behemoth alive at the zoo or in death at the museum. I do know that for many years Bushman followed my every sleeping moment, terrorizing my subconscious.

I remember now the small bedroom and the small dresser at the foot of the bed. I recall how the Bushman sat on the right hand corner of the dresser…except on stormy nights. On stormy nights it would sit where ever it wished to.

I recall the first terrible storm after the great ape was brought home. A storm with heavy winds and drenching rains was mauling the city one late summer night. The wind, whistling and screaming through the old wooden window panes, brought a chill into an otherwise overly warm apartment.

The old oak tree outside the bedroom window scratched and clawed at the glass, as the wind helped it try and get into my room. The lightning flashed quickly and loudly as the storm continued to grow.

The thunder from the great storm rattled and shook the entire building. Between flashes of lightning I could see the bank on the dresser looking in my direction. The great ape, down on his haunches, teeth showing over a curled pair of lips, was menacingly looking right at me. I found the covers a frail but necessary protection from this king of all monsters.

I tried to sleep, but the storm, and the tree, and the great ape, refused to allow me to clear my mind enough to fall away from this evening's terror.

After a huge crackle of lightning lit the bedroom, my worst fear began to take fold. The instant light and then darkness brought on by the storm showed Bushman had moved to the center of the dresser. Another flash of light and the great ape was now on the left. Still another and the ape was gone.

I held my breath as I clenched the blankets tight against my throat. The storm had let the monster loose and I feared it was coming for me.

At the next flash of lightning that held for several seconds, I looked for the demon but could not find it. My relaxing was for just a moment, as turning my head to the nightstand, I saw the creature sitting there, just a foot from my head. In the darkness, it was still visible, its red eyes and mouth full of razor sharp teeth, almost in a smile.

I bolted from the bed and ran into the kitchen of the long shotgun style apartment on Sheffield. The Bushman bank didn't follow me. It didn't need to.

At the front of the apartment, through the kitchen, dining room, hallway, and around the turn to the coat closet, I could sense that the real Bushman lurked in those shadows. I felt myself compelled to move from the kitchen into the dining room, ever nearer to the giant shadow at the turn at the end of the hall.

I remember trying as hard as I could to stop my trek towards instant death, but there was a force pulling me ever closer and closer to its massive being.

Finally, after fighting the pull for hours as best I could, I was compelled to enter the long hall way. I grabbed hold of the doorway of the bathroom and hung on for dear life. The shadow, now only ten feet away, mentally continued to draw me towards its clutches. It wanted me to come to it, at the turn at the end of the hall.

My parents were awakened by my screams as their bedroom was just past the bathroom and just a few feet from the end of the hall.

I remember dad shaking me and telling me to wake up. I bolted upright, finding myself in bed. I told him that somehow Bushman was alive again and he waited for me at the turn at the end of the hall.

Dad shook his head and told me I had been having a nightmare and to go back to sleep. I told him the storm had brought Bushman back to life. Dad looking out the window asked me what storm I was talking about as a calm sky held a full moon in its hands.

I told dad all about the evening and what had happened, never once admitting it could be a dream. Dad went over to the dresser and picked up the Bushman bank. He placed it in the closet and closed the door, telling me that now I was safe and to get some sleep.

I persisted and begged my dad to let me sleep in their bedroom. There was little room for another, but I promised to lie on the floor and not make another sound.

My dad, never seeing me this scared before relented, and I spent the night at the foot of my parent's bed, feet against the closed bedroom door.

Every night for the next several years brought the same terror to my sleep. On some nights I was able to remain in the kitchen or dining room. On others I would get pulled all the way past the bathroom to my parent's bedroom door and my last cling hold before death.

Always I hung on to something for dear life, as I could see the shadowy figure lurking at the turn at the end of the hall.

Always, somewhere in the dream, I would wake in a cold sweat and chastise myself for being so stupid as to keep dreaming the same nightmare. If it is a nightmare, I would quickly point out to myself.

Finally, after years of torment, the night came where I was too weak to fight the thing at the turn at the end of the hall.

Again in a storm that had the great oak slamming against my window, I found myself up and in the kitchen. This night I was not ready for the ordeal, and within moments found myself slipping past my parent's bedroom as I was pulled to the turn at the end of the hall.

That night was the night I was going to die.

I remembered how with every bone in my body tensed, I closed my eyes and awaited the end of my young life.

When I reached the turn, I felt a small sigh of relief at the fact there was nothing there. No shadow, no Bushman, nothing but my own reflection staring back at me in the mirror at the turn at the end of the hall.

The feeling of being pulled again hit me as I realized that Bushman wasn't at the turn, but lived in the cloak closet just ahead. Fighting as best I could, I was compelled to open the closet door and meet my doom. Ever so slowly, I turned the knob. I was being forced to face this demon from the past few years, and I could do nothing except open the closet and face my worst nightmare.

Resigned to slaughter, I opened the closet door.

Nothing. Nothing but the coats the family wore, resting on the pole. Nothing but dad's fedora on the shelf, and an umbrella on a hook on the back of the door were inside the closet.

I awoke from the nightmare and found myself in bed again. This time I realized there really was a terrible storm outside, but I found no fear in my heart. Jumping out of bed I ran down the hall, flung open the coat room door and yelled at the top of my lungs.

Dad, not very happy, stumbled out into the hall to see what all the yelling was about. He shook his head as I explained that there was no monster at the turn at the end of the hall. Dad said something about there could be a beating at the turn if I didn't shut up and go to bed.

That was it. The dream never came back again. The Bushman bank sat on the right hand side of the dresser until I was twelve years old and we moved away. Bushman never moved again.

I wrote this little remembrance for the 1998 *Lincoln Courier* Balloon Fest supplement. Perhaps lost among the pages of real stories and advertisements, those who did read this little blurp all asked the same question. Is it true? Of course this tale is true. Stuff like this is too hard to make up.

The Reason I Can't Fly

I was nine years old the first time I had an aerial mishap. Or should I say almost had one. For my birthday, I got my very own Superman costume. Superman of course was the number one, greatest superhero in the world right then. The man of steel carried far more import than those mere mortals, Hopalong Cassidy, Roy Rogers, or Gene Autry. The man of steel was not only the ultimate good guy, but he could fly too.

I recall for years having dreams about running down the block, sticking my arms out in front of me and taking off into the heavens. My nightmares were the dreams in which I had problems taking off, or if lucky enough to become airborne, quickly drifting back to earth. To this young boy, the importance of being able to fly was the central theme in my childhood.

My parents decided that buying me the rather expensive Superman suit for my ninth birthday was in fact a wise decision. For years I had stolen bath towel after bath towel, stuck them in the back of my tee shirt, and whooshed around the neighborhood. Since the towels rarely came home with me, and those that did had become suitable for the rag bag, my parents probably felt the uniform was an investment, rather than an expense.

I still remember the incredible feeling I had when I first donned that uniform. Standing in front of the mirror, in all my splendor, with hands on hips, I decided it was time to fulfill my destiny.

Going into the living room and removing the third floor window screen, I prepared to leap out into the wild blue yonder. At just that moment of historical import, my mom grabbed me by the cape and pulled me back into the world of mere mortals.

The remaining years of my childhood were split between lectures on doing my homework and explanations of why I could not fly without mechanical assistance.

As the decades have passed, I have had my turns being above the Earth. From commercial jets flying to and from vacations, to Cessna's and Piper Cubs in the Army, I have had my time in the air. Always, I have felt terribly uncomfortable being subjected to the whims of a "man made" flying apparatus.

I have passed on several opportunities over the years to go up in a hot air balloon during the Balloon Fest. To be honest, I never will. My wife and son assume it's because I have become a wuss in my older years, but it isn't.

They don't understand that in an open gondola, I probably wouldn't be able to fight the urge of 45 years to prove I have the ability to fly without any assistance but from the winds themselves.

You see the reason you rarely see me in shorts or without a shirt is because I still wear that suit under my clothes. I still believe I can fly.

I'm also old enough to fathom the repercussions in the event I am wrong.

This was my *Lincoln Courier* column for the Christmas of 2005 edition.

The Christmas of 1960

In October of 1960, my dad took the plunge into becoming a homeowner. We had been Near North residents in Chicago since I was born, but the neighborhood surrounding Wrigley Field had slowly grown too dangerous to raise a family. When it got to the point my dad had to pay an older kid to walk me and my younger sister to St. Mary of the Lake school to prevent getting pounded on by one of the neighborhood gangs, my father decided it was time to leave.

My father, then a truck mechanic, found a classic Chicago style bungalow on the northwest side of the city and decided it was time to move west.

The house, badly in need of repairs, carried a price tag of $16,500 due to its condition. The $101.50 per month payment made my mother cry every time someone said it out loud, but my dad was determined to work longer hours to pay this huge monthly bill.

The weather gave little chance for my father to dig into house repair that first winter. It didn't stop him from starting a tradition of Christmas decorating that eventually would become legend. The Christmas of 1960 showed the first signs of things to come.

Although needing almost everything at the time, the house boasted strands of Christmas lights around all the damaged windows that first season. On the small lawn appeared the first tacky hollow plastic figurines of a snowman, Santa and reindeers, and of course, a pair of three foot tall angels. They all had light bulbs inside them to beam through the dark nights leading up to Christmas.

Neither my mother nor I knew that this decorating would continue to grow every year until people from Kentucky and Nebraska would eventually be seen slowly driving by the house to see this incredibly gaudy display of house decorating. Urban legend has it that the managers of Marshall Fields would drive by our house to get ideas for their State Street store, but I can't confirm nor deny the tale.

I do remember my Grandma Treacy mentioning that she could have used the electric meter for a meat slicer when dad turned all the decorations on every Christmas season. All of this started in the year 1960.

One day in mid December, when my father came home from work, he stood at the back door without coming into the kitchen. When mom asked him why he wasn't taking his coat off and getting ready for dinner, he said he wanted to clean up a few things in the decrepit old garage first. Looking at me, he said he could use my help. I could see in dad's eyes there was something else going on, and knowing that look always produced interesting results, I grabbed my coat and ran out the door after him.

My dad, smiling as he entered the garage, told me he wanted to show me something he had found at work. As he began to open the rear of the old Plymouth wagon, he gave me that dad look that meant I was being sworn to secrecy. Nodding my head and peering into the back of the car at the same time, I was shocked to see a bomb in the car. The bomb, about four feet long and more than a foot in diameter was distinctive by its back stabilizing fins. It was obvious this blockbuster bomb was the kind I had seen in hundreds of movies and newsreels being dropped over bad guys during the wars.

Dad reached in and pulled this huge bomb out with one hand. Banging his knuckles on the side of the bomb I could tell from the hollow metal ring that it was just a tin shell. This alleviated my fears that dad had decided on blowing the house up and starting over, rather than remodeling room by room.

Dad explained how this was known as a practice bomb. The shell, filled with water or sand, was used by the air force to help novice pilots practice their bombing without errantly blowing something up, such as a neighborhood, in the event they weren't quite ready to be given the real things.

Dad, rummaging through the company's scrap heap, had found this marvelous bit of junk and he started explaining to me what he thought we should do with the bomb. His idea was to cut the front of the bomb off, from left to right, at an angle that matched the slant on the roof of the house. Then bolting the bomb to the roof, it would look like it was sticking into the house. Behind this "ornament" would be a sheet of plywood with lights strung on the board saying: "Merry Christmas, The Russians are coming".

It only took my twelve year old mind a few seconds to realize this was one of dad's best ideas yet. It also only took another moment to wonder how we could get this idea ratified by mom.

In the ensuing days, I could tell dad was just waiting for the perfect time to spring the idea on mom. One night, at dinner, when mom was in a totally good mood by not burning the meat for the thirtieth consecutive night, dad sprung the idea on my mom.

It only took a heartbeat for mom to tell us both we were crazy and that there was no way she would allow us to put a bomb on the roof as a Christmas decoration. Mom finished her lecture by leaving a loophole for dad that over the years he would exploit to the fullest. Mom said dad could do whatever he wanted with decorations, but no bomb.

Over the years, I failed to ask my father if he ever thought we actually would use the bomb for Christmas. I do recall it being in the garage for a decade, and every year when he brought the subject up, mom would tell him to do something else, which is exactly what dad did.

As time went on, dad revised Christmas history on our front lawn to include Santa and his thirty reindeer as well as Frosty the snowman having a mate and twenty or so baby snowmen.

I will never know if he planned on using the bomb or just used the threat as a means to continue embellishing his Christmas decorating ideas without being slowed down by mom. I do know that I will always remember those days as if they were yesterday, and I imagine they are a Christmas gift unto themselves. I do wish I knew where that bomb went to.

One lazy Sept 1998 day, I was in the back yard of Jeff Nelson, managing editor of the *Lincoln Courier*, sipping sodas. We were exchanging sports stories of memories long past. I was surprised that I mentioned the story you are about to read since it has always been embarrassing to me. Jeff thought the tale was great and said I should put it down in words.

A few days later I turned in this copy with the joke that if it were printed, the back page of the paper would be a great place for it to be situated. The next week, as Sosa and McGuire closed in on 60 home runs, my story made the paper. On the front page.

The Things We Throw Away

It's time to open a closet door that I have been leaning against for 35 years. I have told this story to only a dozen or so individuals, and then only when my guard was down. It happened in the spring of 1964 at the almost brand new Gordon Technical High School on Chicago's North Side. Gordon was a sprawling campus of 1700 all boy, Catholic students. It hasn't been that small since.

I sat out my freshman year of sports due to an act of humanity. As a freshman football player, I tried to catch a falling behemoth fullback who had just tripped over the yard line marker. As the monster fell into my arms, I caught him and watched as he proceeded to drive himself and me into the frozen turf. My act of kindness had turned my right arm and wrist into an accordion that meant the whole year of sports was over for me, let alone the football season.

As a sophomore, intelligence told me that since I was far better at baseball than any other sport, perhaps I should concentrate on this far safer recreation. How I rue the day of that decision.

At the time, Gordon Tech was an integral part of the Chicago Catholic League. That meant that the only three sports worth any merit were football, basketball and bowling. As a member of the just christened frosh-soph baseball team, my teammates and I were advised that there was no budget for a secondary sport such as ours. Our schedule was even made up on the fly, with games scheduled against any school at any grade level that would play us.

With no budget and even less school interest, our school was delighted that they had been able to finagle "hand me down" uniforms from another ball team. When we were given our uniforms, there were no questions about the size of your chest or waist. Brother Frank simply said:

"Your tall, here's a tall one; your short and dumpy, here's a short and dumpy one."

Those uniforms precipitated the season from hell.

The major leagues in those days had switched to lean, cotton uniforms, with a higher stirrup sock than before. Our hand me downs were drab, baggy white and blue pin stripes, made out of 100% itchy, scratchy wool. We hated those uniforms so much that I don't recall a single player asking his mom to tailor them to size. I seem to recall now, that a few guys on the team didn't smell like they ever bothered to take them home to wash.

The first game we played was against the all boy, 7000 student, just down the block arch-rival, Lane Tech. How well I remember the hatred we had for them when they got off the team bus in their fancy uniforms. Many of them laughed at us in our oversized woolies. That was a mistake. In the first game of the frosh-soph Gordon Tech team, Lane Tech went home with a major league spanking from a group of angry 15 year old Catholic boys with only two practices under their belts.

I'm not sure if we won because we were out to avenge ourselves, or because the Lane Tech team couldn't stop laughing long enough to play ball. I will never forget the locker room after the game, when varsity coach Wynn came in and apologized for forgetting we had a game. When Brother Frank told coach it was no problem, that we had won easily, Coach Wynn had the most unbelievable look on his face.

At that moment, Brother Frank was christened a baseball genius by the varsity coach. Seeing a long season still before us, none cared to argue the coronation.

Brother Frank was all of five foot five. For several days, however, his head scraped the ceiling tiles as he paraded around school.

A lot of the season is lost to me. Like the name of a date long ago who told you not to call her again. Many things have been swept into dark comers of my memory. One thing I will never forget is that those damn uniforms cost me my baseball career.

As an eighth grader at St Bartholomew's, I had a 750 batting average. It was easy to remember, because I went 33 for 44 at the plate. During that summer, before my sophomore year, I made two park league all-star teams as both a pitcher and catcher.

My sophomore year at Gordon, however, was awful. I must have batted something like 3 for 40. It was so low that the team manager refused to figure it out and post it on the team bulletin board. His act of kindness is something that I will always be indebted to him for.

"It" drove me to retire from high school sports. "It", is not my performance, but that awful uniform I had to wear. I wish I could tell you how many times I came up to the plate and seeing that bat in my hands, stuck it down my back to scratch an itch as a pitch sailed past me for a strike.

Once, I remember wearing long underwear to see if that would help. It stopped the itches, but I got so dehydrated by the heat that one inning I ran out to left field without my glove. Thank God Brother Frank was observant enough to notice in time.

I recall clearly the end of the season. After personally securing, I am sure, the lowest batting average in organized baseball history, Brother Frank came into the locker to cheer us all up.

""Boys, thank you for a great first season. I know some of you will be moving on to the varsity. (This said as he looked away from me). And some of you will be back here with me again". Either way, we will have new uniforms, just like the varsity wears".

With that statement, Brother Frank rolled out a 55 gallon garbage drum and smiled at us as we all slam dunked those hated uniforms into the garbage. My career was over, but at least I felt the satisfaction of sending that uniform to the dump to dwell forever with my batting statistics, which also belonged there.

Now you may wonder what the point of this whole story is.

This is the part that causes so much embarrassment to me. You see, I have to this point, left out two important facts. First, the team that donated uniforms to our team was The Chicago Cubs. Secondly, the number I wore that year and threw in the garbage was number 14.

Yes, I threw Ernie Bank's old uniform into the garbage. To make the memory even worse, I stood over a garbage drum that had the uniforms of a dozen of my childhood heroes in it. I could have taken them all home with me, but instead I just walked away from owning a marvelous chunk of Cub history. Lord help me for being dumb enough to tell you this story.

A person can't have stories about one's life without including the pets that were an integral part of their lives. Here, in random order, are tales of animals that graced or ruined a portion of my life. A condensed version of this little tale was carried in the *Lincoln Courier* in the spring of 1999. The marked response to this simple story showed again how much in common we all have with each other, especially with our love for our pets.

Murphy the Cat

When people drop me notes or call me about something, I make a little note on the old floppy disk. Eventually enough information or common remarks from many of you cause me to try to render your thoughts into a coherent article. One of these days I hope I do one.

My file on pets and pet stories is full to the gigabyte so it seems it's time to tell a pet story. The problem is there are just so many heartwarming tales of pets and the people who live with and care for them, that I can't do justice to some without doing injustice by omission to others. Let me tell you a story and see if all of you who own pets can relate to it.

As a child my gathering of pets was typical of the era. A half dozen parakeets and canaries, turtles, goldfish, and an occasional batch of lightning bugs in an old mason jar, were always a part of my upbringing. The principle pets for my family of course were the family dogs. Sparky, Skipper, and ever reliable Rusty helped raise me in Chicago during the 50's and 60's. It seems the only animals I never called my own were an alligator, which was a craze back then, and a cat.

My wife Sharon and I were married in 1979. We had talked about a pet dog, but realized that with both our families living in Chicago, leaving a dog at home while we made weekend visits up north just didn't seem fair to either our rugs or the dog's bladder. We talked about getting a cat because they can be left for a few days with a good bowl of food and a clean litter box.

One day, when I came home from work, a little multi colored baby kitten was in the garage. Sharon knew folks who were looking for homes for their litter of kittens and she just couldn't resist this little ball of fuzz. The kitten's head showed markings in the shape of the letter M that caused me to think of a good friend of mine, Mike Murphy, so we named the little cat Murphy.

That first summer we bought an unfinished home in Eureka, Illinois and I took the summer off work to finish out the home. It was during those days that Murphy and I would begin a bonding process that would fulfill me for the next 17 years.

I would be working outside, painting or sawing. Murphy would be in the huge back yard, chasing grasshoppers or butterflies as all kittens do. Never would she stray too far from me. Always she would come at the run when I called her. A trait other cat lovers tell me is rare in this most independent minded of pets.

We had lunch together and would read the newspaper together. That is after I moved Murphy off of the part of the paper she was laying on. This habit of being right in the middle of things never left Murphy's personality. Ask my son how often we would play board games and old Murph would come in the room, plop down in the middle of the board and start purring. It was impossible though to ever get mad at that darn cat.

Murphy had a remarkable trait that I have never seen in any other feline. She would purr so loud that you could hear her in another room. Many were the nights when Murphy, asleep at the bottom of our bed, would purr so loud she would wake my wife and I from a sound nights sleep. Sometimes a "Murphy shut up" would do the trick. Other times, Murphy knowing she couldn't shut off her purr machine, would just get up and walk out of the room. Yes we could hear her purring all the way down the hall.

As the years went by and Murphy slowed down, she began to gain weight. Her life became simple and basic. Take a little nap, eat a little food, and find somebody's lap to lie on and get a good scratch job. In later years it got to the point that as soon as I sat down anywhere, there was old Murphy on my lap, ducking her head under my hand looking for a little attention. You could never give that cat enough scratches.

She also had another very strange habit that I have never seen before. When you picked her up she would open her forepaws and place them around your sides. Many are the witnesses who would say;" Is she hugging you?" She was, and I miss it terribly. In 1998 I had to have Murphy put to sleep.

She began losing weight. Her legs wouldn't work as they should and she couldn't keep her food down. Ever the good cat, she used her litter box when she would loose her meal.

Because she couldn't keep her food down she was always starving and I couldn't bear to see her so miserable.

After procrastinating for weeks, I took Murphy to the vet to end her suffering. I remember sitting in the car in the parking lot, trying to tell myself this was the right thing to do. I remember Murphy sitting in my lap, her paws again hugging me. I wondered if she knew what was happening as I sat there blubbering like an idiot, trying to gain my composure. I wondered if she too felt that it was time to leave the world and her now sickly body.

After what seemed an hour, I sucked it up and went in the veterinarian clinic. Everyone understood the agony I was in and tried their best to help me through this. The Vet explained what was going to happen as if he were telling me about an operation I was about to have performed on a loved one or myself. I held my little buddy while she was given the lethal sedative and used every ounce of manhood I had to remain stoic.

I almost changed my mind a dozen times, but Murph was too sick. She needed peace.

In only a moment, 17 years of living experiences were turned into just memories.

I had built a little cypress casket for my buddy and placed her in it. Rushing out of the vet with the wooden box, I made the drive home disconsolate. I brought Murphy back into the house so that our new kitten, Smirky, could see Murphy and not spend the next two weeks sniffing about the house looking for her mentor. You could tell from the new kitten's reaction that she understood what had happened to Murphy. The instincts of the animal world include somehow the understanding of death.

I remember sitting on the kitchen floor, my back against the refrigerator trying to explain to Smirky why I had done what I had just done. I remember telling Smirk that I hated myself right then and asked the little kitten who made me the judge of life over one of God's creatures. Smirky just sat on the floor, looking strangely at me and sniffing the air around Murphy from time to time.

I had decided to bury my pet in the front yard next to the soft maple. The day was cold and rainy, the ground, hard and unforgiving to the blade of my shovel. I recall being thankful for the rain. It shielded my emotions from many the motorist who honked as they drove by. As the last tuft of grass was laid back over the simple grave I recited a verse used often by the author and Veterinarian James Herriot.

"All things bright and beautiful
All creatures' great and small
All things wise and wonderful
The Lord God made them all."

I believe there is a heaven. I don't know if I belong there or not. But I need all of you to know that if there is a heaven, a little cat by the name of Murphy is up there, no doubt sitting on someone's lap catching a few scratches.

Every Christmas I write a Christmas story for my column. This one was for Christmas 2004.

Jackson's Christmas

The December winds blew hard and cold at the farm on top of the hill. The two kittens huddled against each other by the back door of the farmhouse. They were trying to catch a little of the heat escaping from the bottom of the door before it was mixed and lost forever with the cold. It was under these circumstances that the old man with the raspy voice first met the two kittens.

The old man, working at the farmhouse, came upon them as he arrived for work one day. It was apparent that the male tabby, about 7 weeks old, had been through a real scrape with something that he couldn't handle at his young age. Cuts along the face as well as ears showed a fight that had gone badly. The old man assumed that an argument over territory with one of the older cats, living with the horses, had led to the kitten being banished to the open harshness of the winter.

The other kitten, a female oyster shell about three months old, seemed to have taken on the responsibilities of helping the younger cat survive. The oyster cat lay over the younger kitten, using its body in a feeble attempt to keep the injured kitten warm in the 20 degree temperature.

The little yellow tabby, although badly beaten, was as outgoing as any cat the old man had ever seen. Sitting down with the kittens on the back stairs, the tabby immediately ran into the old man's arms and starting purring. The oyster kitten came closer to the old man, but laid next to his leg, seemingly preferring attention be given to her injured ward.

The old man with the gravely voice fed the kittens a doughnut he had and watched as the two gulped down the food. He knew he had to do something to help these kittens or this winter would be their last. He found a cardboard box, and placing it behind a sheet of plywood leaning against the house, laid his flannel shirt in the box. Without any need of direction, the two kittens climbed into the box and huddled together in the shirt, the older, oyster kitten again lying on top of the tabby.

In the next few weeks, the old man and the two kittens became good friends. The arrival of the red truck in the driveway each morning brought the two kittens flying out of their box and climbing immediately into the front seat of the old truck. On a paper plate waited a can of cat food that quickly was gobbled down by the kittens.

The old man had named the kittens, since all good friends should be on a first name basis. The little tabby, who was constantly wailing for attention, was given the name Whalen. The oyster kitten looking like a Jackson Pollack painting gone bad was named Jackson.

The old man was worried what would happen to the kittens when the job closed for the Christmas holidays. He was afraid a week alone might be their undoing, and was planning on coming back whenever he could regardless of the job site being open for work.

Just before the holiday, the situation changed between the old man and the kittens. Arriving one morning, only Whalen came running to the truck. The old man looked everywhere, but Jackson was nowhere to be found. He had always admired Jackson and the way she had decided to mother little Whalen. He thought perhaps she had decided that only the barn, with its bales of hay, could save her from the winter and had abandoned her little adopted child.

"She toughed it out as best she could." the old man decided.

He never went to the barn. He feared he wouldn't find Jackson there, and that meant she had met her demise in the harsh reality of a country winter.

The old man knew he couldn't leave Whalen to fend for himself and knew a couple who were thinking of getting a kitten. Bringing Whalen to town, the kitten and the young couple really hit it off immediately and Whalen had a new home. The old man was glad, but he often wondered and worried about what had happened to Jackson.

The story was over until mid January when the old man, arriving for work, saw a very thin Jackson come flying down the lane towards the truck. The kitten didn't even need the door opened for her as she came leaping through the window and began nuzzling the old man. Again with only a doughnut, the old man rubbed the kitten as she devoured the food in quick gulps.

The old man found out from one of the other workers that before Christmas, Jackson had somehow ended up in one of the worker's vans and had been transported to Lincoln. Jackson, not as friendly with people she didn't know, had taken off when released from the truck and had begun a great Christmas journey back to the cardboard box she knew as home.

It had taken nearly a month for the kitten to make the thirteen miles back to that old box, but here she was with the man she considered her friend.

As the kitten curled up in a ball on the man's lap, the man thought of what the little kitten must have gone through. Thirteen miles in the cold snowy farmland was a trek by itself. Where did she find food and shelter? How often did she come close to being killed by a farm dog or a coyote during the travail? What empowered her to face any and all dangers just to get back to a cardboard box with an old flannel shirt stuffed inside it?

As the kitten slipped deep into sleep, the old man's eyes welled up with tears for the young cat. She had been through so much and all she ever asked for, all she ever got, was that old box behind a sheet of plywood.

Stroking the kitten's head, the old man remarked to his friend how sorry he was she had such a rough Christmas.

The old man and Jackson became very close in the next few weeks. Upon the man's arrival, Jackson would jump in the truck, eat a good meal, and then sleep the day on the dashboard of the old truck as the distant sun gave off heat through the windshield.

During breaks and lunch, the old man would sit in the truck and visit. Jackson, getting stronger, started to act like a kitten for the first time in her young hard life, and they had great times chasing string or a catnip toy that the old man had bought her.

Always at the end of the day, the old man would take Jackson out of the truck and place her in the box. Always Jackson would chase after the man, and follow the truck down the road, as he left for another day. It was a hard time for the old man as he looked in the mirror at the little cat trying to catch up to the truck. He knew as the job was winding down that he couldn't just leave his little friend in that old cardboard box.

In mid February as the old man packed up his truck to leave the job for the last time, he didn't take Jackson off the dashboard. Instead he started the truck, and told the little cat to get ready for a new adventure. Jackson now sitting on the man's shoulder bent over and licked his nose. It was her way of saying she trusted him.

This Christmas Jackson doesn't have a cardboard box for a home nor is she ever hungry or cold. This Christmas, as she has for nearly a year, she will find a good, warm night's sleep in the folds of a blanket at the bottom of the old man's bed.

"Goodnight Jackson and Merry Christmas. I'll see you in the morning."

I don't know how I can have a book with pet stories and not include a story about the family dogs. I love all animals, including man's best friend, so I believe a little recollection of the dogs in my life is appropriate in this compilation.

Dogs in My Life

My first dog was a mutt. Actually all my dogs were mutts, but since I am Croatian and Irish with a smidgeon of Polish ancestry in me, I suppose I also am a mutt. I don't find any necessity in having purebred dogs as pets. I'm not against that practice. I just don't see any requirement for a dog to have a parent's lineage on a piece of paper in order to be a great friend.

Anyway, my first dog was a cocker spaniel mix. That is the kind way to state you don't really know who the daddy was who talked a cocker spaniel into a few moments of conjugal bliss.

The dog was named Sparky. I know that isn't a very original name but considering the other two dogs in my life were named Skipper and Rusty shows my family never got caught up in fancy names for pets.

In fact, one of the only pictures to have survived of my grandma, Louisa Fak, is a 1930 picture of her on a stairway with a huge German shepherd next to her. The note on the back of the picture denotes grandma is sitting with King, another non original name to be sure. I suppose the message was to help viewers understand the shaggy looking individual next to grandma wasn't the then missing Grandpa Tony who bore a remarkable resemblance to a German Shepherd.

Anyway, my first dog was Sparky and that is all I can tell you about that first dog. Sparky was only a member of the family for a few months and then he was gone.

I do recall being frantic, looking for Sparky as a call out to the yard on Sheffield was met with silence and no dog in the back yard.

I remember dad coming home from work and walking the neighborhood with me looking for Sparky and getting nowhere.

One night, soon after Sparky disappeared, dad showed me an article in the newspaper about some family telling how their dog was kidnapped and held for ransom. Dad didn't fool me into thinking Sparky had been kidnapped since I knew we didn't have enough money for a new Wilson baseball mitt, let alone pay off kidnappers to get a mutt back.

Nonetheless, I remember getting excited and then saddened every time the phone rang for the next few weeks. It was always Grandma Treacy and never the head of an international pooch theft ring wanting to make a deal to give Sparky back.

I recall dad telling me the apartment wasn't a good place for a dog anyway, and with his plans for the family to buy a house heating up in his mind, he promised that as soon as we moved we would get another dog.

When we moved to Waveland Avenue, dad kept his promise and got us a mixed Lab, which we named Skipper.

I don't have many fond memories of Skipper either, as he came into my life, ate all the furniture, and then abruptly left almost as quickly as Sparky.

I do remember that Skipper loved to jump when he wasn't eating the legs off of the dining room furniture.

The dog would go flying out the back door and start jumping over the cyclone fence that marked the boundaries of our yard with our neighbors. Back and forth Skipper would jump, easily clearing the four foot tall cyclone fence until he stopped long enough to go to the bathroom and then he would start jumping again.

The neighbors never really liked Skipper since he always landed in the flower garden they had planted directly on their side of the fence. Every time Skipper did his little fence jumping foray into their garden, old man Westlake would have to come out and fix or pull a few of his favorite flowers that Skipper had demolished with his antics.

I remember the next spring that Westlake had planted a series of rose bushes along the fence line and that cured Skipper from jumping the fence on that side of the yard.

We didn't have enough money to get Skipper fixed, but I think Skipper did the job on himself that first time he jumped into old man Westlake's rose bushes.

I can understand now, looking back on it, that dad wasn't as mean or tough as he pretended to be. Skipper was a chewer and in the few years he was with us, every leg of the dining room table as well as the chairs were gnawed into nothingness by that dog. Any other dad, would have killed Skipper or had him put down, but dad would just curse and yell at the dog and at mom and at me and that would be the end of it.

One day Skipper went outside, jumped over the fence adjoining the alley and never jumped back I'm not sure where Skipper ended up but I think he decided he needed a new family to take care of him as ours was almost out of wood furniture.

For several years we had a dining room set with gnawed legs and a few of the chairs, damaged so badly, were thrown out after being considered unsafe to sit in.

I believe the dining room table had a brick, or block of wood under one of the gnawed off legs of the table until dad could afford to buy a new one. I don't recall anyone who visited our home thought that was unusual. Maybe that was because Skipper was living with them.

I don't know why, but in my mind, I kept seeing Skipper jump the back fence just as the garbage truck was pulling into the alley. I pictured Skip flying into the front of that truck and meeting his demise that way. There were no tell tale signs of this on the truck, which I checked the next time I saw it, but I have always had this notion in my mind that is how Skipper ended up. Maybe that really happened and I have repressed that portion of my life. I guess we will never know.

A trusty Irish Setter by the name of Rusty then entered the family's life, and Rusty, who might actually have been a pedigree, would be a part of the family for 16 years.

Rusty was a classic Irish Setter, big and happy, full of love and loyalty, dumb as a box of rocks.

Rusty was everyone's dog and he had so much affection, I'm sure every member of the continually growing Fak family thought for sure they were Rusty's favorite.

Rusty didn't eat furniture, wanted to be outside when it was time to go to the bathroom, and was content on sleeping at the foot of the bed without demanding any scratches or covers

With all those praises, Rusty did have his faults. Again, the family not being able to afford a Veterinarian's bill meant Rusty was still "all there". This didn't cause any problems for the family except when guests would come over, and sitting down in a chair or the sofa, would have to fend off Rusty's amorous endeavors. Rusty never saw a leg he didn't love. A quick admonition would send Rusty sulking into the kitchen and mom would spend the rest of the visit apologizing to our guests.

When I got out of the service, I spent a few years living in the basement and often had the guys over for an evening. Rusty became a member of the group as we would all gather to eat a few burgers, drink some beer, and watch low budget, garbage movies on Channel 32 all night.

Rusty would of course mooch a chunk of food from each of us, but what the dog truly enjoyed was his beer time with the guys.

Rusty would have his bowl in the middle of the room and from time to time, one of us would pour a few ounces into it for him. The dog loved to just sit by the bowl, take a couple laps of the brew and then listen in on our conversations.

The dog truly savored his beer, lapping, then sitting, then lapping again until a look at one of us told us he needed a little more.

By the end of the night, it was time for Rusty to be let out in the yard and then he would stagger upstairs to find a place to pass out. I'm not sure how many times mom would yell down the steps that she was going to kill someone for getting the damn dog drunk again, but it was a lot.

In the later years, Rusty became such an integral part of the family that the dog food was replaced with a pound of ground beef that mom fried up for him every night. There were a lot of things the Fak family could have spent that money on, but like any other important member of a family, Rusty deserved this one simple recognition of his value and worth in the Fak household.

The truth be known, I think Rusty was dad's dog more than any other Fak member. Dad used to think he was hiding his box of chocolate cream drops in his underwear drawer, but we all knew where they were and so did Rusty. When dad would go into the bedroom to watch his White Sox on the tiny television and to savor a few of his special treats without all the Fak kids clamoring for their share, Rusty would go quietly into the room with him.

I remember peeking in and seeing dad and Rusty on the bed, the two of them savoring another chocolate cream drop together as the Sox tried to win enough games to prevent my dad from getting mad at them.

As my dad started to decline in health, so did Rusty. Dad was dying from Alzheimer's, the faithful dog from a full, loving life. In Rusty's last days he stayed with my father faithfully and constantly. I'm sure he knew something was wrong with his old friend as well as himself and he had decided they would stay together till the end.

Rusty didn't make it as long as dad, dying the year before.

They say you meet everyone you knew and loved when you die and go to heaven. Under those conditions, I'm sure one of the first people dad saw was Rusty, no doubt with a box of chocolate cream drops in his mouth. I hope the White Sox were on.

When I wrote my first compilation of stories in "One Hour 'til Dawn" in 1999, I found myself just short of my goal of 250 pages. In a hurry to get the book to press, I remembered my friend and managing editor of the *Lincoln Courier*, Jeff Nelson, telling me people always loved animal stories. Since I already had a few in the book, I quickly pasted this story into the text and rushed off to the printers. Over the years I have had more comments on how readers enjoyed this true but simple story than any other in that book. Here again is my true story of visiting the realm of the big game hunters.

The Great Raccoon Hunters

I have had to wait several years to write this story. I have had to wait because I needed the statute of limitations to run out before I could give this self incriminating confession.

I recall how in 1983, with the assistance of my wife, I made the monumental blunder of buying our house on Union Street. I remember wondering if Union was going to be too busy of a street to live on. Union as it turned out is too busy of a street, but not from cars and trucks. Union, for some reason, seems to be a crossroads where all the wild animals known to man come for a while, drive me up the wall, and then depart. I assume Noah sent scouts into this strange neighborhood when it was time to fill the passenger registry for the ark.

During my sixteen years in this unauthorized game preserve, I have been harassed by rabbits, squirrels, possums, owls, deer, and once a baby pig. Don't ask about the pig. You wouldn't believe that one in a month of Sundays.

The basement of our home has seen bats, mice the size of Dobermans and spiders, so big and mean, that they have tattoos on their arms, or is it legs None of these unauthorized neighborhood inhabitants however ever drove me as crazy as the raccoons.

I promise you this tale is a true story. That is of course unless you carry a game warden's badge. Under those circumstances, I will admit this is just another tall tale. Or is it tail.

144

Like all nightmares, this story started very late at night, perhaps three or four in the morning. Sharon woke me to tell me something or someone was in our attic. In a half comatose state, I listened for the sound of a bird caught up in the eve somewhere. I bolted upright as I heard the footsteps of something really big walking across our bedroom ceiling.

I felt a pang in my ribs as Sharon elbowed me. I effect she was saying "See, there's something big up in our attic". In my underwear, ball bat in hand (you have to keep one available if you live on Union). I crept up the stairs to the attic, checking briefly if the label of the bat was up. No sense breaking a good bat on an intruder's noggin, I thought. The room was empty except for the shadows dancing in and around the boxes of everything we didn't need downstairs right then.

I was about to go back downstairs when I heard footsteps coming from the roomed off storage area to the back of the attic. Slowly I opened the door and reached inside for the light. Slowly I peeked around the corner of the door to see what was so big to make that much noise. In the comer of the attic, going back out the eave, was a twenty pound burglar, I mean raccoon.

It stopped for a minute before it squeezed between the soffit and downspout, turned towards me and gave me that, "who the hell are you" look that all the wild life on Union has given me over the years. I didn't give it an answer with my own look. Instead I turned off the attic lights and went back downstairs to bed.

Sharon asked me what it was that had made so much noise, Murphy, our cat, with a fat tail of hair standing on end also looked at me for a reply.

"I don't know, I didn't see anything", I said.

As the three of us curled back up to sleep, I hoped that perhaps I had been just so tired that I simply had a nocturnal hallucination.

A week went by with no further sightings or bumps in the night. I was beginning to think that I had indeed just had a bad 3:00 a.m. nightmare. That was until Sharon yelled at me one morning to come to the bathroom. There, as Sharon toweled off after a shower, was a thirty pound raccoon sitting on the window ledge, knocking to get in.

My wife, ever so calm said:

"I think he needs to use the toilet".

I made a quick gesture towards the window, in an attempt to scare the behemoth away. The male raccoon stood up on its haunches and clawed at me through the glass.

In the event you ever see a thirty pound animal on its haunches you will be able to ascertain their sex. This was a male.

"Great", I thought. 'This animal is bigger than the one I saw before'. "I have a family of raccoons moving into my house and now they want bathroom privileges".

As the raccoon turned and shimmied back down the drainpipe, I had no idea how accurate my thoughts really were on the subject.

Time passed with no further sightings until Memorial Day Weekend. I had promised myself to get back to work on the front porch and was preparing to tear out a rotted section of the eave on the western corner of the porch roof. As my hammer dug into soft, chewy wood, a large amount of straw and twigs drifted into my face before cascading down the ladder to the ground. I thought it was just the remnants of an old birds nest, as more and more twigs and dried grass clogged the back of my tool.

On Union, we have every type of bird from a sparrow to the South American Condor, so I didn't think much of the continuous debris that fell to the ground before me.

"Must have hit an aviary hotel", I thought to myself.

Getting a good bite on a rotted board, I pulled hard and was hit on the head by something much heavier than a twig. As I brushed the dried grass from my eyes, I saw a little raccoon lying on the ground at the base of my ladder.

Looking back up, I saw five more babies, their heads bobbing and weaving as they looked at me and wondered what the hell happened to their nest and to their little brother. I know it was a little brother since I had run down the ladder and picked the tiny interloper up to see if it was hurt. It growled a funny, baby animal kind of growl and peed all over me. That is how I knew it was a boy.

I held the little critter with mixed emotions in my heart. I was busy checking it for injuries. I was also mad at it making a home in my porch eaves and peeing all over me. I grabbed an empty bucket and gently placed it over the little troublemaker.

Calling Sharon for a glove and some type of cage, she responded rapidly and well. There is no need for delays or for asking questions if your spouse yells for a cage real fast. Not if you live on Union.

Sharon was back in a heartbeat as I waited, staring up the ladder, at the ruins I had made. She had given me a pair of garden gloves and an old antique chicken coop that neither of us had yet refurbished into a potential coffee table.

With gloves on, one critter in the coop, and Sharon watching half inside the door, just in case she needed to run away, I climbed the ladder. There in the nest, staring out over the edge down at me, were three more baby raccoons.

"There were five," I recalled. "Where did the other two go?"

As I reached in and grabbed another boy, yes, it peed on me, I saw the mother in the shadows at the back of the enclosure. One baby on her back, one in her mouth, she looked at me for just a second, as if to say; "asshole", and then she was gone.

Two more trips up the ladder, two more boy raccoons and I had four little bandits in the coop. I also had a shirt ready for the garbage.

Sharon had remained half in and out of the house. Murphy the cat, nose twitching in the air, tail again thick as a tree, also kept herself inside the doorway.

"Cowards" I thought to myself.

As the day progressed, I continued to search through the porch roof for mom and the two wayward youths. I had read somewhere that a raccoon will mate and return to where it was born to give birth to its own offspring. I felt it was essential that I catch these vagabonds before I ended up with a whole herd of raccoons in and around the house.

I couldn't find a sign of where mom and the kids had disappeared. I really didn't care to find the dad. He was a big fellow and might still be holding his bladder since I wouldn't let him in to pee a few weeks ago.

That night, in reaction to my master plan, I set the chicken coop with the four baby raccoons in the middle of the yard. Well fortified with a bowl of milk and a paper plate of tuna, (Hey, I'm not a monster); I waited to see if mom and the rest of the family would show up to try and spring the prisoners. Later, I would recall this plan had no contingencies if in fact they did appear.

Nothing happened. Nothing happened all night. The next morning, Sharon ran the four little buggers in the cage over to the Vets office. She had called and asked if they could make sure these little pissers were weaned and ready for the world. I also made them promise that they would drive for three days in one direction before they let them go. I wasn't about to take any chances on a return engagement.

Just two days later, another interloper fell into my clutches. Working down in the basement, I heard a great deal of noise coming from the old chimney. A chimney that had been part of the kitchen's venting decades ago now was used just to vent the hot water heater. Hearing a great deal of ruckus in the brickwork, I unhooked the exhaust pipe and removed the coffee can lid that everyone uses to cover a chimney hole.

Immediately upon removing the cover, out plopped another baby raccoon onto the floor. As I picked the little sucker up, I noticed it was a girl. I was still dry. I also noticed an argument going on inside the chimney as mom and the other baby climbed back up and out to freedom.

"So that's where you've been hiding", I mumbled to the raccoon.

Another call to the vet, another run over to their office and I was elated. Five babies down, one baby to go. The joy was tempered by the knowledge that I still had mom and dad to deal with and dad was just a little smaller than I was.

In the event you think my ordeal had been trying up to this point, you haven't got a clue. The next several months were a torment I wouldn't wish on anyone, and I mean anyone.

Every night, with no time out for weekends or holidays, mom and the baby would visit the house. Sometimes you would hear them walking on the roof. Sometimes you would notice they were on the porch roof, just outside our bedroom window. Sometimes with power tools in hand, you would hear them cutting and ripping and sawing their way into the house.

One time a neighbor called and asked me if I knew a raccoon sat on top of my chimney every evening. He told me the animal sat back on its haunches surveying its domain. Sort of like Batman on a steeple top looking down on Gotham City. I asked the neighbor if he noticed if the raccoon wore a tool belt around its waist.

One day, a morning inspection of the house showed a huge hole cut in an eave I had previously repaired. That was it. The die had been cast. I was prepared to exterminate the little bastards.

That afternoon I went to Wal-Mart to purchase a BB rifle and ammo. I looked at the BB guns on display and picked the one with the maximum stopping power. The cardboard case the gun nestled in showed a picture of a dead grizzly bear, its tongue hanging out, as a small boy raised his BB gun in the air in triumph.

"That's the one I need", I exclaimed.

Nervously, I took the rifle and the box of BBs' up to the counter. This was my first gun purchase. I kept myself from having eye contact with the clerk in case she ended up being a witness. Without a glance, the clerk rang up my purchase and placed it in a large brown paper bag. I didn't want a plastic bag that would show on store cameras that I had purchased a high powered rifle from the BB gun section of the store.

That was it. In just a few moments time, I had chosen and then purchased a weapon of destruction with no questions asked. As I walked out of the store, I thanked the Lord for the NRA.

I told a good friend of mine, after a blood oath of secrecy that I was going to "smoke" the raccoon family who were destroying my house. Thinking nothing of it, friend X (I want to keep him out of this,) said that he had a "Have a Heart" trap that I was welcome to use.

Being civilized, I thought trapping these interlopers was better than blasting them into oblivion, so I accepted his offer. That turned out to be a mistake.

The first night, I set the trap up on the porch roof. I baited the trap with some of the best cheddar cheese chunks money could buy. I slept well that night for the first time in weeks. The morning showed I had slept too well. The trap was where I had placed it. There were no creatures of the night inside it, and the cheese was gone.

For several nights thereafter, I baited the trap with delicious morsels previously planned for my own dining pleasure. Each morning, the delicacies were gone and the trap lay empty. Finally after a week, I went to merchant Y and purchased a can of poison gopher peanuts. This time, I felt sure, I had outfoxed the trespassers.

I whistled as I spent the early minutes of dusk baiting the trap. A couple gophers' peanuts here, a couple delicious morsels of tuna there: The enemy was mine, I surmised.

Sleeping like a log, I awoke to realize that my adversary was of a greater intelligence than I. The trap sat as it always did, empty. The tuna was gone; the poison bait was still there.

I went into the attic and searched for my old army helmet. This meant war.

For a week I stayed up all night. Helmet on head, trusted BB rifle in hand, Murphy the cat by my side, sniffing the outside air to warn me when the intruders were approaching.

Nothing. Murph and I saw nothing. We heard nothing. We smelled nothing.

I was starting to be convinced that the raccoons had sensed the party was over and had moved on to greener pastures. No doubt the vision of me in full army gear, weapon in hand with faithful and trusty cat on my shoulder, had been a vision that had scared them into leaving the neighborhood. The night of the storm would show me otherwise.

Sharon and Tim had gone up to Chicago for the weekend. I had to stay in town and finish a job that Saturday. That night, Murphy and I dozed on the couch watching violent movies that we had wanted to see but hadn't because of young Timothy being in the house. I had my chips and beer. Murphy was purring on my lap from an overdose of tuna that I was no longer feeding to the raccoons.

As I dozed, the storm that night was a dandy, with heavy rain, thunder, and lightning. Murphy stayed close to me as we gathered ourselves for a good nights slumber in the bed. Murph took her place on Sharon's pillow. She loved it when Tim and Sharon went somewhere.

It was about 2:00 a.m. when Murphy woke me up. Her growl was deep and her hissing was sincere. Amidst the thunder and rain, I could see the raccoons standing on the porch roof just outside the window. Ignoring the rain, the mother raccoon and her now bigger, fatter baby (I wonder how) sniffed and searched the roof.

"Looking for a meal?" I whispered. "Well you're going to get a lead brisket in just a minute."

Quietly, I pumped up the BB rifle that had been under Murphy's pillow. Gently I slid up the sash of the window to cause no concern to the thieves. Ever so carefully, I slid up the screen just enough to clear the barrel of old Betsy. I felt my heart racing as I brought the weapon to bear. I felt Murphy's heart racing as she sat poised on the back of my neck. I could tell she was peaking out from behind my head at the unwelcome visitors. I could feel her breath in my ear.

The raccoons knew we were there. They also didn't seem to give a crap.

"Big mistake girls", I whispered as I moved the barrel out the window and into the field of fire. The fat baby raccoon looked at me, at Murphy, and at my gun. What it did next was a complete surprise.

Walking up to the gun barrel, the youngster took it into its mouth, and started to suck on it as if it was a giant teat. The mother noticing her child's dumb maneuver, looked at Murph and I, and started to growl. I definitely had a clear shot. I also was shaking so bad, I could hear the baby raccoon's teeth chatter against the steel gun barrel. I took a deep breath, and aided by Murphy, who was growling in my ear, I pulled the trigger.

Nothing happened. The gun had misfired. The click however, had been enough warning for the mother raccoon, who came growling and running at the window. The baby, not knowing that it had just missed a golden opportunity to go to coon heaven, chirped and ran from the older beast. Murphy ran under the bed and remained there for a week. Slamming the window just in time, I watched the mother stop short of bouncing off the window pane. Giving me a nasty look and slowly, as if daring me to do something, she walked away.

Hindsight, if you will pardon the pun, is always 20/20 but I often regret not pumping my rifle again and sending a BB into mom raccoon's kiester as she arrogantly sauntered off the roof.

That was the last time the raccoon family bothered our house. Perhaps they were run over by a car. Perhaps they found better pickings at some other idiot's house that had a "Have-a-Heart" trap baited every night. In my mind, the reason they never came back was because mom raccoon knew that she and the baby had dodged a bullet that night.

I still have nightmares about the eventual confrontation I must face with the father raccoon someday. I will let you know what happens.

In the event I survive of course.

My parents were an integral portion of my life and although they have been sprinkled throughout the previous stories, their deaths hold a more significant place in my mind then their lives. I suppose that is because I realize now I didn't have a deeper relationship than I could have with both of them. I regret deeply these next few stories need to be included in this book, but they are what they are, and I can only tell you how I feel about these two very important souls in my life.

This first story, shortened to column length, first appeared in the *Lincoln Courier* in 1996. I received a greater response to this article than any article I have ever written. In 2005, *U.S. Legacies Magazine* published this story in their Father's Day 2005 issue.

Remembering the Tough Guy

This Father's Day I would like to tell you a story of a man and his family whom I have known for many years.

The man, born in 1920, was one of five children in a broken home. Growing up during the depression, he was forced to quit school after the sixth grade to help support the family. In those days there was little time for personal goals. The need to help one's family survive the harsh economic times was more important than an individuals own personal dreams back then. From the age of twelve until his death in 1983, the man's life revolved around nothing but work.

After serving in World War II, the man came back to the states and took a job as a grease monkey for the largest ice company in the Midwest. His job was simple. To keep the fleet of some fifty odd junker trucks running. Workers at the plant told many stories of how this man could get an old truck operational when no one else could. In later years, the workers would often tell the oldest son, who had begun working at the plant that his father was the best mechanic they had ever seen. The comments never surprised the son. His father seemed to have the knack of doing anything he set his mind on better than anyone else.

As the years went by, the man had married and began to grow a family that would total five children over eighteen years. Needing a higher salary to sustain his ever growing family, the man took a home study course on how to be a heating and cooling engineer.

The man passed the test easily and became a refrigeration engineer for the same ice company. In the following years, men told the oldest son that his father was the best engineer the company ever had.

For thirty seven years, this man gave all he had to make the company thrive and prosper. He worked afternoon shifts as well as nights. Holidays, including Christmas, almost always found him on the job earning overtime pay to give more to his children.

The oldest son recalls how for many years his father worked seven days a week to provide a solid middle class life for his family. All of the children from time to time have told me that they wish their father had been home more often. Somehow the man had been caught up in the struggle to give his family all they needed. He never realized that what his family could have used the most was just his being home with them. The man had determined he was in charge of supporting the family. It was left to his wife to raise them.

The man who was quick to temper but just as quick to laugh loved to talk. His favorite hobby in the world, it seemed, was to argue with someone. On more than one occasion the sons have told how their father, when seeing the other person starting to agree with him, would change sides just to keep the argument going. The sons always laugh when they tell stories of his more famous debates.

Although the man loved to talk, he was not one to sit down and give sermons on life to his children. His fatherly advice came instead in little vignettes of recollections by his children.

Two of my favorite stories come from the oldest son who worked for a few years at the ice factory with his father.

It seems the son could really play baseball. At lunch each day the son would stand in the middle of the yard and challenge all the workers to try and hit one of his fastballs. Many a worker grabbed a bat. None of them could come close to hitting the tennis ball as it blazed past them, bouncing off the icehouse wall. Always the young man berated the workers, bragging incessantly that there wasn't anyone who could get a hit off of him.

One day, as worker after worker went down swinging, the son's bragging became too much for the father. Putting down his sandwich, the man ignored the bat, grabbed a janitor's broom and unscrewed the handle. Stepping up to the mock plate, the father didn't say a word. The man just stood there. His eyes telling his son to deliver the best he had to the plate.

The son recalls how with everything he had in his strong arm he fired the ball at his father. The son also recalls the solid sound of the broom handle meeting the ball true and square as it soared over the fence and adjoining factory's roof.

The old man looked at his son and said; "too much mouth" and walked back to continue eating his lunch. As the work crew howled with glee at big Mike showing up little Mike, the son sheepishly went over and sat down next to his father. His dad immediately started talking about an idea he had to get more air pressure out of the factory's compressors. Nothing more needed to be said about his son's arrogance. The lesson had been given. The lesson had been learned.

The son also tells of the day his father had dropped a 400 pound cake of ice on his foot.

That evening, in the locker room as they cleaned up to go home, the son remembers his father's foot was discolored and so badly swollen that the toes were hardly distinguishable from one another. The father gave that look to his son. The man never did tell his wife. The son never told his mother. For two months the man hobbled around the plant. For two months he never took a day off work.

The man, who never lectured, gave all his children their own lessons in life. All the lessons carried the same basic tenets. You don't steal, you don't cheat and you don't lie. You always take seriously what you are doing, and you do it as best as you can.

The man who loved to grumble about the world never could be remembered as grumbling about his lot in life. The oldest son wishes he knew what his father thought of his life. He wishes he had asked just once what his dad had once dreamed of becoming before he got caught up in the tide of raising five children.

As the father approached the age when many begin to think of retirement, he was struck with Alzheimer's. His last two years on Earth were sad memories to a family who remembered the man with the most powerful of minds being mentally laid to waste. The man's last year of life was spent in bed. His mind was completely gone. His tougher than nails body refusing to give in.

Finally in December of 1983, the man's body gave up. After 63 hard years the man could finally rest.

The oldest son recalls after his father's death of going through some of his father's papers. Included was the military DD214 form of his father's service record. Under campaigns: were listed North Africa, Sicily, Normandy and the Battle of The Bulge. The father had never bragged about his military status. Once again the father was telling his son how to be humble.

At the father's funeral, the son remarked how frail the once 6 ft, 190 lb man had become. A sad reflection on his father's last worldly appearance, the son thought of what the funeral directors must have done to that gnarled old body for it to lay peacefully in the casket. For months the dad had been locked in a fetal position, his hands clenched into fists. One last tough thing for his dad to have to do, the son thought.

As the wake went on, family and friends as well as co-workers came to pay their respects. All that the son could focus on were the flowers displayed around his father's bier. A dozen magnificent floral wreaths adorned the parlor, giving off that strange sweet smell that we have all come to associate with a wake. In the corner sat a small rubber plant in a clay vase. It was distinctive for its lack of elegance when compared to the more beautiful and obviously more expensive arrays.

The little plant carried a tag saying it was from the owners of the company the old man had given the best thirty-seven years of his life to. It was the only respect the man would receive from his employer. No one representing the company had enough time to say "goodbye" and "thank you" to a man who had given them almost four decades of selfless effort.

The son vowed to always remember that little plant and always understand that everyone who ever would work for him would always receive the dignities of respect and appreciation. Even in death, the father had one last lesson to teach his son.

This Father's Day, it is a given that the five children will tell stories about their dad. There no longer is a need or a purpose in remembering the man's faults. It is to the point that recalling the best essence of what he was is all that is required. The oldest son will have his own thoughts on his father.

"Happy Father's Day", dad. I will always miss you.

A shortened version of this article ran in the summer of 2004. I received a great deal of response from people who have had this disease strike their families. I was glad to hear I was not alone in my feelings, as were those who contacted me.

Ghosts of Alzheimer's

I will leave it up to the historians to gauge the mettle of President Ronald Reagan. In truth, it takes about a century for a person's greatness or failures to be looked upon objectively. Right now, both friend and foe of the former president are too close to the story and carry too much personal baggage to honestly determine where the man should be placed in the history of our chief executives.

That being said, I would like to spend a moment talking about the cause of the man's death rather than talking about his life. Ronald Wilson Reagan succumbed to complications from Alzheimer's disease. His tomb and every article ever written about the man will show his final day on earth as June 5, 2004.

That date will forever be wrong.

You see, with a disease as insidious as Alzheimer's, it is impossible to know the day a person really dies. Oh, the body is still there, but there is nothing else. There are no feelings, no cognizant skills, no sentient thoughts or awareness of the world.

Throughout the week long eulogy to Reagan, I experienced two distinct feelings of sadness. First, I thought how all of us were robbed this past decade of having him on the airways. Whether you liked the man or not, his wit and his intuitiveness would have made him a great pundit for every cable news show in America. I can just imagine how much fun it would have been to hear his comments on the issues of today.

The Alzheimer's robbed us, as well as him, of those years. He stopped public appearances in 1994 and gave up all outside visits to his office as early as 2001, no doubt because his mental skills just didn't allow him to be himself anymore.

I also felt my heart go out to Mrs. Reagan, a classic wife if ever there was one. I felt for her sadness of saying goodbye to her husband, fully knowing that perhaps for as many as three years, she had done so every day.

The final stages of Alzheimer's, where a person becomes totally unaware of the outside world, can last from a few months to many years.

As I watched her shed her tears over the President's casket, I knew from experience that those were just the latest drops in a tearful journey that encompassed the last few years. I knew how she felt and my heart went out to her because I had been there myself.

My father died from complications due to Alzheimer's in 1982. His death certificate says Dec.16th, 1983, but it was somewhere during 1982 that he actually stopped being truly alive. A child of the tough Gold Coast in Chicago during the roaring 20's, he had survived the streets as well as four years with the Third Armored in North Africa, Sicily, Normandy, and the Battle of the Bulge.

Tough as an anvil, my father, who never went to a doctor after the day he was born, began noticing something was wrong in 1981. Returning from work, he couldn't remember the way home and ended up in the northern suburbs before his mind snapped back to the present. Other things at work, such as forgetting how to start the huge machines he had built using his incredibly gifted mind, caused him to make the personally monumental decision to seek medical advice.

In 1982, there was not much known about the disease, so tests showed there seemed to be nothing wrong with him. My father knew there was.

Ready to be sent home from the hospital with a clean bill of health, my father, in control of his wits that day, had asked me to come and drive him back home from the hospital. As I watched my dad get dressed, I asked him if there was anything I could do for him. Still being the tough street kid, he told me to go find his old colt 45 pistol and put a bullet between his eyes before it was too late.

Tearfully, I told him I couldn't do that. Ever the pragmatist, he told me then there was nothing I could do for him.

In the next year his mind wandered in and out of sensibility. On one occasion he visited me downstate and seemed a bit slow in conversation but was still definitely my father. Getting up to go to the bathroom, he stood in the corner of the rec room, relieved himself, flushed an imaginary toilet lever and sat down again as if nothing unusual had occurred.

That night, as I washed the urine off the wall and floor, I knew that I had little time left to spend with my father.

In the ensuing year, my father became a wanderer in his house. Constantly in motion, he would cry if someone tried to sit him down to rest. Back and forth through the house, 24 hours a day, until, exhausted, he would fall in a heap for my mother to drag to bed.

For several months he would go to the door and fuss for hours with a piece of rope wrapped around the doorknob. The rope, originally placed their by mom to keep him from being able to turn the knob and go wandering outside, became an incessant project for my father's mind to work on. He would un-wrap the rope, tie it, untie it, then wrap it around the knob, and then start the process all over again.

I can only surmise that somewhere in his mind he was fixing something as he had his entire life. I'll never know. My father was already gone in those days. He had no awareness of anyone by then. He just walked back and forth and worked on the rope and then went back and forth some more. He would walk around you and never notice you. He didn't see anyone anymore. He had already died, but his body still lived on.

Back on the television, as I watched Mrs. Reagan say goodbye to her husband, my mind wandered back to a very sad day in my life. I recalled the night my brother John and I went to the house to give our mother a night off from the hell of trying to make my father's shell comfortable. She had been invited to a baby shower and my brother and I had volunteered to watch dad so she could spend a little time reveling in the birth of a new person rather than continually dwelling on the aspects of a death.

Soon into the night, a visit to our now continually bedridden dad found he had soiled himself and everything else in the bed. I remembered the incredibly putrid odor that had my brother and I both gagging as we carried the now 140 pound man into the bathroom. John turned on the shower so that we could wash the feces off of dad. Impossible to hold him up from outside the tub, my brother quickly took off his shoes, and still dressed, climbed into the tub to hold dad up as the waters washed away the filth.

As the water washed away my brother's tears as well as my own, a myriad of emotions ran through my mind. I recall as if yesterday that I never did and never will love my brother more than I did at that moment in time. I remember feeling so terribly sorry for my mom who was going through this hell every day without a complaint passing her lips. I also remember being terribly angry ay my God for allowing this ordeal to happen to my father and this family.

Ronald Wilson Reagan has been put to rest. What is more important is that the hell Nancy Reagan and her family have gone through these past years has also been put to rest. Alzheimer's is the most insidious disease a person can imagine. It is darker and more evil than the worst horror movie and is beyond understanding except to those who have been subjected to this ordeal.

As I watched the Reagan's all hug each other as the service ended, I mouthed to no one in particular: "Damn that disease, Damn it to Hell."

When a writer faces personal tragedy, the only thing we know how to do is write. This little story was written the morning I received the phone call that my mother had unexpectedly died during the night.

The Phone Call

You know the call is going to come. You put it out of your mind as many times as it pops into your head but you always know it will happen one day. Always, when the thought crops into your head you ask God: Not today. Not next week. Not next year. The call is as inexorable as life itself. It comes in its own time, not ours.

My call came at 6:45 a.m. Sunday May 25th 2004. My sister Patricia made the call to tell me Mary Catherine Treacy Fak, our mother, my mother, had died.

Mary Catherine, age 76, had not been feeling well for a long time. She was getting around enough to complain about feeling poorly, and since at age 54, I have such days myself, I didn't give it the import that it seems I should have. I should have called one last time. I should have taken the time from a totally mundane and thus unimportant life to go visit her just one more time. But I thought the call wouldn't come today, not next week, not next year.

She had been in the hospital. A guinea pig for a battery of tests that showed perhaps she had a mild stroke somewhere along the line. Nothing too serious, the doctors said. Not good was the prognosis, not bad either was their determination. Seventy-six years of age carries its own medical baggage. Nothing to get too worried about I surmised. Not today, or next week, or next year.

She had just come home from the hospital the other day and was getting ready for a grandmother's bonanza of family pride. Grand daughters and grandsons were about to graduate from grammar school as well as high school, and she was determined to be there in person for all of them. She had birthed five children, Michael, Mary Ellen, Ann, Patricia, and John, but her ten grandchildren were what were truly important in her life. None of the five children ever minded of course.

162

Somewhere along the line she had become grandma not ma, and her five children accepted the change as the natural progression of life.

In the past few years, my calls, or my mother's calls to me, had always ended in I love you. I don't know why it started, but somehow that ending phrase became more important than the conversation did. Such a simple thing to say. So hard for some of us to get out of our mouths. I didn't say it often enough to mom because I didn't talk to her often enough.

Mom, always one to just talk on and on, had developed a true love for Sharon and Tim, often I would see Sharon just hold the receiver in the air and ask me if I wanted to talk with mom. Too many times, I waived her off mouthing silently I wasn't home right now. I always thought I had tomorrow, next week, next year. I will now live with those failed chances for as long as I go on.

I told Patricia I would make the call to Mary Ellen. I remember sitting there just looking at the phone. I rationalized that I should wait until I was sure that I would not wake her and Mark with such sad news. I knew all along she was an early riser, but as long as I didn't make the call, one of us believed mom was still alive. One of us didn't have to plan a funeral for their mother.

Finally I called. I was quiet and Mary Ellen was as well. The"what happened", "when", "what are the plans", kept us from becoming emotional. Quickly she said she would see me the next day and I hung up without a thought to really talking to my oldest sister about what we felt. Perhaps tomorrow, next week, next year.

My sister Ann, who had to make the call in 1983 that my father had died, called around 9:00 a.m. She started out fine and then she lost it. I found out right then that I had a very short fuse regarding mom's death. I was fine just as long as you were. You lose it, and so will I. As I hung up I regretted not telling her I loved her and how much I appreciated all that she and Mike and Michelle had done for mom over the years.

I talked to my sister-in-law Audra that afternoon, and as she handed the phone to my brother John, she blurted out that she loved me. I replied in kind immediately. It's so easy to tell someone you care. It gets ignored so readily. We always think we can wait until tomorrow, or next week, or next year.

John was solid and stoic, but I could tell that if one of us lost it, we both would. His conversation told me that he regretted being ten minutes late to the hospital. A 2:00 a.m. drive trying to see your mother before she dies probably set off a series of demons in John's head. I will talk to him about those thoughts. I need to find the symbiosis between his thoughts and mine. He was just a few miles away from talking to mom one last time. I was just the pickup of a phone away. Neither of us made it.

As the conversation ended, I blurted out that I loved him. He snapped back the same, and I wondered what terrible stigma is there to telling someone you care or that you appreciate them. What makes it so hard to say affectionate words to someone you care about that you decide to wait until tomorrow, or next week, or next year.

I find myself walking around the house today talking to mom. That makes sense doesn't it? I could have talked to her every day for hours if I cared to, but I waited until she was dead and now I feel the need to tell her everything. I feel like an idiot, but I know, although she is listening, she isn't judging me. That just wasn't her style.

I have always been angry at my father's death. Just 63, he never lived to enjoy the fruits of retirement. He never had the opportunity of seeing 8 of his grandchildren become, and then grow before his eyes. I'm also angry that I really don't know the day he died. The date his body died is December 16th 1983, but his life force was gone long before that. How long was the body, curled in a fetal position, with no understanding of life, just a body. How long before that last day did my father actually die? I will never accept Dec 16th as the day my father died.

With mom, I feel more sadness than anger. The suddenness, the unexpectedness, the "if you had a brain you could have figured it out" of it, will always be in my thoughts. I fear that I feel sorrier for myself than I do my mother. Today, you see, I don't have any parents anymore. In a way I am an orphan, and the thought makes it very hard to see the keyboard right now.

Sharon asked me to feed the digital camera pictures into the computer today. She had taken a picture of Tim's award wall, with all the ribbons, and plaques and trophies he had won in speech these past two years. It was apparent that it was important to her to have a print of that picture today. When I asked her why, she said she wanted to place it in the casket with ma so she could show it to my dad and her dad who also was cheated out of so many good years.

I told her that was a lovely thought and enhanced the photo to get a really good picture for mom to show off in heaven. When Sharon went back downstairs I went into the bedroom and blubbered like a baby. All three of them, my dad and mom, as well as Sharon's dad should still be here. At least for one more day, one more week, one more year.

I will be going up to Chicago tomorrow. A couple really long days are ahead for a lot of the people I care about. I have made a promise to ma that I won't be afraid to tell everyone how I feel about them.

I find myself dreading the thought of having to discuss mom's estate in the next few weeks. A house to sell as well as 40 years worth of grandma stuff filling the rooms and walls needs to be removed. Not really an estate I suppose. But it was her stuff and it should be dispersed according to who thought something had special meaning to them. I really don't want anything. I want my mother back instead. For just another day, another week, another year.

Ma loved St Bartholomew and I'm sure there will be a lot of priests and nuns visiting her at the wake. I'm sure that out of affection they will lead us in prayers for ma many times these next two days. They will be doing it out of respect for her and how active she was in the parish. Rain, snow, sleet, hail, you name it, a little old chubby lady who couldn't walk worth a damn was in that same side pew almost every Sunday.

I will keep quiet, but I wish I could tell them we don't need to pray for Mary Catherine. Instead we need to pray to her for ourselves. That little old lady doesn't need any help from us to get into heaven. Mary Catherine wasn't a saint, but she was damn close and I will miss her today, next week, next year, forever.

Ma, please tell dad happy "Fathers Day" for me. I'm not sure if my messages have been getting through.

Well, now we are into the last portion of my life and I have included a few columns and short stories to let you know how things have been going with me these last few years.

I expected the pictures of me on vacation would show an old man. I didn't expect them to show a dumpy old man.

Our trip to Tennessee had been the last straw in my gradual ascent into fat world. Looking at the pictures, I saw a 6 foot 3 inch man with roughly 40 pounds too much weight hanging about in all areas of his body. I couldn't allow that to happen of course, so I embarked on a monumental diet to get back to the point of just looking like an old, unattractive man in photos sans the extra poundage. This is my story

How to Lose 50 pounds in 90 Days

…Without Cutting Something Off

The first things diet experts tell you to do when embarking on a weight loss program is to write down what you consume in a day. So I did.

For breakfast, I had a grapefruit plus three cups of coffee, and I washed that down with two beers and a glass of wine.

For lunch I had two greasy cheeseburgers plus fries and washed that all down with two beers and a glass of wine.

After work I stopped to hang with the boys and had four beers and two glasses of wine and then went home.

For supper I had four 8 ounce steaks, a vat of mashed potatoes and gravy, and a bowl of green beans. I washed that all down with two beers and a glass of wine.

My night time snack was half an Eli's cheesecake and a box of chocolate donuts and I needed to wash that down with three beers…I ran out of wine.

Writing down my daily food regimen showed a glaring problem in my eating habits. Yeh, that grapefruit in the morning was killing me.

Alright, I was joking with you, but the meal menu I just hit you with isn't far from the truth. Let's look at a real day before I started my diet.

Morning: nothing

Lunch: nothing

Supper: Let's start with a giant belly bomb pizza. One of those kinds that has everything but raw sewage on top of six pounds of cheese. I don't eat it all, Jackson the cat gets half a slice, but in the event I can't eat it all right away, I just wait a while and then nail the rest cold.

After an hour or so, its snack time, so I grab a can of mixed nuts. It isn't a big can. It's one of those cans that say family size on the side. I don't feel guilty since I assume they mean a small family. What I normally do is eat all the cashews and walnuts and almonds first, leaving only the peanuts, which I then eat so I can throw the can away. During all of this, I have sucked down a half dozen beers of course since all that salt makes a guy thirsty.

That pretty well takes care of my food consumption for the day except for a couple slices of cheesecake, a Hershey bar, (family size of course,) and a couple 12 ounce tumblers of Merlot to kill any possible cholesterol thinking of growing inside my stomach..

That mealtime massacre was not "make believe" and as I look at it now, I am grateful I was only 250 pounds when I started this diet. I deserved to be 500 or more.

I have been big my entire life and must attribute my insatiable hunger to my parents. The Fak family members are all genetically predisposed to start craving cheeseburgers two hours after birth. I remember mom telling me she used to get honked off at strangers asking if I was retarded since I still wore diapers and drank from a baby bottle. My mother would have to explain that I was eight months old regardless of the fact I was thirty two pounds and could walk around.

I really did learn how to walk when I was eight months old and could open the refrigerator within a week of that. I was almost a year old however, before I could make a Dagwood sandwich for myself.

The first thing an obsessive compulsive does when going on a diet is to read everything that has ever been written about weight loss programs, nutrition, and food group substitution. I read everything the internet had from A to Z.

Some of the programs made a lot of sense. Calorie reduction and exercise will cause a person to lose weight. Most of the diets however, were beyond the realm of reality.

A person who can eat three Big Mac's without feeling full is not going to replace those items with tofu or celery stalks or non fat yogurt. People who are sedentary are that way by choice and they aren't going to join three health clubs the next morning to get slim by next weekend.

My research told me one glaringly obvious fact. Most diets probably would work. Most diets also don't work because people are asking the impossible of their victims, I mean clients.

As always, being the king of the do-it-yourselfers, I decided to do my research and devise my own diet. A diet that I actually could follow without waking up in the morning with heartburn and noticing the cats as well as my pillow have disappeared.

The very first bit of information that made me excited was the discovery of negative calorie foods. These are foods that use up more calories to digest than they originally contain in themselves. They all were fruits and vegetables of course, since a thousand calorie burger couldn't possibly be digested at all. Thousand calorie burgers of course are immediately directed by your stomach to your belly for nurturing and cultivation.

Some of the negative foods made sense. Broccoli, and celery, as well as apples were on the list. I could see how these crunchy "hard ass" things would make the stomach work overtime to digest. Other foods however were totally surprising. Watermelon and Cantaloupe also were on the negative foods list. I found this hard to believe since those items are already squishy and after chewing them, which I sometimes would do, they would enter the digestive system as schmush. Still, since I liked both those items I wasn't going to question their being good for a diet.

I now had to go on an "in person" fact finding mission to determine for myself what other foods I would include on my diet besides fruits and vegetables.

The trip to the local IGA took several hours and I had to explain myself to the staff that I was not in fact a price checker from a competitor. I slowly walked the aisles and checked the calories on all the foods I needed to give up or start to eat.

Immediately I found out my eating habits mirrored those of the entire crew of the K-19 Widow Maker.

Chili, any kind, was over 700 calories. Corned beef hash was the same, as well as deviled canned ham and beef stew. All the things I used to consider just a side dish told me they contained half the calories a sane adult should consume in a day.

I found out there is no such thing as a potato chip that won't destroy a diet. Because they are all made with potatoes, which have high calories to start, every brand came in at 150 calories per serving. Looking at the brands I would consume during a quarter of a Bears game, I realized I had been nailing between 1500 and 2000 calories just on something I didn't consider food.

Oh, there were a few sneaky companies trying to trick me into thinking they were better. The bags said "low fat" or made with soy oil or "baked". Every one of those chips still had almost 1400 calories per bag anyway. Now I know a bag has 10 to 15 servings but if I open a potato chip bag, I eat the potato chips contained therein, so don't tell me I could eat the ten chips or so that comprise the 150 calorie per serving crap they put on the back of the bag.

As I continued my research, it became apparent there was no such thing as a low calorie snack. Oh, the pretzel and nacho and cruncho companies all had bags claiming they were low calorie. But a look at what their opinion of low calories meant was over a thousand if you like to munch.

I did some research on juices, as I knew they were about to become a huge part of my life.

Most were all right, at about 100 calories per eight ounce serving. Some were not. Little things like sugar and sweeteners made some of these juices no better than drinking a can of lard. Grapefruit juice, which almost every diet claims to help digestion, wasn't too bad at between 60 and 100 calories per glass. I liked grapefruit juice so I loaded a shopping cart full of it and parked it next to the shopping cart full of fruits and vegetables.

Meat, my lifeblood, also showed me I should have been too fat to squeeze through the grocery market's doors. Every meat I picked up told me I was over the thousand calorie range, and in most cases flying by 2000 calories due to the quantities I consumed regularly. Now I know meat in small quantities is not too bad calorie wise. I found a rule of thumb of an ounce of meat being about 80 to 100 calories. Remember, when I eat meat, I eat at least two pounds or I only count it as a snack.

Turkey seemed to be the champion for calories, especially calories from fat, which my research told me, were worse than calories not from fat. Although how someone could figure that out is beyond me.

My studies also told me soups weren't bad for calories. Although soups that had more than "essence of meat", were pushing the range of a solid meal at 300 calories or less.

I imagine I need to back up for a moment here and explain my new strategy. Research had told me that a 1500 to 1800 calorie diet would work wonders on my flab. My studies also showed many experts believe eating six small meals a day is better than three large ones. This frequent stuffing of my mouth would help alleviate the withdrawal pangs of not being able to open the refrigerator and taking swigs of creamy garlic or bleu cheese dressing. Thus, I divided 1800 calories by 6 meals and came up with a diet "budget" of 300 calories per meal.

I found a real friend in the "cream of" soups. Most were right around 200 calories per can and I imagined taking a can of this mush, adding broccoli, or mushrooms, or asparagus, or all three, and making a stew that might end up as zero calories because of all the negative calorie ingredients I was adding to the slop.

I also found the "frozen food" section was a great help. There was tons of Lean Cuisine or Weight Watchers or Healthy Meals that all are less than 300 calories. I noticed how small the portions were, but took comfort in the fact I could eat six of them and still be following my diet. All I needed to do was make sure I didn't eat all six at once.

I found out that pizza, a staple of any carnivore, just doesn't have room on a diet. Even the weight loss meals that offered a pizza slice in a small box came in at 500 calories. Those little snack size ten inchers in the frozen food section ranged from 1500 to 2000 calories, so I resigned myself to skipping pizza for at least a while.

I have never been a breakfast person except when there is a pound or two of bacon lying around, but I found comfort in the cereal section that day. Many breakfast cereals, which I had never eaten before, claimed only 100 calories per serving. I liked this since I knew I had to start eating breakfast for the first time in my life on a regular basis.

The closest I ever came to eating "The most important meal of the day" was when I was a kid and mom made me a bowl of oatmeal every morning before school. Of course, every morning when mom went downstairs to iron my clothes for school, I took the oatmeal and flushed it down the toilet. I could always bank on mom never having my clothes ready the night before, so this ruse worked well for all the years she fed me that garbage. In later years dad had to completely replace all the plumbing in the house and I will always believe it was because of mom's oatmeal.

For the most part, when I left the grocery store, I had a real battle plan devised for losing the flab that hung all over me. Now I just needed to do two things. The first was to consume all the Italian beef my wife had made for me for Father's Day. I couldn't imagine looking at the leftovers every day and not ripping into them, so I got rid of the beef the only logical way I knew. I consumed it, all three pounds of it.

The second thing, and I believed this would be the hardest thing to do, was to get rid of all the beer and wine in the house. I had made up my mind that eating less but still drinking tons of calories and carbs would just protract the time frame of my diet. Feeling better about myself, I washed down all the Italian beef with all the beer and wine there was in the house. When I went to bed there wasn't a trace of alcohol left in the house. I felt good about my first day on a new diet plan.

The next morning as I began my diet in earnest, I poured myself a bowl of Total and added just a smidgeon of skim milk to the cereal. I came home for lunch and took a can of cream of mushroom soup and added a half pound of mushrooms and swirled it all into a non recognizable stew. It tasted good however, since I love mushrooms, and I felt I was on my way. That night I had a big salad with all kinds of negative vegetables mixed in it and added just enough dressing to keep it from being dry.

During the day, I drank club soda with a little lemon juice in it, and I really didn't feel too hungry until about 7:00 p.m. when my stomach demanded I feed it. Most of my incredible measure of calories was stuffed down my throat right around that time of night. A 250 calorie bag of popcorn helped, and I went to bed before my stomach realized that it had been screwed out of its meals for the day.

I had weighed on Father's Day and came in at 250 pounds. I decided to give it the week before I weighed again because I didn't want to be discouraged in the event I didn't lose much weight.

I was perfect all week. I ate my meals and had tons of veggies. I was elated by how low in calories many fish are and almost hired a marching band when I noticed giant gulf shrimp only have 9 calories per shrimp. The cats also were delighted with the fish products as they not only begged for scraps, but felt no doubt relieved that such foods might prevent my catching them and putting them on a spit when Sharon and Tim weren't home.

At the end of the first week, I stepped on the scale and weighed 242 pounds. Yep, in just one week I had lost eight lbs.

When I told Sharon I measured my glee with the footnote that I realized there was going to be a big loss the first week since I was dropping my calories by about 4000 a day and my metabolism still was on full tilt from my previous eating habits.

The next week I had lost another 6 lbs. 14 pounds in two weeks and I was on my way.

I have to be honest and admit those first two weeks were monumental to my continuing the diet. If in fact I had lost a couple pounds, which I can do anytime I go to the bathroom, I might have shucked the whole deal and went out and bought a case of beer.

Because I was down to 236 pounds, I found myself getting more and more into learning the dynamics of the human body.

The best way I can explain what I was visualizing is to use a boiler room of an old steamship. Just for an example, let's say my stomach is the boiler of the Titanic. It is hot and burning furiously from all the coal being fed into the hopper. Even when the coal stops being thrown in, the fire still burns ferociously from the coal previously added. Now as time goes by, this consumption will begin to ease off as the fire dies down. Sure the small amounts of coal added keep the process going, but it is consuming less coal than it did previously as it becomes used to the new quantities it is being fed.

I hope I didn't lose you on that analogy. My metabolism, much like the Titanic's boiler, had been at maximum burn trying to keep me from being bed ridden from obesity. That is why I had such an extreme weight loss in only two weeks. Now with new improved, lower burning quantities going down the pipes, my metabolism was slowing down. For a week it slowed down to the result I didn't lose a pound my third week.

I'm proud of myself that I didn't go crazy and shuck the whole idea. I examined everything I had been doing and noticed two gleaming faults in my strategy. First, I wasn't always eating breakfast, and secondly, my six meals were all getting stacked up between 3:00 p.m. and bedtime. I was also drinking too much coffee and everyone says caffeine slows metabolism.

The next week, with a better strategy, I lost another six pounds. Twenty pounds gone in one month was damn good in my estimation.

I found I was now able to go to the bar and drink club sodas while everyone else swilled down their brewskies. This was important as I was now starting to get comments that people could tell I was losing weight. When I told them I had lost twenty pounds in a month I received several retorts that such a weight loss so quickly sounded unhealthy. I explained I was still eating a lot but eating a lot of good things rather than bad. When I was stilled questioned about my loss being too fast, I told the person to shut up and that they were drunk. Nothing worse than a reformed anything is there.

Things did slow down after that. The next few weeks I lost a couple here and a couple there, but when it became extremely hot and I sweated up a storm at work, I dropped another chunk big time. At the six week mark I was down 30 pounds coming in at 220.

It was at this period in time that I went and bought a small pair of solid, fifteen pound dumb bells to work out with. I did plenty of heavy work during the day, but I wanted the hand weights to help me try and sculpt muscles I normally didn't use. I also bought an Ab-Lounger II for a hundred bucks, since I knew sit ups would help but I was damned if I could do more than a few on my own. With the machine, I could do twenty-five good ones at each rep.

In the next ten days I gained two pounds. Normally that would have caused me to go buy a brisket of corned beef and a gallon of Merlot, but I believed it was times to double check my habits. The one glaring difference in those ten days was I was sitting at home, writing the story about Timothy and a few other articles, and downing a dozen diet sodas each day as I did so.

Sharon told me my weight gain could be from the artificial sweetener, Aspartane, now used in diet sodas. Sharon has always known her stuff about eating and nutrition, so I took her advice and did some research.

I found out some people are in effect allergic to Aspartane. The possible side effects of the stuff seemed as if they were interviewing me. Slow down of metabolism? Check. Headaches? Check. Dizziness? Check. In a nutshell I realized I was one of those few people who didn't take Aspartane very well.

Let's go back to my "boiler room" analogy.

It became apparent my heavy consumption of caffeine and Aspartane when the furnace was at full throttle had little effect on my body. Like anything else thrown into the inferno of my stomach, it was disintegrated into nothingness in moments. Now with a smaller, leaner burn going on in my body, it was apparent that caffeine and Aspartane were slowing down the burn process with the steam of these chemicals being sent up the headache and dizziness pipes all the while they dampened down the burn rate.

This all made sense, and with a new concept of what to do, I dropped the diet soda and coffee. In three days I had lost another five pounds, plus the two I had gained back.

Further research told me that a lot of my problems at losing weight (now that I'm at a reasonable weight to start just trimming down) might be because of all the chemicals we ingest into our bodies each day. I'm not talking about steroids or pot. I'm talking about all the preservatives added to foods and the hormones added to animals. There is a broadening school of thought that all these things that are proven as non lethal, might actually cause us to have a slower metabolism.

All this time I thought those pictures of thin people in the Middle Ages was because they were starving to death. Maybe they were all thin because they didn't have any crap added to their food by manufacturers.

Whatever the effect chemicals have on me, I forged forward. I wasn't going to go over to any type of organic nuts and berries diet. Not in this lifetime.

The eight week mark came and I officially came in at a 35 pound weight loss.

The next week, as I ended my 63rd day on a diet, I weighed 213 pounds.

People have asked me and continue to ask me why I wanted to lose 50 pounds. I don't really have an answer. I know I needed to lose at least 40 or perhaps a little more just so I wouldn't be embarrassed to take my shirt off in public. I guess 200 pounds sounded better than 215 or 210.

I have made myself a promise to just continue eating healthier with a smattering of "sinful" foods for the rest of my life. Somewhere along the line I found myself deciding to permanently give up the booze as well. I have been shocked from the first day that I haven't missed my ten beers or half gallon of Merlot more than I have. I stop by the bars to shoot the bull with my friends but find no problems drinking club sodas while they sip their beers. I'll be honest. I never thought that would be the case.

I will always miss my institutional size bags of potato chips and will savor the few strips of bacon I will have from time to time as really special. I don't seem to miss chocolate so I guess that means socks for Christmas instead of ten pound boxes of chocolates that have never survived to New Years Day.

You might ask yourself why this is the end of this story. Yes, I currently have lost 37 pounds in 63 days but that is a stupid sounding title for a short story. Thus the "50 pounds in 90 days" is the tag for this compilation of words. Besides, in the event you read this a year or two from August of 2005, you might find out I have lost another 50 by then and I'm not going to keep changing the title of this story just to keep up with my current weight.

Author's Note; at the time this book was submitted for publication, in April of 2006, I weighed 196 pounds. I debated changing the title of this story to; "How to lose 54 Pounds in 214 Days" but decided to leave well enough alone.

An article in the fall of 2005, a lot of people told me they understood exactly what I was going through.

In Search of...A Set of Choppers

It is a natural progression of life on my side of the family. We don't get to keep our teeth our entire lives, even when those lives are short lived. My choppers are long past the time of needing to be replaced by a store bought set. But you know, having every tooth in your head pulled isn't exactly an event one puts on the top of their "to do" list. It's my time however so I thought I would share my feelings and worries with you in today's column.

I have lost 45 pounds. The lines in my face, no longer being supported by a major influx of beer, have for the most part dissipated and I have shaved my moustache. These changes have made me look much younger, or so I have been told. Much younger, that is, until I open my mouth and smile. I honestly have a smile that would make Sue the Dinosaur at the Field Museum cringe.

My teeth have not only lost their enamel but have begun shifting around in my mouth. The other day when I was brushing my teeth, an old pot roast from months ago fell out from between a couple molars. I know it's time to say goodbye to these poorly constructed, non operational, chunks of calcium I have had in my mouth for 57 years, but I tell you that isn't easy... nor cheap.

I find it fascinating how much it costs to have teeth removed in this day and age. As a kid, a bad tooth cost ten bucks to get yanked. Now ten times that amount won't get the job done for one and I've almost got a mouth full. I have never been one to question inflation when I was getting something for my money but it seems strange to have to spend so much just to have something permanently taken away from me.

I guess it's like paying to have a dead tree removed from your yard. You're not really getting anything, but the yard will look better when the tree is gone. Of course, unlike your yard, you can't leave your mouth empty. Well I suppose you could. My dad never liked his fake teeth, and I remember his sitting at the dinner table gumming his meat to death as if it were yesterday.

There is something about a set of teeth that seems to be the finishing touch on a human head, so I don't think I could go around smiling with a vacuous pit in my mouth.

I have been debating removing my teeth myself since I am a classic do-it-yourself kind of guy, but I think I should have done such an operation before I gave up drinking and not after. I tried the string around the doorknob and then around a tooth. So far I still have all my teeth, but only one doorknob left in the house that's operational.

I tried to yank them with a pair of channel locks wrapped in tape, but my nose keeps getting in the way of a good grip so I have given up on doing the pulling myself.

Buying new choppers also has many dilemmas attached to their purchase. I fear getting a set that looks so fake, that as soon as I open my mouth, it is obvious my teeth came from somewhere other than my own mouth. I don't want to get a nasty yellow set either since what would be the point in doing that. I already have a set of those for free. To have a realistic look, I thought maybe getting a real nice set with a piece of plastic broccoli permanently stuck between two of the teeth as the way to go. The broccoli would probably cost extra and I'm on a tight budget so I've given up on that idea.

Over the last few years I have asked older friends, about my mouth size, to leave me their teeth in their wills. So far, no one has, so I can't go the donated route. There are no sources for repossessed or refurbished false teeth. At least I can't find any.

I took some measurements of my mouth and ordered a set of false teeth from China. When they arrived, they needed braces and I'm too old for that, so I've given up on internet, mail order choppers. Surprisingly there are no sites on the internet telling how to make your own, so I guess I'm stuck ordering a set from a dentist's catalogue.

I also have to decide if I want a local or to be put to sleep when it's time to get my teeth yanked out. I don't mind a local. Blood doesn't bother me. Over the years I have had more stitches put in me than there are in a football. The thought of hearing all that pulling and digging and yanking tend to make me think I might want to be in "lah lah" land when all this is happening. I also don't think I want to see how the dentist gets my nose out of the way while he's pulling my choppers out.

Getting knocked out is its own problem however, as over the years when I have been "put under" I have had a tendency to wake up during the operation. I don't want to scare a dentist into pulling out my tongue after he is startled by my sitting up in the chair and asking how he's doing. I could live without any teeth. I couldn't live without having my tongue to wag.

Since the demographics of my readership shows a strong following in nursing homes and cemeteries, I'm sure many of you out there have your own stories about what I will have to go through. Send me a note or an E-mail telling me a few "do's and don'ts" about what I should prepare myself for. In the meantime, I'll just keep smirking when someone asks me to smile.

Normally around the end of a year, I write a column about my resolutions for next year. Since I never keep any of them anyway, I suppose writing about my Christmas wish list will do just as well. This was my resolution wish list for 2006.

Wishes Over Resolutions for 2006

Personally I wish I could be a vegetarian. I'm finding myself more and more sensitive to the plight of animals all over the world these days. Although my diet consists mainly of cows, pigs, and chickens that I have never had a familial relationship with, I find my eating such animals makes for a fine bit of hypocrisy on my part. Granted my meat consumption is down at least 90% from my "pre health nut" days, but every time I do eat that infrequent steak or strip of bacon, I wonder if I'm gnawing on some youngster's farm pet.

Eggs are a principle source of my protein right now. Eggs of course, would have turned into chickens, which would have turned into pairs of scrumptious chicken wings. I guess I'm just ending a chicken's life before it gets a chance to grow up and become fearful of my eating it someday. Like I said I wish I could be a vegetarian.

Now I don't wish to become a radical about animal rights either. I mean I won't demand sportsmen shows on television display a disclaimer: "No worms were hurt in the filming of this fishing show." You won't see me picketing outside a business with a sign saying "bug whackers are inhumane" either. I guess what I'm saying is, I wish I could find a happy median in all of this, but I'm afraid I won't. I picture myself harboring guilt the rest of my life even when I'm just eating a gummy bear.

I also wish I didn't live in this current era of computerization. Of course these things are amazing, but they also do untold screwy things at the very worst possible moment, that cause all of us to have high blood pressure, create stress, and of course, curse. They consistently are getting better, but it will be years before all the bugs are worked out of these things.

I wish I could have been born later on, since I'm fearful I have some answering to do someday for the nasty verbal barrages I have directed at these machines over the past decade.

I already have my holy defense prepared showing an analogy between the early automobile and the computer. When automobiles first were invented, they were considered truly remarkable machines. That is until they broke down and no one could figure out why, nor how to fix them. Looking at history, a person can readily note that stress, high blood pressure and cursing were yet to become a part of the American landscape until automobiles were invented. Thus, using a little bit of modern day extrapolation, it's obvious the same thing has happened to me with computers.

As my defense exhibits, I will produce hundreds of books, song sheets, and short stories pre 1890 which have not a word of cussing in them. I will also show as many books and songs written since the car was invented, displaying a language that would have made an early American scalp hunter faint.

In my defense, I will try and prove the computers caused me to say some of the stuff I said, and that it really wasn't my fault. I wish I knew if this will work for me or not.

I also wish I had the time to read more. I have all kinds of reading material stacking up, waiting for my eyes to see and my brain to digest the contents thereof. I've been so busy writing that I haven't even had the chance to read the last six months of my columns in the *Lincoln Courier*. I wish I knew if any of them were any good or not.

I also wish I had taken seriously my candidacy for governor. A think tank located in Goofy Ridge has come out with a poll sampling showing I'm already within eight million votes of locking the election up. It appears my comments concerning the spaying and neutering of some Illinoisans has hit a home run with many potential voters. Jumping on this unexpected bandwagon, I will be coming out with a bumper sticker stating: "Mike Fak will fix this state...and many of the people in it."

On an ethereal note, I wish to make it known I want to have my remains cremated. I wish to have this done to me after I have died and not a moment before. I still have a problem with this thought and wish I

181

could talk to someone who has experienced this event personally, to be absolutely certain that it doesn't hurt. I wish I had some really poignant or impressive notion on what to do with my ashes, but I don't. Maybe, since I have spent so much of my life on the toilet, perhaps I should spend the rest of forever in it. I wonder if the city sewer system charges extra for flushing a person.

On the political front, I wish we had a Governor I really liked these past seven years. Although both Ryan and Blagojevich have given me a wealth of material for articles extolling how little I think of both of them, I wish that wasn't the case. Believe it or not I love to write about great people making great decisions that I totally agree with. Well, at least I wish I did.

I also wish people didn't take their opinions or the opinions of others so seriously. I love opinions. In fact this little job in the newspaper depends on them, but opinions are just like noses, (I'm already improving my cussing) everyone has one.

The problem I see is that too many individuals are totally and firmly convinced their opinions are always right, and everyone who disagrees with them is always totally wrong. I wish people could see the other side of some things. It would make for a better world. Everyone getting along with their opinions of course means there will be no further need of opinion pages. I wish you to know if that happens I will survive just fine. I can start concentrating on writing the biographies of Lincolnites who perhaps want to tell the story of a childhood farm animal that they loved. An animal I no doubt probably ate at some time or other.

This column in the fall of 2005 shows my body getting into becoming physically fit even if my brain isn't

I'm in the Senior Olympics

People tell me my thinking isn't unusual. It is sort of a mid life crisis or something that has caused me to believe I need to do something out of the ordinary before my body just folds up tent and tells me to forget it.

I first had this urge to do something physically unique when the fund raising effort for local 644 was under way. At that time I tried very hard to find a company that had a grizzly bear for hire. Yeh, I thought my wrestling a grizzly bear would be a great fundraising event, plus quell this strange urge I have had lately to do something off the wall. I had seen pictures of bear wrestling in the older days and thought I at least could last long enough to make people feel they got their monies worth before I got massacred.

Members of the fundraising committee believed the possibility of seeing me crushed by a bear would be huge for ticket sales, and encouraged me to find a bear. Unfortunately, I found out bear wrestling in America is now illegal. You can ask anyone on the 644 committee how crushed I was (figuratively not literally) finding out I couldn't wrestle a bear.

I have entered a new thought process on trying something before it's too late. It isn't quite as exciting as getting body slammed by an eight hundred pound bear, but I think it will be enough to quell this urge I have to prove myself one last time. I intend to enter the 2006 Senior Olympics.

Next year's Olympics will have state finals in Springfield this summer, with nationals in Mobile, Alabama this fall, so I have time to train for the games. I will have to decide soon however, which events I intend to devote my training to, since I believe I will have a better chance to win if I pick a sport I can still actually perform.

Some of the events are out of the question for me. The 5k and 10k runs for example. Looking at last year's finals in the 55 to 60 year old bracket, it seems runners are almost as fast as kids. Just to be certain I tried a 10k jaunt and fell exhausted before I was done with the whole distance. Thank goodness I was still in my car or I might have been run over by a pair of runners using the county road at the same time.

Running is definitely out, except perhaps for the 100 meters. I was as fast as the wind as a kid, constantly running a 4.5 in the 40 yard dash, so maybe that inherent speed is still there. Surely I can run 100 meters without needing a defibrillator standing by so I will give this a try in the next few weeks. The time to beat is 13 seconds. If I can't get close to that time now, say under a minute, before I start training, I need to junk the idea of running in any event.

There are some other events that I could become good enough in that are special to the Senior Olympics. There is bowling and horseshoes for example. The problem with both of those endeavors is a person can have a bad game and then that's it. I want a sport where I know I have a chance and can consistently be near the mark every time. There is badminton, but to be honest, I wouldn't feel any urge to brag if I was a badminton champion. There aren't many books on the shelves about the greatest badminton champions ever, are there. Besides, one bad shuttlecock and your season's over, so I'll scrap that idea along with swimming, which I can't do since I'm allergic to water.

The track and field events also have tests of strength and that is where I believe I have my best chance. There is the javelin, the discus, and the shot put in the event schedule and this is where I believe I need to concentrate my training. Of those three events, I believe my best shot is with the shot put, so that is what I will train for in the event I can find a shot put to train with.

I looked through my attic of sports equipment and couldn't find any puts. I did find an old bowling ball at an equal weight, but I fear people seeing me putting a bowling ball around town might be the final event my wife needs to have me sent to an old soldiers and sailors home. I thought of borrowing one of the cannonballs off the County Building lawn, next to the cannon, but they are all welded together so that won't work. Someone must have had that idea already, I suppose.

With all due respect to area merchants, not one of them has a shot put for sale, let alone a selection to choose from, so I will be forced to buy my put out of town. Bloomington has a "Shot Puts R Us "store so I imagine I will go there for my ball.

I will need a few sponsors to help with bills while I train for my events. I have a real good idea on who will help me with that. The entire Senior Olympic field will be people old enough to croak at any minute, so having a funeral home as a sponsor is a natural in my opinion. I can have a track shirt printed out that says on the back: "I intend to be cremated by so and so funeral home". I can have patches on the jersey ala NASCAR that support my principle sponsor. There can be a patch from the crematorium oven people saying they are the "only way to go". I can also get the utility company as a sponsor since for years their slogan was "Things cook better with gas".

I will keep all you readers abreast of my progress of course. Right now I have to go. I have been practicing with the old bowling ball and its rolling down the street heading right for the sewer. I don't want to read an editorial about plugging up someone's sewer in the paper.

A column from the spring of 2005 shows how much fun research on the internet can be.

In Search of Fak

About twenty years ago a young man came to my door. He was a traveling salesman from Michigan by the name of Gary Fak. To break the monotony of his travels, Gary would look in city phone books to see if there were any Fak surnames listed in that town. He advised me I had been the first Fak he had ever met outside of his immediate family in all his travels.

At the time, my son Tim had not been born, my brother John was unmarried, and had not sired any children, and Gary advised me he had three daughters, so we commiserated each other on the probable doom of the Fak family name from the face of the Earth.

The other day, I decided to use the web to see if the Fak lineage had improved in the last twenty years, or was I eligible to be on some endangered species list.

I went to Ancestry.com to see what they had to say about my lineage. Using the widest parameter settings of "anywhere" and "anytime", I came up with about 200 Fak surnames being recorded going back to the early 1800's. Ancestry.com charges you for information, but they do list the names and locations for free, so my research was not obstructed by capitalism.

I believe the site to be very accurate. All my family: father, grandfather, uncles and aunts, as well as my brother and I were listed.

I found great interest in some of the Fak first names on the web. There was Tippo Fak who lived a century ago in New York City. I wonder if his wife's name was Tippsy. There was a Moses Fak at about the same time in Miami, Indiana. Pong Duk Fak still is alive in Maui Hawaii as well as Yatu Fak and Takashige Fak in San Francisco. Also in California are Leong and Chu Fak. I'm not sure how the person relates to me, but I would like to someday meet the man or woman who was stuck with the moniker: Chu Fak.

Sadly I found no Fak with a first name giving some hope to the possibility of a little Native American lineage in my past. There is no Scratching Beaver Fak or Pelican Nose Fak which means I have no chance to claim my fair share of a casino's profits somewhere in the U.S.

Further searching tells me my name will forever be ensconced in the modern scientific world. FAK, Focal Adhesion Kinase, is a new something or other that bio geneticists have found to be anti-aptotic. Japanese researchers appear to be very excited about FAK and I can only wish them luck in their fight against aptotics. Unless of course aptotics are good things, which would mean Fak's are bad things.

There are dozens of German language web sites that carry the name FAK. My German is poor, but I can translate the beginning of this paragraph from one of the sites. The FAK is a national networking organization that meets as kernbesigheid on vestiging, samesnoering, handhawing and bevordering.

Now I can accept my surname being considered important in Germany for samesnoering and handhawing, but I have got to put a stop to my name being used in conjunction with bevordering. At least I think I do. The German to English dictionary doesn't show any of these words so I assume they are slang, or perhaps FAK is a German organization formed for poor spellers.

There also is a Finish recording label called FAK Records. They offer techno music from such heralded bands as the Latin group Super Ape as well as recording artists Cotton Chesterfield and "She Said Sofa". The major artist on this label appears to be Wells Wartknuckle, but with so many big names under house, who can be sure. The FAK Records logo is the skeletal remains of a three eyed dog with two mouths, which is a marvelous picture to have looming over one's family name. There is an E-mail address that I could use to find out how they came to use FAK, but the more I think about it, the more I think I don't want to know.

There is one very interesting thing I did find out about the name Fak. It seems that in the country of Papua, in New Guinea, there is an entire regency named Fak-Fak. Reading about Fak-Fak, I was initially excited that an entire area of an obviously English speaking country was named after me. I had visions of flying to Fak-Fak. I saw myself getting off a plane, showing someone my driver's license, and immediately being lifted up and carried away amidst a cheering throng, as the keys to the province, and the long emptied castle were handed to me.

Unfortunately, after further studies, I found out that the 90,000 inhabitants of Fak-Fak are aborigines, many who have yet to get over such mundane problems as genocide and snacking on each other. My new vision again saw myself being hoisted into the air, but this time the crowd was delivering me to a cooking pot rather than a luxurious castle. To further make the point, the New Guinea Tourist Bureau advises a traveler not to waste time carrying credit cards, as they have no value except as potential ornamentation around the neck of a no longer hungry Fak-Fakian.

I might still gamble and go there someday. There is a picture of one warrior from the area with two wild boar tusks sticking out of his nose. There is an alarming resemblance between him and an uncle of mine. My uncle of course doesn't wear wild boar tusks in his nose. Unless, of course, there's a formal gathering of the family.

Written the last week of April 2006 this is just my latest foray into a life long argument with computers.

Raw Fish in Havana

I had heard about voice recognition software but had never seen it in action until I noticed *Lincoln Courier* Editor, Jeff Nelson talking into his computer screen a few weeks ago.

He was new to the program himself, but was having fun teaching the computer program his vocabulary and vernacular to assist it in becoming more proficient.

My immediate thought was how much does something like this cost and Nelson said he wasn't sure as it came from the main office at the *State Journal Register*.

Running home, I immediately went to the web to see if I could afford to:"Get me one of them."

At first I was disheartened as I saw price tags running into the thousands for such programs. Finally on about the tenth page of my web surfing, I saw a site promoting an IBM software program on sale. The site stated the program, now outdated and having newer, better renditions available, was being marked down to a mere $29.95 while supplies lasted.

That was too good a price to pass up so I purchased the voice recognition software and went out on the front porch to await its delivery.

I had mental pictures of buying a headset with a hundred foot cord. I saw myself walking around the house dictating to the computer and knowing my words were being transcribed while I opened the refrigerator door looking for a snack. I could just see great novels spewing out of my mouth at record speeds.

I pictured frying a couple eggs while I told readers:

"Blackie quickly reached into his trench coat to pull out his piece before the one eyed Olaf could pull his. The night was filled with bullets as Blackie popped Olaf right between the eyes. Oh, correct that, right next to his one eye."

In my mind I saw myself writing two or three books a week with this new software. I could even leave it on to find out what I talked about in my sleep. I always have felt I have created and lost great works of prose in my nocturnal mumblings and now I could find out for certain each morning by looking at the computer screen when I woke up.

It only took two days for the software to arrive and I couldn't wait to install it.

The computer kept asking me to say words not in its vocabulary so it could better understand my voice pattern and relate my voice to those words. It then asked me to read a 5 minute chunk of "Treasure Island" to gather more information. It had an option for a much longer reading, which no doubt would have helped. Being in a hurry, as always, I opted for the abbreviated lesson.

When I was done, I was amazed and disappointed at the results. I was amazed because every time I said something, there it was being typed on the screen. I was disappointed because sometimes the computer typed a different word or didn't do anything.

I found out a bit of this problem was I had overly annunciated in my reading and now was talking my normal "Fak talk" and the computer couldn't figure out what I was saying. Annunciating more clearly and a little slower, the computer did a much better job. I pictured needing to change my novel:

"Blackie slowly pulled out his piece before the one eyed Olaf with terrible hand-eye coordination could reach for his."

There would be concessions I could see, like maybe only doing one novel a week, but it still was all good.

What happened next is something everyone can relate to. You know when you get something neat and new and want to show it off how it always screws up when you are trying to show how cool it is? Well that happened when Sharon came home from work and I pulled her up the stairs all the while asking her if she had time to see something.

My demonstration started out fine. I said Hello dear wife. How was your day? There it was on the screen. I said a few more things and there it was, almost. I said a few more words and different words that made even less sense appeared on the computer screen.

190

Finally, as is my nature, I shouted out "What the %&%$#&* is going on here."

Without a pause, the computer printed out "Raw Fish in Havana."

I have no idea how the software decided to use those words. I don't recall ever saying raw or fish into the vocabulary file. I'm sure I never said Havana.

I wondered if the computer meant Havana Ill or Havana Cuba so I said:

"Que tal amigo, este es Cuba por Illinois?"

Nothing popped on the screen so I assume I didn't get the Spanish version of the software.

I have pulled the program from my hard drive and will do it over again using the longer version of "Treasure Island" and talking as I normally would to help the program be more accurate. In the meantime, my collective morality will get a little redemption as I have decided to use the computers interpretation of my cussing whenever possible.

From now on when I want to say:

"What in the $^&*$%$# is going on here." I will use raw fish in Havana instead.

Let's see how it will work.

Exxon gave their retiring CEO a $400 million retirement package. Raw fish in Havana.

Ex-governor Ryan had his sentencing postponed for four months. Raw fish in Havana.

The ICC approved a 35% electric rate hike to Ameren Cilco. Raw fish in Havana.

You know this works pretty well. I wonder if the creators of South Park and the Sopranos could use this.

The Great Latrine Fiasco

The following is the lost chapter I mentioned in the foreword of this book. It is part of another of my great, unfinished novels. The book which currently has the title: "Stateside Soldier" is a collection of memories of zany but true events that either happened to myself as a U.S. military policeman, or my friends while in the active military during the height of the Vietnam War. There of course is a little embellishment and extrapolation in this story. I consider this entire book more of a historically based lampoon of the silliness of the Vietnam era military machine rather than some type of document bound for the Library of Congress as a definitive narrative.

Even as a 21 year old young man, I could notice that a lot of things in the U.S. Army didn't make a lot of sense back then. Having a sense of history, I decided to keep track of many of the stories that fell upon me, and my fellow soldiers, with the intention of someday bringing them all together in a book. Needless to say, since I was discharged from the Military in 1971, and the book is still unfinished, it is apparent I have not given it the priority a book would demand if it is supposed to be completed in my lifetime.

I have changed the names of many characters in this chapter, and the book as well. I'm not sure how many of these men are still alive, and I would rather not embarrass them. In a few cases I left the names the same but will never tell who is who. As for the military base, I have changed the name of it and left the location vague on purpose. In the days we were stationed there, any comment by a soldier that the base housed nukes would get you in the brig and out of a cushy job in a heartbeat. That actually was funny since everyone in the towns around the base knew exactly what was going on out there.

I remember when I was discharged. I was told I had a stop on getting a visa to a foreign country for a time period I can't quite remember. I do remember being nervous in 1979 when I applied for my visa to go to Ireland on my honeymoon. I feared someone would stop the process. No one did.

I noticed on a website that the base has been closed. Interestingly, the history of the place mentions munitions storage several times but not a word of anything else. It appears the government doesn't want the truth out about the depot even after it's gone. Since I don't want to get in trouble with anyone in our government I will remain vague...this is easy for me.

The book, written as a third party narrative, is sort of like a ride at Disney's Epcot Center. The story moves right along, but from time to time, comes to a stop to expound a certain bit of information in much greater detail. When the little vignette is completed, the book again moves on and repeats the process until of course, the saga is over. If the saga ever gets done to the point I can recognize that it is over that is.

I believe it is important to touch base with a few of the central characters in this chapter, as readers are entering a book "mid stream". Mitchell Flynn is a composite of me and two of my friends who were in the service at the same time. Needless to say, I was a handsome, six foot three inch, 180 pound, pasty white, half Croatian, half Irish kid from Chicago.

First Sergeant Pettus, can best be described as a moderately thin James Earl Jones. In fact that fits his appearance to a T.

Hall is a 22 year old black from South Philly. The six foot two inch, 200 pounder, was a marvelous physical specimen, looking like he was carved out of oak. Since I am into giving descriptions of the characters right now, I would say Hall looked a little like Erique LaSalle from E.R. fame. Hall, however, had a four inch afro and was thinner. I'm sure he would add that he is better looking.

Contino on the other hand has been reincarnated with Christopher Meloni from Law and Order SVU being a dead ringer for this soldier.

I believe the rest of the characters can be left to your own imagination to determine what they looked like. Just keep in mind all of them were so very young.

I have changed the language to PG-13 in this story to maintain my social awareness of younger readers. I found a distinct enjoyment when One Hour 'til Dawn's review by Lincoln Public Library Director, Richard Sumrall, gave that book a "suitable for all ages", rating. To be honest, if I ever finish the entire book, I think some of the language will have to go back in. Realistically, to assume 21 years old soldiers say "gosh darn" all the time, won't cut the mustard.

The following chapter is out of the center of the incomplete book, and in the event I receive any positive response to this little tale, I might be encouraged to go back to work on this story and bring it to the point of being one of my great, nearly finished novels.

The Great Latrine Fiasco

The last day and night of Flynn's reign as acting platoon sergeant was a disaster made in hell. Staff sergeant Contino had gone home to ask his "Miss Vicky" to marry him, thus leaving Flynn in charge. The two weeks had gone rather smoothly for the most part. Pena got too drunk to drive perimeter, but as always, there were plenty of volunteers to take his four hours around the fence line. "We're all screwed together" was the motto of the Fifth Platoon.

There was one incident at Post 7 with a truck carrying coal into the complex. Flynn got a hurried call from Spec. 4 Bullock that Spencer had gone "John Wayne" again and was threatening the coal delivery driver with dumping the entire truck of coal to check for bombs under the tons of heating materials. A quick admonition by Flynn explaining to Spencer that the idea was past department regulations for inspection didn't seem to be working. Flynn's explaining a dumping would require everyone stay past duty switch to maintain surveillance practices backed Spencer off in a heartbeat.

Like I said, everything those two weeks Contino was gone had been relatively smooth. And then came the day and night of August 18th, 1970.

The post had been furiously preparing the past week for an Inspector General's visit on the 19th. Everyone had been given the word to clean up, clear out garbage, and have everything standing tall in the entire complex before some swag general from the Pentagon walked around the base.

Only a few of the E-6 and E-7's had been around long enough to remember the last I.G. the base had. First Sergeant Pettus, the company's E-8 and ranking NCO on base, had seen a half dozen, and didn't seem to be very worried about the whole affair. At least not like the 250th Company Commander, Captain Vincent Mendoza, who was a "basket case" according to First Sergeant. The inspections came randomly, about every three years or so, which meant most of the men, including officers, had rotated out since the last inspection.

Third Platoon Staff Sergeant Elmore, in his twentieth year on base, almost all of them as an E-6, had told everyone in the 250th that the inspection could be a real "Ball Buster" if you got the "wrong" general conducting the inspection. Like everything and everyone in the army, there were good generals and bad generals. There were generals who understood that the base was inhabited primarily by 21 year old draftees just counting the days until they could go home. And there were generals who thought everyone in the army should love everything about the service and really took great pride in finding everything wrong with every base they inspected.

Sergeant Elmore said that phone calls to his buddies at other bases had told him things were tense right now and the I.G.'s were the toughest ever.

In 1970, besides the all too constant cold war with Russia, Vietnam was reaching new heights of troop deployment and casualties. Opposition to the war was gaining momentum, and the armed forces were starting to worry about demonstrators becoming militant in their protests. Since the base carried hundreds, if not thousands of nuclear warheads and missiles, the Pentagon feared these groups, finding out what was really going on at Area 11, might try something crazy.

The I.G. was scheduled for a Saturday morning, which was perfect and terrible all at the same time. Being on Saturday meant the base and its inhabitants had a whole week after another no doubt hellacious and messy weekend to clean up. This was good. The Saturday inspection also meant the boys were going to have to give up a Friday night on the town to make sure every last detail on the base was perfect. This was bad. Most of the "long timers" had worked their way into weekends off, and telling them they had to give up a Friday night didn't go over very well.

The grumbling had been short lived after Captain Mendoza's notice of all passes being revoked for the 18th was put on the bulletin board.

The captain's words weren't that important of course. The little hand written blurb by First Shirt Pettus under the notice was. In the First's obvious handwriting was the simple sentence: "Don't make me come after you". Everyone on base knew what the First meant, and although an old man by the young soldier's standards, maybe 50, no one relished getting in a brawl with Pettus.

The cleanup of the 250th barracks was going impressively well. Even the Captain and First Shirt were impressed by how well everyone was chipping in and clearing out a barracks that usually looked like a dorm room building at a cheap college.

Closets were being emptied and washed. Walls were being wiped down, and the floors were actually cleaned before adding three coats of G.I. wax to the floors. The puke in wastebaskets was being washed out, and tons of garbage filled the "roll off" dumpster to the point the captain finally ordered a garbage truck to just stay at the barracks until everyone said there was no more trash to haul. Then Moore and Hastings, again in the Captain' crap house for sleeping on duty, climbed into the company's freshly emptied dumpster to scrub and hose it out.

The sight of the boys scrubbing out the garbage container rang home with most of the troops. This was different than just the Captain or Base Commander Thomas, calling for an inspection. This time things were going to be real. They were all back in the army after so many months of living large.

Early afternoon on Friday of the 18th was the time where Flynn's foray into hell began. The platoon, off duty that day, was not only making sure everything in the platoon area was spotless, but many of them were making good money cleaning up things in other platoon areas where the guys were on duty and couldn't finish. Hall, of course, was the big money maker. He made the deals with the on duty guys, and then sublet the work out at a lesser price to guys like Demaso and Tripp who had no lives and were always ready for an inspection.

It was while many of the Fifth Platoon were wiping down the community bathroom area for both the Fifth and Sixth Platoons on the third floor of the barracks, that Flynn allowed his better judgment to go right out with the trash.

It was Demaso and Tripp's fault.

Demaso, trying hard to scrub a wall behind one of the toilets, started complaining how dirty the walls in the entire bathroom were. Tripp also chimed in that they were polishing a turd and that what the bathroom needed was a fresh coat of paint.

Now, in those times, a fresh coat of paint was the Army's answer for everything. A wall is dirty? Paint it. A ceiling looks a little yellow? Paint it. The U.S. Army had more paint than they did soap and it was this mentality that helped Flynn make a monumental blunder.

"Is everyone up for giving this place a coat of paint?"

"Hell yeh," came the chorus.

"Hall, can you get me a deuce and a half?"

With a grin, Hall plopped his ball cap on his totally non regulation afro and went out the door.

Flynn spent the time waiting for Hall to get back with the truck by going down to the office to tell Pettus of his decision. The First, with his head down, scribbling on a pile of papers, just nodded and kept saying "Uh hu" as Flynn told of his decision. In mid sentence of one of Flynn's explanations of why he thought a coat of paint was needed, the First pulled open his middle drawer, pulled out a set of keys and said.

"The paint and supplies are in hut 456 at the east end. One of these keys will open the door."

A horn honking outside the window showed Pettus and Flynn that Hall had found a truck. On the side of the big deuce was stenciled 1123rd Headquarters Company. Pettus went back to his papers as Flynn left the office. The First had a smile on his face as he continued work on the dailies.

"That boy Hall is something else" he remarked to himself.

The trip down the access road was uneventful. Flynn tried to make conversation about who should paint what, but Hall just kept driving the rutted gravel road faster and faster without any replies. Flynn noticed Hall's ball cap kept bouncing higher and higher off his head until it was just laying there; ready to fall off at the next pothole Hall hit.

As the truck screeched to a halt before Quonset hut 456, Flynn asked Hall why no one had told him to get a haircut before the inspection.

"No one's got the balls." Hall replied with a grin.

"No one but Pettus" Flynn replied with his own smile.

Quonset hut 456 was just one of many World War II buildings setting in a neat row on the east end of Army Base 11. They were huge by anyone's standards, being about 100 feet wide by 300 feet long. Not many knew what the dozen or so monoliths contained, but the contents couldn't have been of much importance since they were only checked hourly by the Department of Defense cops rather than every fifteen minutes or less by the M.P.s of the 250th that guarded the bunkers full of missiles and nukes.

After about the tenth key on the ring finally opened the lock, Flynn threw open the massive, twin steel doors and fumbled inside for a light switch. He had to dart out of the way as Hall came barreling into the structure with the deuce. Flynn really didn't need the lights. The years had made so many holes in the rusted away thin corrugated metal of the hut that, coupled with the doors being open, plenty of light from a bright summer's day filtered into the building.

Two hundred feet into the center of the hut, Hall slammed on the brakes of the deuce and popped out of the truck. He, like Flynn, was speechless for a minute as they looked at the contents inside 456. On both sides of the quonset hut, stacked fifteen feet high, the entire length of the structure, were pallet after pallet of five gallon buckets of off-white and O.D. green paint.

"There must be a million gallons of paint in here." Flynn mumbled

"No shit" replied Hall.

"We couldn't use up all this paint if we poured it all over the base" Flynn quipped. He didn't realize his comment wasn't far from what was going to happen that day.

While Flynn kept walking around the interior of the building, Hall started throwing canister after canister of paint in the back of the truck. Flynn, who had a background in home repair work, knew that two five gallon buckets of off-white and one of O.D. green would be more than enough but he didn't stop Hall until a dozen of the fifty pound containers of paint were in the back of the truck. Rather than tell Hall he had loaded too much paint, Flynn decided the extra could be stored in the company storage hut, out behind the barracks, for another day.

Hall was having fun while Flynn mulled over these thoughts, throwing a huge box of paint brushes and rollers and pans into the truck.

"We got enough Sarge. Let's hit it"

Flynn didn't say a word. This was the first time Hall ever called him anything but Flynn. Smiling, he locked the doors of the quonset after Hall barreled the truck out into the daylight.

Back at the barracks, heads popping out all the cranked open windows looked down at Hall and Flynn as they dismounted from the deuce. By the time the two had the truck's tailgate down; a dozen soldiers were there to grab the paint and supplies. Everyone was way too anxious to get going on this project, Flynn noticed. He didn't know it was because not a single soldier, save himself, had ever swung a paint brush. The guys all thought they were in for a couple minutes of fun, the bathroom would be perfect, and then they could all start getting snockered for the morning's inspection.

The five gallon cans of paint were not easy to carry. A full 50 pounds of dead weight, the thin metal handles quickly dug into a person's hands as the parade of soldiers carried the paint up to the third floor. Hall, to continue to keep his legendary status up to date, was carrying two of the canisters effortlessly while everyone else struggled with one. The point wasn't lost on anyone. Hall was definitely a bad ass.

As the soldiers started to pry off the lids, Hall tapped Flynn on the shoulder.

"I need ten bucks to pay off Mendenhall at the motor pool for letting us use the deuce".

"Ten bucks!"

"Yeh, it was the only deuce left and it isn't ours you may have noticed"

"Alright" Flynn grudgingly replied.

As Flynn looked in his wallet, he saw the thirty bucks he had until the 1st. Losing a ten spot was going to mean using the chit books at the

NCO club a little sooner in the month than usual. Normally Flynn didn't go into hock for his booze bill until around the 25th of the month.

At first Flynn started to pull out the ten he had, but thought better. Hall probably had promised Mendenhall a fiver, and as always, Hall was taking a cut on the action. Just because Hall had called him Sarge, Flynn took out two fives and handed them over. He could see in Hall's eyes he had figured correctly.

"Be right back. Don't finish without me" Hall said as he went down the stairs.

Flynn turned to the latrine door and should have changed his mind about painting the bathroom right then and there…but he didn't. The lids were off every bucket of paint. A half dozen of Fifth Platoon sloppily stirred the old paint that had set through God knows how many seasons freezing and then thawing. In line, almost like they were waiting for chow, another half dozen soldiers waited with pans and buckets to get their share and to start painting.

"Everyone stop what you're doing." Flynn yelled.

Since most of the platoon liked Flynn, they did.

"Painting can be a messy job guys. I want all of you to go back to your rooms and put on old fatigues and shoes. I don't want to see any of you have to spend the night cleaning this crap off your clothing. Pick out stuff you wouldn't mind throwing away after we're done Just in case you're a slob"

Flynn didn't know it yet, but the entire platoon, even Demaso and Tripp, were slobs when it came to painting.

As everyone walked out the door and back to their rooms, Flynn caught several high fives or slaps on the shoulder.

"Good idea, Sarge." was the principle remark from all of them.

Flynn decided to go back down to the office and give First Sergeant Pettus the keys back before he lost them somehow. He was afraid some of them might be to something actually important and he didn't want to get court marshaled for losing the keys to a building or two full of Pershing missiles.

Pettus was finishing up for the day as Flynn walked in.

'"Get the paint"

"Yep"

"Got the boys going already"

"Well, I told them to go throw on some old clothes first"

Pettus smiled. He liked Flynn and still had hopes he could keep him in the Army and at Army Base 11 after Flynn's time ran out.

As Flynn started to walk out of the office the phone rang.

Quickly Pettus yelled at Flynn.

"Contino's at the main gate needing a ride. Take my jeep and go pick him up."

Flynn for a moment thought of telling First he needed to get back upstairs, but the thought of most of the painting being done while he followed orders and went for Contino was an appealing thought.

"Sure First. Will do"

Contino wasn't due back till tomorrow midnight, but Flynn wasn't going to question this little stroke of luck.

The main gate was perhaps a mile at best from the barracks and Flynn found himself wishing it was a lot farther away. The longer it took to grab Sergeant Contino, the less painting he would have to do.

As Flynn pulled up to the gate he could see his platoon leader sitting on his half filled duffle bag. Hands to his head, it looked to Flynn like he was crying.

"Oh shit" Flynn thought to himself. 'Things didn't go well with Miss Vickie."

Now most soldiers would have been heartbroken if they found out their sweetheart gave them the axe. Then after a few days, they would either get over it or store it inside somewhere and let it out when they were alone. Contino was different. The 24 year old Italian took everything to heart, and just couldn't let go of anything. Stories of how in Nam he had sobbed heavily for every soldier he saw die were all around the base. Once when his platoon's captain took an RPG that blew off his head, stories of how the emotional Italian then proceeded to single handedly wipe out every gook within a one mile radius were all around the base. The action had given Contino a staff sergeant stripe and a silver star as well as an early dismissal from the front line.

Contino could have gone home, since the army had decided he might be nuts, but he thought that would be a disgrace, so he took a nice safe assignment at Army Base 11 for his final year of service.

Contino had gone home to ask the love of his life to marry him. It seemed obvious to Flynn that request had been rejected.

As Flynn pulled up, he didn't doubt his sergeant had probably been sobbing for two weeks straight.

"Hi Sergeant Contino." Flynn tried to say pleasantly.

Contino looked up and with eyes as red as a glass of burgundy wine muttered.

"Hi Acting Sergeant"

"Sarge, are you alright?" Flynn knew the answer.

"Miss Vickie is marrying another guy." Contino muttered between tears.

"Oh crap Sarge. I'm really sorry. What happened?"

Flynn really didn't want to know, but Contino was a good guy who cut him and everyone in the platoon more slack then they deserved, so he sucked it up and sat down next to the morose soldier.

For the better part of an hour, Flynn listened to his Sarge tell about his leave. "Miss Vickie" had changed. She hated soldiers. She didn't wear a bra, and walked around in a robe with sandals. On and on Contino told Flynn about his dream girl until Flynn couldn't take it anymore.

"Hell Sarge, it's her loss not yours. Besides it sounds like she's gone nuts or something, so the hell with her."

Flynn braced for a tongue lashing but it didn't come'

"Maybe your right buddy, maybe this is for the best."

As soon as Contino finished the sentence he started bawling again.

Suddenly Flynn realized the latrine job wasn't being supervised.

"Sarge, we're painting the bathroom and I've got to get back and see how the guys are doing."

Contino jumped off his duffle bag.

"You're what? Whose painting the bathroom? Oh, dear God, don't tell me you left those idiots with five gallons of paint in a room?'

"Actually Sarge, it's more like 60 gallons.'

Contino was in motion. He had his duffle bag in the back of the jeep, and was yelling at Flynn to get in.

"Oh Jesus, Flynn, don't you know you can't let those kids anywhere near paint? It's bad enough they guard the nukes. That's safe enough, but letting them loose with a truck full of paint. Oh, my God."

In just a minute, the jeep was screeching to a halt in front of the barracks. Without a word, Contino, with Flynn right behind, were up the stairs and at the doorway of the latrine. What they saw was beyond anything that their minds could have envisioned.

The bathroom, in the center of the third floor, is roughly 25 feet by 25 feet square. Down the center, is a wall that has a half dozen sinks on each side. To the right of the wall are a half dozen toilet stalls. To the left of the center wall, a half dozen urinals line the room. Around behind the wall the urinals are fastened to, is a shower room with a half dozen shower heads all in common to the small room with a central drain.

I am explaining how the latrine was set up because a new observer wouldn't be able to tell exactly what this room was, nor what it was supposed to look like at that moment.

Flynn, looking into the bathroom, had started to mull whether being killed by First Shirt or getting sent to the brig would be better. He quickly decided he would probably end up with both happening to him very soon.

As Contino and Flynn walked through the bathroom with Contino screaming, Flynn took everything in.

The O.D. green stalls on the right where painted. You could tell because under the bottom of the wooden stalls, a small stream of green paint was snaking itself towards the middle of the floor. To the right, three of the urinals were almost completely covered with new fresh paint. In one urinal sat a half filled, half tipped over bucket of green paint. The octagon shaped white and black ceramic tile floor wasn't discernible under what Flynn could best call a pool of white and green paint.

As Contino continued to scream, Jonesy, looking more like a KKK member than a young black, cheerfully told both sergeants the job was almost done. Contino received puzzled looks from the guys as he continued to rant. In their minds the job was almost done and after a little cleanup they could start knocking back some brews. They chalked his rant up to just another fiery Italian blow up, which he was famous for, and went back to sloshing paint.

Contino, with paint on his boots and trouser leg from brushing against a sink, had his head around the turn into the shower area.

"What the goddamn hell are you people doing/" he screamed.

Inside the shower, Bullock, Muller, and Root stood covered in paint. They were only wearing skivvies and their boots. Early on they had decided not to ruin any of their clothes by getting paint on them, so they went with the minimum allowed at the time by a bunch of "straight" army guys. As Flynn gingerly tip toed his way into the shower area, he noted perhaps one small victory. At least these guys had found a tarp to cover the floor with before they began sloshing.

Between Contino's screams, Flynn asked Root where they found the huge canvas drop cloth.

"Out in the shed, Sarge. Pretty good idea, huh."

Before Flynn could answer, his eyes noticed the heavy grommet rings that circled the edges of the drop cloth. Picking up one edge, he noticed the other side that the boys hadn't looked at as they unrolled the tarp. In huge, professionally done block print, under a pair of antique crossed pistols, were the words: "250th Military Police Detachment"

Saying nothing, Flynn laid the tarp down as Bullock bragged.

"Almost done."

Flynn tried to smile.

"Great, let's finish it up guys"

Flynn grabbed a still screaming Contino by his now paint speckled civy shirt.'

"Sarge, I need to see you outside. Right now."

Contino could tell Flynn was dirt serious and stopped yelling long enough to ask him what the hell he needed him outside for.

"Trust me Sarge, This is really important. Outside. Please"

As the two sergeants neared the bathroom door, they faced a real dilemma. Outside of a few minor paint speckles, the freshly scrubbed and waxed hallway floor didn't need them or anyone else walking out there with shoes full of paint." Pulling his fatigue shirt off, Flynn took off his boots, and double checked his trouser legs to make sure no paint was dripping off them. Contino followed suit as Flynn yelled back into the room.

"I don't want anyone leaving the bathroom area and messing up this hallway. I'm going to get some towels so you guys won't drip paint all over the damn place. Got it!"

A "Yes Sir" resonated from the men.

Flynn, scared to death of what might happen to the whole barracks if those screwballs started walking around dripping paint, waited as a few of third and fourth platoon members looked up the stairway to see what was going on. He smiled at them and told the soldiers that everyone in the Fifth was busy and to please stay off the third floor while they were working.

As the G.I.'s turned and went back down, Flynn took a deep breath and turned back to Sergeant Contino.

"The drop cloth in the shower room is the company tent."

Contino didn't say anything. His face appeared to be taking in the words but refusing to accept their meaning."

"Sarge, the company tent, the tent we put up on the front lawn during an I.G. inspection is totally covered in oil based, green and white paint."

This brought a response from his sergeant.

In a calm, almost scary tone of voice, Contino replied:

"You're screwed. The guys are all screwed, I'm screwed, the captains' screwed and First Shirt is screwed. Flynn, they're going to send us all to jail."

Flynn didn't dispute his sergeant's opinion.

"I'm sure your right Larry"

Flynn never used Contino's first name, out of respect, but he needed help and he needed his sergeant to understand they were the only two sane people in the entire platoon right now. They needed to be more than soldiers. They needed to be friends.

Flynn told Contino his plan.

"Sarge, in a few minutes those idiots in there are going to figure out the paint doesn't just wash off."

To prove the point, Flynn pointed to Root, furiously washing his hands and arms in one of the sinks. A quizzical look on his face as the paint just smeared around, but didn't come off. Jonesy was rubbing the side of one of the urinals and was beginning to panic as the paint just smeared and smeared after the shirt he was using became soaked.

"Larry, we need to get enough towels to wipe everything and everyone off. We need to get gasoline, maybe five or ten gallons of it. We need a trash container we can pitch all the clothes and towels in and then destroy or hide from everyone else. The company tent needs to be buried or destroyed. And we need to do all of this now."

Both sergeants looked at each other and chimed in together.

"Hall."

The shock of what Flynn had observed initially had caused him to not notice that Hall wasn't in the bathroom with the other platoon members. He immediately turned and jogged towards Hall's room at the end of the floor. Flynn could hear loud music blaring under the door of Hall's room. Knocking and entering simultaneously, Flynn started right in on Hall, lying on the bed, a pillow under his head.

"Soldier why aren't you in the latrine with the rest of the platoon." Flynn barked with authority.

"Man have you seen what those crazy bastards are doing in there Sarge. I ain't going to the brig. They all are. You are. But I ain't."

Flynn couldn't fault Hall's logic. If he could run away from this he would. He had already pondered making a dash for the Canadian border but decided to stay and try to help the platoon… and himself.

Flynn swallowed hard and made his plea.

"Will you help me? Help us?"

"Whaddya need." Hall asked.

Flynn then went over his list of things, while a grinning Hall made a mental note of what his Sarge was asking for.

"How soon you need this stuff?"

"An hour ago."

"I'm on it."

With that, Hall was out the door and down the stairs. Flynn felt a little better. He had a plan that would get them out of some of this mess. They were still all screwed, but maybe they wouldn't be shot.

Walking back towards the latrine, Flynn could hear that all of the men were starting to panic. They had found out the paint they had all over everything, and themselves, wouldn't wash away. They started yelling and Flynn stood in the door, blocking any slob from running out of the bathroom with paint dripping from their bodies.

"Listen to me, men. We are all screwed right now...but I have a way to get us all out of this mess.

Flynn noticed everyone staring at him with pleading eyes.

"I will be right back, and don't worry, I know what to do. Things will be alright, but we've got to stick together on this. And no one, not anyone for any reason, can leave the latrine right now. We have one room screwed up but if you leave the area, we will have the entire third floor screwed up."

The group of soldiers all either nodded or replied. They were scared, but Flynn said he could fix things and they believed him. They had zero alternatives.

As he turned to leave he could hear Tripp, sitting in one of the toilet stalls, complain that the toilet paper he had just used was full of green paint.

Flynn wondered what had happened to Contino and walked down the hallway to the platoon sergeant's room. As he approached the door he could hear Contino inside talking to himself amidst sobs about his "Miss Vicky" and his platoon all going to jail. He decided he better leave Sarge alone. This was a mess he would have to handle on his own.

Flynn walked back to the latrine and after putting his boots back on walked into the bathroom.

"Listen up; Hall will be back in a couple minutes with stuff to help clean up this mess. The first thing we need to do is make sure the job is done and done right."

With that, Flynn walked around the latrine pointing out drips and missed spots. Every time he mentioned what needed to be done, eager soldiers, fearful of losing their cushy army jobs, did what he asked. Finally, the room was well painted. Unfortunately the toilets; sinks, urinals, and floor also were well painted.

"O.K. Listen up. I want all the paint containers sealed up and I mean good. I want all the brushes and rollers and pans stacked over here. I want the tarp in the bathroom rolled up, paint side in and brought out here. Let's go people."

With that command everyone started in motion. They felt good about doing something that might actually bail them out of trouble. Flynn knew the soldiers in the shower room were about to find out what their drop cloth actually was, and he knew he needed to be calm lest everyone just start screaming and running out of the bathroom on their way to foreign countries. It was Muller who started yelling.

"Oh no, oh crap no. This is the company's tent. Oh, sweet Jesus, we're gonna die."

Flynn grabbed Muller.

"I know it's the company tent. We're going to get rid of it. No evidence? No one will ever know what happened."

Root, Muller and Jonesy all asked what to do at the same time.

"Look it's too full of paint to walk out of here, so I want you to roll it up as tight as you can and we're going to throw it out the window." Flynn directed.

The soldiers liked the idea and proceeded to follow their sarge's orders.

Flynn was immediately dismayed by the fact the old, crank out windows in the latrine only opened half way, making the fit of a tent very tight. He had never noticed this before, as he had never had to attempt to throw a paint soaked company tent out of one of them before. Checking to make sure the Captain's and First's jeeps were gone, and no other vehicle was anywhere near the window, he gave the command.

"Alright, get it tight men, and bring it over here to the window."

Muller and Jonesy, each carrying an end, looked at the window and then at Flynn.

"It'll fit. We might need to do a little pushing but it'll fit."

As the two soldiers shoved the tent out the window, it began to re-open.

"Keep going." Flynn barked as the soldiers looked at him.

The other ten Fifth Platoon members all yelled out words of encouragement as slowly the tent went through the window and out into the early evening air.

Flynn knew he hadn't banked on the ancillary problems this action now caused. Immediately he knew the outside of the window and any bricks the fluttering tent might have touched would need to be scrubbed. Wherever it landed on the lawn would make a real mess too. He kept these thoughts to himself to prevent a new panic among the soldiers.

The dozen soldiers let out a roar as the tent disappeared into the night. To make matters better, Hall appeared at the door to the bathroom. In his arms were dozens of army issue bath towels. He threw them into the room, not wanting to get too near any paint that might get on his always impeccable fatigues.

"Be right back." Hall said.

As the soldiers grabbed for towels, Hall came back with two five gallon containers of gasoline. Setting them inside the door Hall smiled and went back down the stairs. More towels, more gasoline came up to the bathroom as everyone furiously started soaking towels in the gas and washing down everything that wasn't supposed to have paint on it.

"It's working." Tripp yelled.

"Yeh it'll work" Flynn agreed, 'but don't anyone even think of having a smoke right now. Open up all the windows as far as they can"

Amazingly, as Flynn finished his command, Hall appeared at the door with one of those huge army fans and a 100 foot extension cord.

Flynn couldn't help his admiration.

"Soldier, anywhere, anytime, you're my main man."

Hall grinned and proved Flynn's faith in him even more.

"I've got a couple old drum barrels we can throw all this crap in."

For the next two hours, a dozen men worked furiously cleaning sinks and stools and floors. The smell was incredibly strong but no one complained. They thought they saw a way out of the "screw up" they had committed, and everyone worked hard as hell to get things right.

Hall had used this time to go to each soldier's room and grab new clothes and boots. He also had a couple old bedspreads laid out in the hallway to protect the floor. No one worried about whose they were.

The plan was to throw away their clothes and for many, their boots, step out onto the bedspreads and put on the new clothes Hall had waiting for each soldier.

The last two soldiers rolled the drums out to the hallway, one full of towels, the other filled with brushes and a few empty paint containers. All paint containers and the drums had been wiped down and "clean" soldiers quickly moved them down to the truck

Flynn kept Jonesy with him as they slowly worked their way out of the bathroom, wiping up any final spots missed by the platoon.

Out in the hallway, the now happy soldiers were making plans for a beer bash to celebrate their reprieve from a firing squad. Flynn told the men to get downstairs and for two or three of the men to roll the tent, still laying on the lawn, inside the not too badly painted bedspreads and to place it carefully in the back of the deuce.

"Everyone must be 'perfectly' careful not to get any paint on themselves or their clothes or the damn deuce. We don't need to start this crap over."

Everyone agreed and the men started moving the mess down the stairs. Flynn took a look back at the latrine. Everything that needed painting was painted. Everything that wasn't supposed to be wasn't, and the room smelled like a tanker truck of gasoline had been spilled in it.

Flynn closed the big swinging door to the bathroom and taped a sign on the door he had already made up.

"Bathroom off limits. Wet paint. Wet floor. Danger flammable materials"

Going downstairs, Flynn decided to make a call to Sixth Platoon Sergeant Hendricks. The sixth would be getting off duty at 2300 and he didn't want anyone stumbling into the bath area full of wet paint and gasoline fumes. He pictured a dumb G.I. walking into the bathroom with a cig in his mouth and blowing the entire barracks to hell. He pictured the general from the Pentagon staring down into a huge hole in the ground full of O.D. green and off-white paint and asking Captain Mendoza what the hell had happened.

Walking into the office to use a phone, Flynn was stunned to see Contino sitting in a chair at First's desk. Behind the paper strewn desk, in a tee shirt with a half burned cigar, sat Pettus.

Before Flynn could say a word, Pettus started talking.

"Contino tells me what happened and he says you got it fixed. That right?"

"Almost, First."

"Whaddya mean, almost?"

Flynn then explained about the company tent and the fact the only thing that could be done was to destroy it. He soon realized Sergeant Contino had stopped his sobbing and had started to look in on the fiasco when Flynn was too busy to notice. Contino had decided to get First Sergeant Pettus involved because he believed an informed First Shirt would be much better than a First Shirt who found out about things while standing next to a general from the Pentagon.

All the while Flynn stammered through his story, Pettus nodded. You could see he was thinking. Finally Pettus got up from the desk, and with Contino and Flynn following, bounded up the stairs to the third floor bathroom.

"Jesus H Christ." Pettus said as he looked in the bathroom.

He had quickly put his currently unlit cigar behind his back just in case. Before Flynn could start pleading for his life and that of his men, the First turned around.

"In twenty years on this base, I have never seen this crap house look that good. Flynn you pulled this mess out of the ashes according to Contino and I agree."

With relief, Flynn thanked First and told him he still had one job to do and that was to burn a company tent and two drums of towels.

Smiling broadly, Pettus told the sergeants to go back to the office.

As Flynn and Contino turned to leave, Pettus pulled out his pen and wrote on the bottom of Flynn's note on the door.

"If you go in here, I will find you."

Flynn, feeling great relief right now, didn't know who to thank more, Pettus, or Contino.

Back in the office First got Hendricks on the phone. He relayed to the Staff Sergeant to make sure none of his men used the third floor latrine and then pulled a real surprise that had Flynn's spirits soaring. Pettus advised Hendricks there was going to be a bonfire out at the east end of the base and not to report it or this phone call in his dailies. He then told Hendricks to meet him at the NCO club after shift and that he was buying tonight.

As First hung up he yelled at the sergeants to get the hell out of his office. As they quickly made for the door, he told them to stop by the NCO club and pick up six cases of beer and a few bottles of Jack Daniels and to put it on his tab.

"Can't have a bonfire without a little hootch, now can you? Go on, get out of here. Flynn, nice job taking care of a real problem"

"Thank you First Sergeant Pettus."

Flynn saluted although army regulations stated you didn't salute non-commissioned officers. In Flynn's mind, First deserved a salute more than some damn general would tomorrow.

Note: Well those are the events of August 18th 1970. The Fifth Platoon, visited after duty by the Sixth, had a hell of a fire out on the east side of the base. Flynn spent most of the evening hugging his fellow soldiers and telling them how much he loved each and every one of them. Contino got drunk and started bending ears about how his "Miss Vickie" had dumped him. A very drunk Tripp kept pulling his pants down and asking everyone if his ass was green. Hall sat on the hood of the deuce, hogging one of the bottles of Jack all to himself. Flynn didn't mind. Whatever Hall wanted, Flynn would gladly do for the soldier who had literally saved the Fifth Platoon from possible court marshals.

At the NCO club, Pettus continued to buy Hendricks drinks and told him how such a good team player as he probably needed to be recommended for another stripe. That would all change tomorrow after Hendricks, still drunk, couldn't stand up straight as the general walked by Sixth Platoon.

The next morning, the supply sergeant for the 1123 Headquarters Company walked back and forth around the laundry truck he had failed to unload the day before. He couldn't be sure, but he thought there had been a much larger stack of towels in the back of the deuce then there were now. But then, why would anyone steal towels he thought to himself.

As for the lawn where the tent had landed, a series of ponchos laid across the grass with the company's 30 and 50 caliber machine guns locked and loaded, covering the sins of the night before. On the bricks of the building, where the paint had hit the wall, the 250th Military Police banner hung proudly.

The 250th Military Police Company and the 1123rd Headquarters Company didn't have their tents out that day. Both First Shirt Pettus and Headquarters Company's Master Sergeant Billings, had advised their captains and the general, that the tents had gone moldy and looked like hell, so they refused to present them for such an important inspection. The general told an aid to make a note to have new tents made and delivered to the base. Pettus had obviously called in a marker from his counterpart at Headquarters Company. No one ever found out what it was.

As for the bathroom, the general remarked to Captain Mendoza that he had never seen a cleaner latrine anywhere in all his days of base inspection…although there was a peculiar smell to the place.

I don't know how I can have a book about my personal memories and recollections without having at least one story about things I personally hate. To be honest, if I wrote about all the things I hate, it would be an enormous book in itself, so for now I will just touch on the principal things in this world that really fry my gonads.

Several of these complaints are pulled from columns I wrote in the last ten years where I was grumping about something. Many more are waiting their turn to hit the op/ed page of the *Lincoln Courier* at another time. I think right now would be a good time to gather a pile of them together and write a little piece about all the things and people who drive me nuts. I imagine that is an appropriate title for this little diatribe so let's get going.

Things That Drive Me Nuts

Why is it that most people working at drive through businesses don't speak English? You know what I mean. Pull up in your car to get your favorite burger or edible and you hear this unintelligible gibberish over the loudspeaker. Now I know a few languages myself, but these people have invented their own language and expect us to have learned it in order to get a mountain oyster taco or baloney noodle salad. Is there a rule, that if you hire an employee who can't communicate worth a lick in the King's English, that you put them at the drive through window?

Urban Legend has it that if you were to record the babble coming out of the loudspeaker and replay it at one third speed, it actually is English. Youngsters, it seems, have learned to speak at hypersonic speed without need of commas, periods or pauses to catch one's breath.

Why do all these junk food establishments require their people to always start out with their planned promotional speech?

"Hi, ya wanna try our new super crunchy meal, or our new get it bigger for a nickel or our extra napkin on orders over $50.00 deal?"

What is wrong with these corporate idiots who are making these kids spit this stuff at us? People know what they want. This isn't a Mercedes dealership. There is no "up selling" to be done. Just let us order our crap and be on our way.

My mother-in-law handles this sales pitch the best. She yells at the voice in the box to shut up, she knows what she wants. It always gets her mean looks when she is handed her bag, but she does get through the line faster than the guy behind her who is listening to page two of all the offers the order taker has to say before; "Whaddya want?" finally can be heard.

Have you ever noticed that, even if your order is bundled and bagged by the time you get to window number 47, you have to hand the money over before you get your stuff? That's because they don't trust us of course. They believe idiots will grab the chicken chunklets and peal away without paying. This is impossible of course because of the five cars directly in front of you, who after paying, were told to pull up and wait for their order.

I have to ask why I should trust these people if they don't trust me. I think the passage of cash for chow should be simultaneous. Sort of like on television, when the dope dealer and junkie both stick out their dope and money, and snatch each other's stuff at the same time.

Maybe a little conveyor system with two belts going opposite ways should be required at drive through windows. Like prisoner of war exchanges, where the two start walking across the bridge to the other side.

Another drive through thing that just sends me up the wall is when I get behind someone ordering lunch munchies for the whole shift at the factory. It isn't bad enough I have to wait now as twenty orders are placed with a youngster who keeps asking for the order to be repeated. Every one of the orders always has to have something added or subtracted from the sandwiches, which makes it impossible to serve the person quickly. I think a law should be passed that anyone ordering multiple meals at a drive through must accept all products as they are originally intended by the fast food franchise.

These people can make the changes to their burgies back at the factory lunchroom. Someone not wanting their pickle can give it to someone who wanted an extra one and so on. If a person is fussy they should go to the Ritz Carlton, but don't make me sit in line, burning a quarter tank of gas, just because Ralphy doesn't like mayonnaise and Buford hates tomatoes.

Inside fast food places there are other customer actions that drive me nuts. It irks me when people waiting in line have to stand ten feet away from the order area. You don't know if their waiting for someone else to join them or whatever, until you decide to walk up to the counter and then you get a: "Hey Buddy, get in line" from the supposed loiterer. Why can't people just get in line and not cause these traffic jams in the middle of fast food lobbies. Are they afraid the person ordering ahead of them will get upset if they get too close and they're overheard ordering a jumbo tater bag?

The people who use a bank drive through also just don't get it. I don't know how many times I have ended up behind someone who doesn't have anything ready to submit for transaction. You can see them fumbling around, looking for a deposit slip, or a check, or whatever else they should have had in their hand before they come up to the window. I always seem to get behind someone who has a mortgage to renew, or needs to transfer three balances from various accounts into two others, and they don't remember whose names they're under or what the account numbers are.

******

Other things that drive me nuts happen at convenient stores. Why do people have to buy scratch cards from the Illinois lottery, and with twenty people lined up behind them, decide right then and there is the time to play scratch and look? Why can't they go out in their car and do that? Do they really think a line of people, holding all kinds of stuff in their arms wanting to get home, are interested in whether they get a free card or five bucks or something?

They seem to think that everyone in the store is mesmerized by their close encounter with financial freedom. These compulsive scratchers will turn around, ignoring the fact they are holding up the line, and yelp out.

"Wow, I almost won a million dollars". Yeh, buddy, and I came within an eyelash of winning a Pulitzer last week.

Another store thing that rankles the heck out of me is; why after paying with a check, does a person feel compelled to immediately determine their new checkbook balance. Often times the person, poor at math, takes forever to determine the new balance. A person shouldn't have written a check if they don't have enough money in their account, and if they do, the balance will still be there after they get out of my way. So get out of my way, go home and have your third grader figure it out for you.

******

Have any of you ever noticed how every television station always sends their reporters out to cover a hurricane. I don't mean from a mile away. I mean they put these people right in the middle of the storms. Just the other night as a hurricane came ashore in Florida, every station had some poor dumb schmuck reporter and a camera man trying to hold onto a building, or flagpole, as the maelstrom swirled debris all around them. Why do television station managers do this?

Someone could bolt a camera to a pole and just take the pictures. Is it really necessary to have someone almost killed just so we can understand how bad things are? I ponder how long it will be before a reporter gets killed. Hit by another reporter flying through the air.

******

Shark attacks always make the news but I have to ask why? Every case of a mean spirited wife doing in her no good, worthless husband doesn't make the news, but have a shark take just a nibble out of some surfer dude's kiester and it's on World News Report.

Why is a shark attack always such a big story that always leads to several ancillary stories about how to avoid shark attacks? I can tell you how to avoid shark attacks right now. Just stay out of the ocean. I feel terrible for people, who are bitten or in some cases killed by a shark, but we are swimming in their world and such possibilities will always exist as long as we believe we are required to swim in potentially dangerous waters.

In the event a person goes for a walk in a lion's den, one might expect to be eaten by a lion, you know. I did some research and to date there have been zero shark attacks in swimming pools or at water parks, so that's the way I would go to get my aquatic exercise.

******

Why does the government continue to take famous or rich people to trial? The trials go on for months, cost millions of taxpayer dollars, and either result in a fine a kid with a paper route could pay, or a time in jail so short that the 'processing in" has to be sped up because the celebrity is late for their "processing out."

There should never be any trials conducted in California. No one of celebrity gets convicted of anything in that state, so why waste the time and money? A celebrity in California wouldn't be convicted of running someone over if the celebrity was caught, still in the car, still on top of the victim.

******

I have to wonder why they keep making square televisions when everything is going to the new rectangular filming called letterbox. I feel gypped every time I have to watch something that has a huge dark space at the top and bottom. I went and bought a larger television because I needed it so that I could have the same size picture I used to have with my older, smaller set. To make my picture even smaller, the networks have to put their logos in the lower right of the picture and the weather people keep putting their huge stupid storm grids in the lower left, so my picture gets smaller still. Wouldn't you think with all that empty dark space, all that crap could be put there rather than on the now smaller picture they are sending at us?

******

Speaking of weather grids, those people really frost my butt. Why, all of a sudden, do we have to have our programs interrupted to tell us a thunderstorm is coming? So what? According to my trusty weather encyclopedia, there are 4400 thunderstorms occurring on our planet at any given moment, so what the heck is so special about the one coming my way.

The voice, which has now interrupted the final one minute of dialogue of a four hour murder mystery I have been watching, tells me the storm could bring heavy amounts of precipitation and high winds. Of course it will. Otherwise, it isn't a thunderstorm. It's just rain, which is occurring at 46,500 places at any moment on the planet.

I can't understand how these weather people can keep telling us to get to safety by running down to the basement, but keep tuned to them for the latest. I wonder how many people have been injured carrying their giant screen televisions down the stairs in an effort to follow the weather person's advice. I'll bet it's a number higher than that of people hurt by the thunderstorm.

These "all important" interruptions, of course, never cut into commercials. They never stop an infomercial to tell us doom is on the way, or a home shopping network. If these storms are so terrible, shouldn't people watching how to buy Gertrude's hard boiled egg maker for only $19.95 know what is happening?

If a storm starts barreling past in the wee hours of the morning, good luck trying to get any information then. Hey, it's late at night, the weather people all went home, and no one is at the studios right now. Why is it that bad weather only deserves pestering us during prime time television hours? Are storms after midnight not as dangerous as ones that come with two minutes left in a tied basketball game at 10:00 p.m.?

The other night around 3:00 a.m., I awoke from the sound of a terrible storm outside. The windows were rattling, so I got up to check what the weather people on television had to say. All there was on any station, was a little W or lightning bolt in the corner of the screen. I thought for certain the area weather channel would have a full report, but as the wind banged my tree against the front room's picture window, and my garbage cans could be seen going thirty miles an hour down the alley, the weather channel was running one of their storm documentaries without a word about what was going on outside. Interestingly, the story was about how a community was sucked away by a massive storm because no one warned them it was coming.

******

219

Speaking of sucking, I hate straws. I always have, ever since I was a little kid. I think they are one of the stupidest inventions in the world, and if I had the chance I would make them illegal. Why is it that no one can drink anything without sucking it up through a miniature tube? What has caused the world to become suckers and sippers rather than slurpers and gulpers?

It can't have anything to do with genetics. I could see the need for straws if the human mouth was the size of a dime. Sticking a stupid tube into the tiny aperture to prevent getting fluids all over one's face would make sense if that was the case. The human mouth, however, is fairly large, and the cups and glasses devised by man over the years are perfect for using both they and a mouth to deliver fluids to the body.

I have to wonder why a person cannot possibly drink anything without a straw…unless it's hot. You never see people drinking coffee from a straw do you? Why not? When I was a kid I was told you couldn't use a straw in a cup of hot Ovaltine because the wax straw would melt. Modern straws aren't made with wax however. The reason must be a genetic link has been established in our progenies DNA code that they must use a straw unless the drink is hot. The world is screwed isn't it? I better go buy stock in a straw company.

Every time I hear someone making that disgusting sound a sucking straw makes as the last fluid from a drink is sucked up, I want to go up to them and slap them.

I remember once telling a waitress to not bother bringing a straw back with my ice tea and she gave me a look like I was addled or something. She got a nickel for a tip.

******

I really wish there was a way I could make "flip flops" illegal. Those nasty, disgusting "semi shoes" are everywhere these days. This foot protection was invented for the armed services to issue to their soldiers. The human foot, being a carrier of many nasty diseases, caused the military to decide wearing a partial shoe that would keep all the germs swimming around a community shower off of everyone's feet, would promote better hygiene. Well now that "flip, flops" are everyday wear, I believe they constitute the number one health problem in America.

Besides the disgusting "suck, plop", sound people make when walking in those nasty things, no one fears what germs are being put in the air by these people and their feet. Just the other day, as I visited my son at college, dozens of students were going back and forth to classes wearing those nasty, cheesy looking things on their feet. A very high wind caused me to wonder what fungi, and other diseases were being blown off their feet and into the air I was breathing.

It's bad enough summers now mean I have to see millions of ugly looking toes and feet, but now I might be getting some kind of cancer off of someone else's toe jam. I'm thinking of starting a non profit group dedicated to making it illegal to go out in public with those hideous things fastened between a person's toes by a chunk of rubber

******

People in cars are a pet peeve of mine. It isn't so much their driving habits, as it is their parking habits that run my blood pressure up the chart. Why is it people can't follow simple painted directions in a parking lot? If an arrow is painted on the ground pointing in one direction, that means you use that lane to go in that direction and not the other. Those arrows aren't suggestions; they are information to prevent cars from running into each other.

The yellow parking lines are also there for a reason, but how many times do you see someone's car or truck parked crooked or sideways in the parking area so that they effectively are taking up two or perhaps three spots.

There of course, are the idiots who have decided they need to get as close to the store's door as possible without actually driving into the store. They are not handicapped, of course. Otherwise they could park in one of those spots. These normal, healthy, people park in the fire lanes, which they believe is all right since they are staying with the car. It seems people don't think they are parking illegally if they are in their car. It is only if you leave the car in a stupid spot that it might not be the thing to do.

The people usually are waiting for someone else in the family to come out the door with something large that they were planning on purchasing…like a treadmill or exercise bike.

While I'm on parking lots, I need to take a jab at all the dolts who can't put their shopping carts back in the shopping cart areas that are everywhere in the lot. These jerks just leave them wherever they wish and don't give a damn about the carts drifting around, putting dents in people's nice cars. If you notice, people who abandon carts all drive junker cars and trucks, have dirty hair, and have few, if any attractive teeth in their mouth.

******

Kids going down the street with car stereos blaring so loud they make the glass in my windows vibrate also really honk me off. These noisy kids don't need to have the sound up that high with their windows down. I imagine that is required lest the sound shatter their windshield. To make matters worse, they always have some type of pure garbage music on that wouldn't be worth listening to even if it was at a proper decibel level. I think kids who drive around with blaring music, and the store owners who sold them the systems, should be arrested and thrown in jail. They should be tied to a chair and made to listen to Gene Autry sing "Frosty the Snowman" for 48 hours straight and that will end this nonsense.

******

Cell phones need to be made illegal. Cell phone usage has gone past the realm of sanity on so many levels I don't know where to start. Have you noticed how many people have to call someone on their cell before they unlock the door of their car? It's like the car won't come out of park if there isn't a cell phone in the ear of the driver. Drivers on a cell, of course, can't drive worth a crap. Study after study shows people occupied with a worthless conversation don't concentrate on moving their one ton vehicles around the roads in a way that will prevent their hitting someone else in a one ton vehicle…who also has a phone stuck in their ear.

Now there is text messaging and picture phones and phones with games and all this other garbage that has no need, nor true importance to anyone except the phone companies who can add more and more charges to a cell phone user's bill.

A lot of cell phone usage is calls to people who the caller didn't get a chance to talk to when they were with them all day. They didn't get a chance to talk to them, because they were too busy yapping on a cell phone to other people who they weren't with.

I often wish that a rumor advising that cell phones are capable of curing hemorrhoids hits the internet. I can then watch as people start pulling those things away from their ears and start sticking them where I believe they belong.

******

I don't understand all these health food fads, and diets, and exercise videos, and "anti obesity" stuff that's going around. The garbage food industry that makes people fat is a near trillion dollar industry. The exercise industry, diet books, diet programs and diet foods that try to prevent or reduce obesity is a near trillion dollar business. Why can't people see that if they stopped eating the junk that makes them fat they wouldn't need to buy any of the stuff to remove the fat and everyone would save several trillion dollars?

I am no longer a chubby man. I am no longer a chubby man because I quit eating things that made me chubby. Thank you. Will someone please send me a trillion dollars for this little tidbit of knowledge?

Seriously, I understand some people have a very hard time with weight. Many don't have as much success as others with losing weight and keeping it off. There is more to the problem than just eating too much, eating too much bad food, and not exercising enough. But don't tell me that isn't a lot of it.

I can understand how stress can lead to serious weight gains. When Timothy went off to college, I was so stressed out; I caused a bacon shortage in Central Illinois. I can see how persons dealing with emotional problems or sadness also can find solace in food. I've been there. I've done that.

There are people in this world who have such a slow metabolism, that pounds go on easier than they come off, but far too many of us use that excuse just to remove any responsibility for our own eating habits. You can't blame it on your metabolism when the owner of the local all-you-can-eat buffet winces every time you walk into his business.

All that being said, to not accept that, on a national level, most people are overweight because they have poor eating habits and don't exercise enough would be ignoring reality.

I am not a harsh judge of my fellow man and I can sympathize with heavy people as long as they understand I don't want to see their personal problems in the flesh. Wearing clothes that show rolls of fat just shouldn't be allowed in public. I don't know how many times I wanted to go up to a young girl wearing low rider jeans with a beer gut sticking out between the top of her pants and the bottom of a way too short top shirt, and tell her there is nothing attractive about showing off that nasty looking belly.

Men, of course are even worse than the women. I would like someone to tell me why men refuse to admit they are getting fatter. When I put on the pounds, I went and bought pants with a larger waist, but it looks like a lot of men won't do that. Instead they just slide their pants down below their bellies and then tell themselves they wear the same pants size they did in high school. I see men all the time who have their pants slid so low off their waist that I marvel the things still stay up.

If you ever really look at these gentlemen, you will notice the barn door of their trousers is somewhere between their knees, and I imagine that presents its own problem when they go to the bathroom. I think there should be a law that states if a man cannot find his "thing a ma bob" when he pulls his zipper down, he is guilty of wearing his trousers too low, and should be required to have someone measure and then tell the whole world what his waist size really is. I believe if you tell a man who is wearing a pair of 36 inch pants down below his groin area, that his waist size is actually a 51, you will see that man start losing weight.

******

While we are on the issue of gonads, I have a gripe with stadiums, field houses, ball parks and the like. There are never enough lavatory facilities at these venues, and of course, there is little opportunity for a man to properly wash his hands after using one of those bathrooms. I wonder how many people realize that during a game, when they are exchanging high fives or getting their drinks passed down the aisle to them, that they are collecting dozens of minute urine samples from every man in the building.

******

I don't understand how these jewelry shows on the shopping networks continue to rake in millions and millions of dollars. There are some of them that aren't too bad. Some of the programs offer necklaces made out of ball bearings painted to look like pearls. Since they're only charging $39.95, I don't see any harm in that. A person buying their own ball bearings and a can of spray paint would almost spend that much anyway. What really frosts me, are these shows that have this gaudy, junky, looking stuff, and offer it for only $2000 or $3000 which is only half what its worth. Sure. And the plastic decoder ring I got in a 1959 box of Rice Crispies is worth a fortune too.

I love how these swank looking people brag how this ring or these earrings are such a bargain that will probably never be available again in our lifetime. One could only hope. They always give a caret weight, of course, as if that makes the crummy thing worth a month's pay.

The stones are always these new gemstones that until a few years ago, weren't even considered gemstones. There are the "junkmolines' and the "Craptonites" and don't forget to buy something made out of a "Buckeyazite" since they are getting harder and harder to find. In the back yard I found a three hundred caret raccoon dropping and I'm offering it for half its normal value on E-Bay.

******

While we are on lousy television, let's not forget all these infomercials selling stuff that any television station with a conscience wouldn't allow on the airways. There are all these pretend talk shows pushing so many garbage things that I can't believe the FCC allows this to happen.

Before every telecast, there is a disclaimer of course, noting that the station doesn't back the product nor offer any endorsement of the outlandish claims that are about to be presented. That's bull. If you don't believe the program is telling the truth and isn't actually offering something of worthwhile value, then you have a responsibility of not airing the show.

Television doesn't allow dope dealers or counterfeiters to advertise, yet they allow people to sell a pill they claim will make you lose pounds while you're standing at a buffet line waiting for a new vat of fried chicken to come out. Let us not forget all the books and tapes that are guaranteed to make you a millionaire. If these books and tapes actually worked, why isn't everyone in America filthy rich…like say the television stations and the people selling this crap?

In the real world someone who profits off of another's crime can be arrested as either an accessory to the fact or charged with "aiding and abetting" a crime. Not in T.V. land. Here, the stations run the ads for big bucks and then when one of these con artists finally gets arrested and prosecuted, the station runs the information on their nightly news and tells people they should be skeptical of businesses like these. What hypocrisy.

******

I don't understand music anymore. I did as a young man, but even then I realized most music stinks. I think I was the only teenager in America who realized that "Love Me Do" by the Beatles, was a poor grammatical foray into telling a girl you have affection for her and would appreciate reciprocity if plausible.

Most music of every generation actually stinks if you look at it. In the 50's you could understand what a person was singing but the words were primarily stupid. "You Ain't Nothin but a Hound Dog" rests my case on that.

The 60's were full of upheaval in the country. The music and words, usually claiming to be pissed at somebody, actually made sense, except they usually were droned out by band members enamored with their new electric guitars.

The 70's and 80's brought about thousands of artists who had one good song in them, but refused to then quit while ahead. They then drowned us with album after album of pure garbage.

The 90's till now of course, have been primarily Hip Hop or Rap music. I'm sorry, but people who can't sing become rappers. Now I was a huge fan of the Temptations, and Diana Ross and the Supremes, and Otis Redding and Sam Cooke and Smokey Robinson. I could go on and on, but the point is none of those artists did rap music. It wasn't because it hadn't been invented yet. None of the great artists of the past did rap because they didn't have to. They could actually sing. So they did. Rap music is like abstract art. If you can't do something right, then do it so bad, with such confidence, that you can fool people into believing you actually are good. It's sort of like my writing.

I find myself gravitating towards Country Music these past few years. The women of country; like Faith Hill, Martina McBride, Carrie Underwood, and let's not forget Reba and perhaps a dozen more, actually have world class singing voices. The songs they sing often are a beautiful blend of vocals and music and message which is missing in the other genres of music right now.

I don't think the same about the male country vocalists however. I think most country songs offered by the males are goofy. I do have to admit I don't like most male country singers because of their stupid hats. Now maybe some of them have ranches and ride horses often, but that doesn't mean they have to wear those goofy hats everyday, everywhere.

There are people in the national guard that from time to time wear a steel helmet, but you don't see them walking around all day wearing one as they go to the grocery store, or go out to eat. Construction workers have to wear a hardhat on the job but they don't wear them to their kid's graduation. If one of those "cowboys" had walked into my Irish grandma's house with their hat still on, she would have lectured them about taking your hat off in the house…while she was beating the crap out of them, of course.

I firmly believe the reason Country Music has their own separate awards events is because most people, including musicians in other disciplines, wouldn't put up with not being able to see the stage because some scrawny male singer, showing off his 10 inch biceps, won't remove his cowboy hat. It will never happen, but if there are ever "joint" music awards and a fight breaks out, I'll bet on the rappers kicking the most butt.

It appears I digressed a little. As I was saying, I don't think the male country vocalists are anywhere near as good as their female counterparts. Their voices for one thing aren't very good, with many of them having a twangy kind of voice that sounds like a beer truck hitting the brakes on a wet pavement.

The male singers also don't offer songs anywhere near the quality offered by the Females. For every "Independence Day" by Martina McBride or "I Feel Like a Woman" by Shania Twain or "Breathe" by Faith Hill, the males offer up such outstanding repartees as "I Spent my Paycheck at the Girlie Bar" or "My Wife Kicked me out fer Spittin Terbacky Juice in the Goldfish Bowl". From time to time the male singers do come out with a sad love ballad. Who can forget the classic: "Why do the sheep run away from grandpa?"

******

I'm really getting fed up with television. The amount of disgusting dialogue, and talking about things that should best be left behind bedroom doors, and showing graphics that can turn the stomach of a goat, has gone far beyond the pale. No I'm not talking about the programming. I'm talking about the disgusting commercials.

Ads showing people's problems with things that grow on their butts shouldn't be on T.V. The advertising about feminine stuff also has no place on the tube. I mean, most people know about these things, but hearing about "spotting" while I'm eating a snack in front of the tube takes the enjoyment right out of the meal.

I don't need to be reminded of itching problems that both men and women have down in their nether regions either. Every time I see one of those ads, I start getting the itches myself. This causes me to get a rash. This causes me to have to go and buy their product.

You notice there are plenty of ads about all the diseases a person's foot can have, don't you? The sponsors don't have the nerve to tell people to wear normal shoes because the "Flip Flop" special interest groups would crucify them.

Why are there so many ads and products directed at men who have had their member get old along with the rest of their bodies? These disgusting ads talk about: Penile Dysfunction, like it's some kind of disease. Your eleventh digit getting smaller and disinterested isn't a disease. It's a natural regression of life. All those pills do is cause more goofy older men to leave their wives of forty years and chase their daughter's friend's children. These pills hurt society more than they help it.

The worst thing is when you go work out at a health club and see nasty old men, with flab hanging everywhere, who look like they hid a ten pound salami in their workout pants. The grins on their faces just give me the willies, and I always shower back at home.

******

I wish disposable diapers would be outlawed. I'm not some type of save the Earth nut but I imagine if all the disposable diapers were placed end to end they would circle the United States and then some. Doesn't anyone realize the reason we are running out of landfill space is directly caused by the landfills being filled with poopy diapers?

The disposables also have put hundreds of thousands of dirty diaper entrepreneurs out of business and that has had an effect on the nation's economy. I remember how a young man would come to the house and pick up the white porcelain pails full of smellies and hand mom a new pile of diapers to fill up for next week. I just realized, America probably lost hundreds of jobs with the closing of the diaper pin factories as well.

******

229

I have a real problem with individuals who own yappy dogs, tie them up outside, and leave for the weekend. The dog, dumber than a box of rocks, can't get it through its pea brain that no one is listening to them, so they bark and bark all night.

I think people who do this should be arrested and taken to the animal shelter. After they are either neutered or spayed they should be sent home and chained in the backyard for a week or two. The dog should be let in the house, so that it can understand how hard it is to sleep with its stupid owners crying outside all night long.

******

If there is one kind of person I can't stand, it has to be the chewer. These people are everywhere. Ever borrow a pen from a pen chewer? God, the thing is awful and nasty looking, and the thought of just having it in my hand makes me feel like puking.

Athletes drive me crazy with their stupid mouthpieces. For decades there were no mouthpieces in sports. Athletes used to pop their partial plates out with pride. They would brag to people that they lost their choppers in the big game against so and so state when they tackled their superstar, as he was running over them.

Mouthpieces aren't really protection of course. I once placed a beer bottle in front of my teeth to ward off a punch from a monstrous looking guy. It didn't work and I lost three teeth and had Budweiser embossed on two others until they finally rotted out. If something as big and heavy as a beer bottle can't stop inevitability, then the idea that a piece of rubber or plastic stuck around your teeth will protect them is ludicrous.

All that will happen is you will loose your teeth, inside a mouth piece, when you get hammered.

How many times have you seen these athletes taking that nasty thing in and out and in and out of their mouth on television? Many of them, of course, twirl it around and chew on it. Why don't these people just go get a pacifier, which also should be outlawed by the way?

******

I don't know how I could have this little rant without mentioning the unwanted phone call problem in America. To be honest I have found the national "Do not call list" does work quite well. Now all I get are calls from some Republican group wanting money to stop some Democrat from getting into office. They are exempt from the "do not call list" of course. The Republicans passed the law with an exemption for political harassment just so they could call me and make my blood boil. I am a fierce independent voter and anyone who starts a call to me with;" Dear fellow Republican" or "Dear fellow Democrat" really sets me off.

I do miss some of those stupid phone calls however. I had a lot of fun jacking with the people who wanted to jack with my personal time at home.

Where I live there is a constant plethora of calls from travel agents telling people they have won a trip to Branson Missouri's "Hill Billy Heaven". I used to get a hang up from these sales people when I would interrupt their spiel by asking them if they thought Dolly Parton's boobies were real or store bought.

Another frequent call I used to receive was from another travel agency telling me I just got picked for a special deal at Disney World. I would quickly steer that conversation to an article I read that said Walt Disney had his head chopped off and put in cryogenic stasis. I would ask if my family could see his head when we got down there. This also always got a hang-up.

Of course there were innumerable calls from people telling me I won a new Mercedes, or a yacht, or a luxury condo by the ocean. I would always tell these people I couldn't make it down to wherever they said I needed to go to claim my prize. Instead, I asked if they would please just mail it to me. When the sales person would ask if I really thought a new car or luxury boat could be mailed, I would reply no. I would then ask them if they really thought a sane person would actually believe the tripe they had just told me. Click.

Well, those are some of the things that really drive me crazy in this world. I'm sure some of you who thought this little story might have been about politics, or the economy, or race or religion might be disappointed. That stuff is too obvious. Trust me. These things I have just mentioned are what really has this world screwed up. I might write a book about all this some day, since every time I look at this story I think of another thing that really drives me crazy.

So many things. So little time left to complain about them.

Thank You

Well, there you have it. You have just finished Mike Fak's defining book of personal short stories. I'm not saying they are any good or not. They are however, what I had in me to convey and I did so as well as I know how, so learn to deal with it as have I.

I hope you laughed a little at a few of these tales. I'm certain the book brought a few tears. Anyone who got this far and now realizes they spent good money for this stuff has to cry a little.

Don't forget my website at mikefak.com. I would enjoy receiving your comments on this latest journey by me into the world of the English language.

I hope to start making headway with at least two other novels of my own, but at the pace I am going, and with other writing commitments, I don't know if I have enough time on the planet to complete either.

That being said, I want to again thank you for your time. I believe it is precious, and for you to have spent just a little of it reading some thing I have written is very special to me.

Thank you and God bless you

Mike Fak

Printed in the United States
50920LVS00003B/82-195

9 781591 139690